LATIN AMERICA
a n d
POSTMODERNITY

LATIN AMERICA
and
POSTMODERNITY

A CONTEMPORARY READER

edited by

PEDRO LANGE-CHURIÓN
EDUARDO MENDIETA

Humanity
Books

an imprint of Prometheus Books
59 John Glenn Drive, Amherst, New York 14228-2197

Published 2001 by Humanity Books, an imprint of Prometheus Books

Inquiries should be addressed to
Humanity Books
59 John Glenn Drive
Amherst, New York 14228–2197
VOICE: 716–691–0133, ext. 207
FAX: 716–564–2711
WWW.PROMETHEUSBOOKS.COM

05 04 03 02 01   5 4 3 2 1

Library of Congress Cataloging-in-Publication Data

Latin America and postmodernity : a contemporary reader / edited by Pedro Lange-Churión and Eduardo Mendieta.
    p. cm.
    Includes bibliographical references and index.
    ISBN 1–57392–911–5 (pbk. : alk. paper)
    1. Latin America—Civilization—20th century. 2. Postmodernism—Latin America. 3. Philosophy, Latin America. I. Lange-Churión, Pedro, 1961–
II. Mendieta, Eduardo.

F1414.L277 2001
980.03'3—dc21   2001016831

Printed in the United States of America on acid-free paper

We dedicate this book to:

Gerardo Marín, for his commitment to Latin America

and to

Jorge Luis Borges, who inadvertently, for better or worse,
made us postmodern "avant la lettre"

CONTENTS

PART THREE. THE "POSTMODERN" APERTURES IN LATIN AMERICAN ALTERITY: POLITICS, SPIRITUALITY, THE POLITICS OF LITERATURE, AND IDENTITY POLITICS

ACKNOWLEDGMENTS

This page, reserved to candidly express gratitude, is insufficient to truly acknowledge the many people and offices whose help and generosity made this timely volume possible. Yet we must, at least, mention those whose sustained support was crucial to us, while we ask for understanding from those whose names we will inevitably omit.

First we would like to thank our illustrious contributors who penned their pieces specifically for this volume: Enrique Dussel, Walter Mignolo, Marcelo Paz, Santiago Castro-Gómez, and Ofelia Schutte. We are also thankful to the other contributors who gave us permission to reprint their works; special mention goes to the Nobel Foundation for allowing us to print Octavio Paz's piece and to the University of Texas Press for letting us reprint the essay by Jorge Luis Borges that, fittingly, opens this volume.

We are indebted to the University of San Francisco scholarly community for their enthusiastic inquiries into our project, but we are most grateful to the Dean of the College of Arts and Sciences, Dr. Stanley D. Nel, and to the Associate Dean, Dr. Gerardo Marín. Not only have they given us the financial support to complete the project, but, most importantly, they have taken a personal interest and pride in our scholarly endeavors; they have given us the opportunity to become relevant teachers and to begin unfolding our scholarly potentials, whatever they may be.

Bless the good ears of our gifted translators and readers José García (Pepe), Cristina Lloyd, Elizabeth Wing, Justin Zavislack, and Martin Woessner. Our infinite gratitude to Rebekah Bloyd for her meticulous and caring editing of the manuscript. And thanks to all our students for being, inadvertently, a source of inspiration. Thanks also to our highly efficient librarians, Marion Gin, Joseph Garity, Eric Paul Ewen, and Hille S. Novak, for helping us obtain some of the materials for the book.

Finally, Pedro wishes to thank Marcelo Paz and Tracy Seeley for their intellectual support, their pertinent advice and their generous caring. Eduardo would like to specially acknowledge Mike Webber's suggestions. He also wishes to thank Jenny, his wife, for her intelligent suggestions, and for her love and patience; his daughter Emily, for being an endless source of motivation; his son Callum who, had we finished this work when we were supposed to, would not be in this page, but who now joins Emily in being a source of unending joy. Words of assurance to "Turtle" Mendieta Farquhar who upon reading this page might feel a tad displaced.

Eduardo Mendieta
Pedro Lange-Churión

Eduardo Mendieta and
Pedro Lange-Churión

INTRODUCTION

The sign that he hung on the neck of the cow was an exemplary proof of the way in which the inhabitants of Macondo were prepared to fight against the loss of memory: This is the cow. She must be milked every morning so that she will produce milk, and the milk must be boiled in order to be mixed with coffee to make coffee and milk. *Thus they went on living in a reality that was slipping away, momentarily captured by words, but which would escape irremediably when they forgot the values of the written words. At the beginning of the road into the swamp they put up a sign that said* MACONDO *and another larger one on the main street that said* GOD EXISTS. *In all the houses keys to memorize objects and feelings had been written. But the system demanded so much vigilance and moral strength that many succumbed to the spell of an imaginary reality, one invented by themselves, which was less practical for them but more comforting.*

Gabriel García Marquez,
One Hundred Years of Solitude

OF MAPS, ENCYCLOPEDIAS, AND ANTHOLOGIES

Anthologies, like maps and encyclopedias, are only successful when they clearly delimit the territory to be covered. Argentine author

Jorge Luis Borges noted repeatedly throughout his numerous fictions that maps—like encyclopedias—wanting to be "perfectly" faithful to their referent would immediately fall into an infinite iteration of themselves. Borges has referred to this cartographical iteration by alluding to Royce's fictional map of England. This hypothetical map of England would contain a copy of England and itself, and itself as a map of England, and so on ad infinitum. He also gave us a glimpse of the "Aleph," which contains all space within the boundaries of a perfect sphere of approximately one inch radius, which, among the many infinite number of things it contains, allows a view "of a terrestrial globe between two mirrors that multiplied endlessly." There is of course the "total library" containing all past, present and future books, the book of sand, containing also all books, and the wonderful antiencyclopedia in "The Analytical Language of John Wilkins." At the base of these Borgesian exercises in extremity and reductio ad absurdum is the insight that representation and structuration are based in some fundamental act of 'epistemological' and 'linguistic' violence. As Borges put it, "There is no classification of the universe that is not arbitrary and conjectural." A map that would be perfect because it is an impeccable reproduction of what it maps would be redundant. An encyclopedia that would encompass the whole of human knowledge would have to contain not just all the books, but also all the other artifacts containing any knowledge. The truth is that a good map, like a good encyclopedia, is the residue of an itinerary already traced at the outset. Maps and encyclopedias can only offer orientation and knowledge from the standpoint of a perspective that prejudges and conditions that which is to be mapped or catalogued. In fact, maps determine territory, just as encyclopedias determine what is worth knowing. To discover new lands, or to rediscover old territories, requires that we dispense with our old maps, just as in order for us to learn something new requires that we dispense with our old catalogues, encyclopedias, manuals, bibliographies. This anthology is no less plagued by these contradictions. This anthology is on the one hand contentious (if not somewhat belligerent) toward the eurocentrism that underpins the postmodern debate; on the other hand, this anthology is cautious of the semantic instability of both terms in the title: (Post)modernity and Latin America. How is the story of these two terms and their relationship to be told? How is this territory to be covered? And now the map within the map, the introduction within the introduction. Hoping to be true to the Borgesian insight into the dangers of naive and self-oblivious maps and encyclopedias, we want to articulate some of the tenets that informed our selections.

WHOSE (POST)MODERNITY, WHICH LATIN AMERICA?

"A place on a map is a place in history," says Adrienne Rich. If that is so, where does Latin America fit in the map of history? The following questions are but a mere sample of the problems raised by the mapping of Latin America vis-à-vis the rest of the world.

Does Latin America refer to a part of the "American" continent? And if so, why has the United States claimed exclusivity to the term "America," preempting everyone else's claim to the name? Does Latin America refer to those countries below the Rio Grande, but excluding Brazil? Is Latin America a subcontinent determined by linguistic identity, the lands where Spanish and Portuguese are predominatly spoken? Where does the Caribbean fit into this linguistic map? Why is Latin America the "Third World" while parts of the south of Brazil are more developed than part of the south of the United States? In what way are modernized cities like Mexico City, Rio de Janeiro, Caracas, Buenos Aires different from Los Angeles, Miami, and New York? Is Latin America the land of vibrant Catholicism, to the exclusion of all syncretism? And if so, what do we do with all the Afro-American religions not just in Brazil, but also in the Caribbean, and the south of the United States? And what of the "mestizo" face of Jesus in Central America and the Andes, and liberation theology, seen by many as a second reformation? Is Mexico part of Latin America? And if so, why is it that in the United States *Chicanos* are not *Hispanics*, while Argentins are *Hispanic* but not *Latinos*? and what is the difference between Haitians, Puerto Ricans, and Dominicans? Or, along the same lines, what are the differences among "New World Africans" in Brazil, the Caribbean, and the United States? How is the map of Latin America to be drawn—demographically, politically, economically, culturally, linguistically, or on the basis of race and religion? Furthermore, when did Latin America become Latin America?

Like Heidegger's *Dasein*, Latin America is defined above all by the fact that its being is always in question. This questioning, however, always betrays the trace of imperial designs. It is with this in mind that this anthology has been put together.

The impossibility of absolute representations is foregrounded by the fact that totalizing discourses are threatened from the outset by incoherence. Such is the challenge we must face in dealing with (Post)modernity (we use this typographical monstrosity in order to underscore the point, addressed later on, that there is a fundamental parasitism between these two cognates.) We begin with the following claim: Latin America is not supplemental or external to (Post)modernity. Instead, it is integral to it. Neither can be thought of without the other. Our conjunctive in the title is less a connective and more an elucidation of an analytical dimension of (Post)modernity. In other words, there is a correspondence between (Post)modernity and Latin America inasmuch as they are both projects and conditions. Our central thesis is that (Post)modernity is no less important to Latin America than it is to Europe and the United States. And, conversely, that Latin America is no less important to (Post)modernity than either the United State or the crisis of the European project. To this extent, those who enter the space constituted by this anthology will not leave it untouched and untransformed. We will have accomplished our goal if we have offered not only a window into how the debate on (Post)modernity has been dealt with within Latin America, but also a window that looks back into the dyad itself: (Post)modernity. If Latin America will be seen as a product of (Post)modernity, whether in terms of its failure or triumph, its point of origin, or its dénouement, then we hope that the reader will also think of (Post)modernity as a significant Latin American cultural and social by-product. In other words, it is not that (Post)modernity has arrived too late at Latin

America; it is that we have failed to note how Latin America has always been there as both subject and object of this global process. Above all, we will have done our job if readers think of (Post)modernity as a dynamic process whereby a society can name itself, a process that is always global and local, contingent and ineluctable.

WHEN AND WHERE WAS (POST)MODERNITY?

We must also begin with the truism—often forgotten—that one's understanding of (Post)modernity is dependent on one's construing of modernity. (Post)modernity is a provisionary category that awaits the elucidation of its root. Who coins the meaning of one is thus also able to coin the referent and promise of the other. It is therefore imperative that we make explicit what we understand by modernity.

Part and parcel of the struggle over the meaning of modernity is the dating of its birth—When did modernity begin? Who is able to give a date to its inauguration has also already prejudged a substantive part of the discussion concerning the meaning of modernity. The selection of a particular set of events or historical processes as being emblematic of the birth of modernity discloses the refraction caused by a particular theoretical perspective. The selection of a particular set of historical events or social processes discloses not only the theoretical angle from which a particular analysis of modernity is enunciated, but also the geographical locality from which it is pronounced. Dates are always a matter of geography, and geography is mapped by history. Evidently, when one gives primacy to the Reformation over the Renaissance, one is also giving primacy to Northern Europe over Southern Europe, just as when one speaks of capitalism without mentioning imperialism, one actually gives primacy to the metropolis while occluding the colonial outpost. Therefore, it behooves us—as editors but also as critics within (Post)modernity—to establish our own chronology, not only because we want to disclose our own theoretical orientation but also because part of the significance we attach to the (Post)modernity dyad is determined by this chronology.

As part of our move to challenge and disclose modernity's hegemonic chronology, we would like to underscore the spatio-temporal coordinates of the following historical events and processes: Above all, the "discovery of the New World" in 1492; the Renaissance; the Reformation; The French and American Revolutions; the scientific revolutions; the revolutions in energy production and harnessing; and the economic or bourgeois revolutions. Although the events just mentioned are intricately related, we would like to agglutinate them under four significant subheadings: the revolution in subjectivities; political revolutions; scientific and energy revolutions; and the economic revolutions. Any one of the above listed historical events may have participated in more than one of these four processes of social transformation and upheaval.

The revolution in subjectivities took place as a combination not only of the Reformation, which represented the liberation of individual conscience, and the Renaissance, which established the dignity of humans as reasoning and undetermined (*exocentric* in the language of philosophical anthropology) creatures who are 'like' God in their capacity to create, but also through the despiritualization of reason and the detranscendentalizing of nature. While the Renaissance implemented the objectification of nature, by inscribing it mathematically, the Reformation made of religion an individual and private experience.

If one considers Bartolomé de las Casas's defense of the "indians" and his debate with Sepúlveda, the issue of individual conscience and religious pluralism is put into greater relief. To this extent, the valorization of 'individuality' and 'subjectivity' usually associated with the Reformation is essential to Fray Bartolomé de las Casas's defense of the indians. It is this type of debate that stands behind the reflections of Francisco de Vitoria, Francisco Suárez, and a host of other Spanish political theoreticians who basically laid the foundations for the theories of international rights and religious tolerance that became seminal for European nation states. Nonetheless, the discovery of individual "conscience" that parallels the objectification and quantification of nature alone would not have transformed European societies. Transformations in the political and economic realms were called for and presupposed. Indeed, rational and spiritual individuality only obtained currency in the context of the assertion of economic independence and political autonomy. The latter, in turn, would not have been possible if the production of social wealth had not expanded exponentially due to the quantification of nature, the harnessing of energy sources for the transformation of raw materials into social goods, and, in tandem, the regimentation of humans into wealth producing entities.

Yet, economic and political transformations of nature and humans would not have been possible without the colonization of the so-called New World that allowed for economic integration and political unification as the simultaneous but converse of economic polarization and political exclusion. The year 1492, therefore, is a *condition of possibility* of modernity, and we cannot stress enough this perspective.

The moral we want to establish is that from its inception, modernity has been plagued by the problem of the other. The other, in turn, has been a coparticipant of modernity, even if in most cases that participation has been represented asymmetrically and solely from the standpoint of the West's effects and initiative. This, however, is not a question of the presence of the other, but of their representation, which is one of the reasons we take this debate to be so important. At the same time, by pointing to 1492 as the date which inagurates modernity, we want to contest the prevalent mapping of modernity that locates it in the center or in the north of Europe (England, Germany and France), while also making suspect the Protestant flavor that has been given to it by the theoreticians who see modernization as secularization. The development of Catholicism as a reactive ideology that contained its particular responses to the modernization of social relations, we want to suggest, is a form of modernity. Not all paths to modernity lead through the doors of the church at the castle of Wittenberg. At the same time, it is not to be forgotten than 1492 marks the expulsion of the Jews and Muslims from the Iberian peninsula. The struggle against heathen and infidel, the reconquest of the Mediterranean sea, the drive to homogenize language are all made manifest in the struggle against the Jews and the Muslims. It is for this reason that modernity as the thrust towards homogeneity and totalization was already presaged in the inquisition, the birth of modern bureaucracy. Note that 1492 is the axis around which purity of blood, belief, and language gravitate. If we foreground 1492, we also will be able to keep in our horizon of comprehension the codetermining role that the "Orient" has had not only vis-à-vis "Europe," but the "West" in general. For modernity has been constituted in a tug of war with the "Orient." Here 1492 stands for the inception of a new global world system, in which "Europe" is able to bypass the Mediterranean Sea and reach the East by way of the West.

Modernity, seen from the perspective of the production, appropriation, and distribution of social wealth has been capitalism: who speaks of modernity must also speak of capitalism. Capitalism in turn is an economic system that is based on integration through the exclusionary polarization of productive localities. Capitalism establishes topographies of subordination (public/private, domestic/factory, city/country, nation/empire, metropolis/colony, etc.), These oppositions exclusively channel the flow of accumulated wealth toward the metropolis, the urban center from which colonial and neocolonial power is exercised and deployed. This dynamic of exclusion through subordination is also true of the different political systems which have accompanied the expansion of capitalism, be it liberalism, socialism, and/or fascism, all of which are in more than one way predicated on the sovereignty of the state and the unity of the nation-state. The history of the political systems constitutive of modernity has been accompanied by the history of imperialism, colonization, and thus of globalization. More explicitly, the constitution of differential geographies (or geographies of difference) is fundamental to political and economic integration through exclusionary polarization. We may therefore define differential geographies as the political economy of gentrification, now, however, thought with reference to all the different levels of human interaction. In fact, these geographies of difference—gentrified localities—map social space at all levels: at the level of subjectivities, at the level of social/communal interaction, at the level of national and international exchange, and at the level of planetary gerrymandering. As examples of these differential geographies, constitutive of capitalism and modernity, let us take the "New World" in relationship with Europe, the "Western" frontier as a trope of salvation and regeneration in the United States, and the relationship between the *mono-cultivos* countries of Central and South America and the United Sates. In short, modernity not only has a *when* but also a *where* within geopolitical space. Any discourse about (Post)modernity, thus, must theorize not only about the convergence of these two coordinates, but also about the occlusion of one by the other. By highlighting the subordination of the spatial by the temporal we seek to unveil the eurocentrism of most theories about modernity that are emerging from the intellectual capitals of the West.

(POST)MODERNITY AS A TEMPORAL PANOPTICON

It is clear that modernity is a complex historical phenomenon that has involved the seismic transformation of all levels of human interaction. To account for this transformation, it is necessary to underscore the global nature of modernity. This is what we intend by focusing on 1492. From its birth modernity is a global phenomenon, one that has entailed the transformation of every corner of the world according to the political economy of its spatio-temporal gentrification. Because modernity maps social spaces according to certain differential geographies, it calls for a *chronotopology*, the science of macromapping time and space. We want to underscore that from the perspective of a chronotopology, modernity appears always as both local and global, plural and heterogeneous. Modernity is *glocal*, an epochal configuration in which the local is produced by the global and the global is determined by certain localities (center/periphery), and in which traditions are retroactively created and innovation becomes routine. Modernity occurs within the coordinates of the local/global, the new/ancient, or innovation/tradition. Modernity secretes both space and time configurations that obey a logic of exclusion and inclusion. This logic can be best named: *spatio-temporal gentrification*. Because modernity postulates universal claims that determine and regiment notions of space and time for the rest of the world, and because these claims are self-legitimating, one could argue that

*modernity wants to be a panopticon whose tower (space) is the the
omniscient eye of time.*

Modernity works in fact as a mechanism for the sundering of
timing (temporalizing) and being timed (being temporalized). It is for
this reason that while every one must write his or her history in terms
of his or her interaction with the West, the West in turn can write the
history of the world as the history of itself. Linked to modernity's
panoptical structure, we discover that modernity is also the epochal
situation in which society comes to the fore as a conceptual structure
for the organization and constitution of agents. Society is born with
modernity, for modernity constitutes individuals as subjects; that is,
selves are individuated through subjection, their becoming subjects,
while their economic and political associations, which aid in their subjection, are incorporated into the totalities of the state and nation. To
be a subject is to be a political, economic, and social individual, possessing certain rights, duties, and economic claims. Modernity, conversely, is the constitution of society according to the regimentation of
the temporal-spatial coordinates that enable or disable subjects to act:
private and public domains, nation, law, and so forth.

Given this geographical fixing of modernity, what can be and must
be said about (Post)modernity? (Post)*modernity* is above all a disenchantment with disenchantment, to use Norbert Lechner's wonderful
phrasing. (Post)modernity is the crisis and abandonment of the pursuit after the unity of reason, selves, societies, and history. Hence its
celebration of the heterogeneous, the hybrid, the Other as total difference. To this extent, the postmodern is also the announcement of
the de-differentiation of social structures, the explosion of the carni-
valesque, the asynchronous, the dysfunctional, the transversal.

(Post)modernity, with respect to epistemic means and machines,
is the denunciation of the impossibility of the purity and trans-
parency of representation and perception, where language is not just
a tool for the faithful representation of the world, but the very condition of possibility of its experience, its naming. Language is not
aleatory to experience; it is its sine qua non. Structure, form, schema
were contaminated by the arbitrariness, refractoriness, duplicity,
and fogginess of language, as Jacques Derrida has established so well.

And mind, at best, is the name of our second order reflection on language, and at worst, a linguistic ghost, a solecism. We are not idle bystanders to reality. We are constituted with it as we constitute it. The real is always the shadow of our gaze: that which we do not see when we are looking at it (as Niklas Luhmann aptly put it). Reality is a detritus of human subjectivity, but no less important for that reason; hence (Post)modernity's announcement of the death of science and the intrinsic impurity of all knowledge. What we have instead are particular, contingent epistemic configurations that obey social imperatives and that reflect images of themselves. (Post)modernity is thus the pronouncement of the death of the innocence of science—this has become no more than our own particular magic; the fetishism of the totem instrumental reason. (Post)modernity, thus, is the simultaneous denaturalization and resocialization of reality and perception. Everything is always, has always been, a second nature.

(Post)modernity, it is claimed, is concomitantly the end of History. As such, (Post)modernity abandons the pursuit of the great teleologies that fueled the modernization of Europe and the colonization of the world. The history of development, enlightenment, technological innovation, and social transformation died, postulates (Post)modernity, with Auschwitz, Hiroshima, and the Gulags of the Soviet Union. (Post)modernity is the collapse of the grand *recits*, the meta-narratives that gave coherence and legitimacy to the homogenizing drive of modernity. Telos turned into eschaton, eschaton into holocaust, holocaust into the end of history. (Post)modernity is mainly the disenchantment of Western society with its own enchantment, its narcissism, its plenopotency.

When did (Post)modernity begin? In contrast to a chronology of modernity, a periodization of (Post)modernity lacks the benefit of temporal distance. Also, the difficulty of addressing the "when" of (Post)modernity is linked with the fact that historical events as temporal markers reflect and sediment a particular ideology. However, regardless of what spatio-temporal coordinates we provided as the markers of inception of the postmodern, these remain determined by the modern, by modernity as an epochal situation. We could begin by offering the end of World War II as the beginning of the postmodern.

Many of the thinkers that were later to become the theoreticians of the postmodern were born and grew up in the shadow not just of the Holocaust, but also of Hiroshima and Nagasaki. Yet, the end of the European age also inaugurated the beginning of the postcolonial. The struggles for decolonization and national liberation marked indelibly the ascendancy of a postmodern sensibility. In addition, and not necessarily as an extension of postcolonial struggles, the political and social mobilizations for minority rights also provided the context for the emergence of a postmodern suspicion of the modern. In contrast to the homogeneous and state oriented political movements of modernity, the New Social Movements brought about a heterogenization of the political. And, without forgetting that May 68 was a world phenomena and not just a "French" experience, we have to consider the intellectual innovations that crystallized during the sixties: poststructuralism, deconstruction, postmarxism, liberation theologies, and feminisms. This explosion of minority discourses vitiated the notion of a homogenous, autochthonous, and continuous Western intellectual tradition, as well as the fetish of a wholly Other.

Along with these Western temporal markers, we also would have to consider not only the Cuban revolution (1959), the rise and fall of the Berlin Wall (1949–1989), the Vietnam war, the 1973 petroleum embargo by OPEC, but also the democratic election of Allende and the Nicaraguan revolution, as well as the struggles for national liberation in Africa. Not unlike modernity, (Post)modernity has been determined by *glocal* events, colonial and postcolonial dynamics.

It is against the background circumscribed by these twentieth century events that we can trace the processes which characterize (Post)modernity. In terms of the subjectivites, (Post)modernity does not mean the end of the individual, as it is mistakenly assumed. Instead, it signifies the politicization of agency in terms of the denaturalization of humanity. Central here is the discovery that individuality is both the medium and telos of the subjection of agents. Agency is not to be taken for granted. The processes of its constitution are the questions of politics and the political par excellance. Postmodern posthumanism is not antihumanism, but rather the call for new forms of agency, the rehumanization of social relations that have been left outside the realm of social determination. Simultaneously, the notion that the unity and stability of selfhood could be traced back to some warrant, such as the psychological, the epistemic, the volitional, the economic, or the social is jettisoned. Thus, the repoliticization of social agency converges with the denaturalization of selfhood. Agency is social through and through.

The converse of individuation as subjection is socialization as totalization. This was a central logic of modernity. In other words, the more agents became individuals, atomatized as economic and political entities, the greater the need to contain them within the totality of the political. The state became the site for the dispensation of autonomy and individuation. This in turn entailed its growth and strengthening. The converse of political individuation and aesthetic subjectification is massification and totalitarianism.

Thus, under (Post)modernity, the repoliticization of agency entails the remapping of the boundaries between the social and the political. At work here is a logic of de-differentiation, of hybridization and detotalization. Power is everywhere, especially where the state is not. The flows of power are to be mapped using a nonstatist strategy. Micropolitics replaces macropolitics, the microagent supplants the meta- and macrosubject (the proletariat, class, race). This entails the plurification of micronarratives and the (re)turn to collective memory, to a memory that is nonstatist and nonuniversal as a point of condensation for political identity (the idea of postethnic identity). Under (Post)modernity identity politics is pursued as a critique of identity brokers and authenticators. To this extent, identity politics are oxymoronic and a performative self-contradiction, albeit to be pursued strategically for the purposes of the remapping of the social and the political.

Similar to modernity, (Post)modernity also presupposed a revolution in energy production and harnessing. Part of this revolution was catalyzed by the petroleum crisis of the early seventies, but also by the use of nuclear energy (and the confrontation with its hazards), the automatization of production lines (the beginning of the end of Fordism), the introduction of the computer, and the mass production of microchips (the informatization of culture as a whole, and the possible colonization of the lifeworld by the hyperreal of cyberspace). These technological changes brought about a revolution in the modes of production that had two clearly related consequences: one, the virtualization of the economy, and the other, the reconfiguration of social relations. In the center, the transformation from industrial to finance capitalism, and the parallel transformation in the periphery from semi-industrialized to industrialized capitalism (mass culture finally arrived to the Third World), reversed the fundamental logic of modernity: industrialization and differentiation in the metropolis, marginalization and homogenization in the periphery. It is clear, however, that this apparent reversal of the logic of the production and appropriation of wealth had as a result the collapse of the progressive conquest of nature and the exponential growth of science. Technological prowess turned into dystopian nostalgia. Science's mesmerizing development turned into stasis. Between the paralysis brought on by technophobia and the dizzying speed in the overturning of scientific paradigms, science and technology discovered their specificity, limits, and ideological character. The end of the metanarratives of emancipation and development were accompanied by the collapse of the metanarrative of the growth of knowledge and the intrinsic benigness of technology. This collapse was not only announced already by the success of the concentration camps and the slaughter machine of World War II, but also in the considerations of Georges Canguilhem and Thomas Kuhn that bespeak the crisis of the belief in the teleological and cumulative development of science.

Whereas the technological sublime of modernity presupposed the strict separation of society and nature, so that nature could be entirely subordinated to society, in (Post)modernity nature is denaturalized in such a way that the boundaries between nature and society are erased. Nature is already society and society is what is not nature, that is, itself in the negative. This is clearly the paradigm under which the ecological movements operate, even if some deep ecologists have turned to nature by remythologizing it, renaturalizing it by othering it. Indeed, just as (Post)modernity announced the end of the natural human being, pronounced as the death of 'man' or death of the subject, (Post)modernity announced the end of nature as nature: nature is the darkness of the negation of our social responsibility; it is a phantasmagoric alibi for manufactured irresponsibility. In Ulrich Beck's terms, the rhetoric of naturalness becomes the rhetoric of risk, which is more appropriate to the acknowledgement that nature is always a shadow of the social. Looked at from the standpoint of technology, the sociopolitical-economic transformation of scientific models and fantasies about the substratum secreted as nature is unmasked precisely as that, just another social imaginary, just another social strategy for regimentation and control. The myths of technology's teleology and its purported neutrality are dismantled. The denaturing of nature is the twin of technology's resocialization. The real of science is the hyper-real of technology and technology is not for the control of nature; rather technology produces it as its excrement and fantasy. Nature is what technology refuses to touch after it has already produced it. It is the preserve of a society that has discovered its permeation of everything.

From the perspective of the production and accumulation of wealth, we also have a redefinition of the economic under the postmodern. Whereas under modernity economic processes were regulated through the nation-state, under the postmodern the territorial nation state has been rendered almost if not entirely obsolete. This has taken place as the metropolis-to-colony relationship has imploded so that now the Third World has come to the First World. Cities in turn have become nodes in global migrations in which relations between international cities are closer than between cities and the respective nations in which they reside. This shift has been registered in what has been called the deindustrialization of capitalism. Heavy industry has been replaced by the service sector, just as high tech jobs get beyond the reach of the under educated. In other words, as the creation and processing of information comes to the fore, labor is pushed down on the economic ladder. Knowledge elites have become the nouveau riches of a postindustrial economy.

The ascendancy of economies of information with its concomitant creation of the over worked and underpaid service sector laborer has resulted in the rolling back of labor's gains at the level of the welfare state. The less capital is accountable to the territorial nation-state, the less labor is able to enter into negotiation with transnational capital. This new economic configuration of social relations has been given the name of disorganized capitalism, but this is overstating the case, not only because capitalism has an intrinsic anarchical dimension but also because regulation and monitoring still take place through international market agreements and national strategies of redevelopment (NAFTA and the European Union). Part and parcel of the displacement of industry by the production of information is the greater role played by "culture" in the economy. In fact, research and development have come to assume equal roles in the actual production of commodities. It is this phenomena which Jean Baudrillard has given expression in his postmodern economies of the sign, in which simulacra is commodification to the second power. This is the triumph of the culture industry, and with it triumphs not just massification, but also the aestheticization of culture. Goods are bought and sold less for their use value and more for their exchange value, a value that exists more and more in its accrued symbolic status. Implicit here is the process of the aestheticization of the economy and the virtualization of money. The fact is that the so-called deindustrialization of First World nations has not proceeded at the same pace in all industrialized nations, to say the least about the industrialization of developing nations. It is also not clear that Fordism is at an end, even as flexible production expands into larger and larger sectors of production. If anything, we have a Fordism that has become global where nations, or global regions, play out the role of subordinate production centers specialized in the assembly of one or two products. Just as the gap between the rich and poor has grown exponentially and preposterously, the life standards and consumption levels between the geographical "Third World" and "First World" has widened scadously and equally absurdly.

Nonetheless, we must speak of postmodernities just as we must speak of modernities. The paths to modernization followed by the United States, Japan, and Germany, as John Urry and Scott Lash have shown masterfully, followed different logics, in which one was not more "modern" than the others. Similarly, the paths to the postmodernization of world economies have been plural; again, witness the differences between Germany and Japan on the one hand, and the United States and England on the other. This same heterogeneity of paths to and through modernity/(Post)modernity is evident in Latin America. It would be entirely inappropriate to try to assimilate to one pattern the experiences of modernization that Mexico, Argentina, Brazil, and Venezuela underwent.

The onus, in fact and to close these reflections, is not on showing whether Latin America is postmodern, but on how a certain path to and through (Post)modernity is Latin American; more precisely, how certain (Post)modernity is very Latin American. Culturally, economically, and politically many Latin American countries have struggled with the issues of the heterogeneity of the "cultural" realm, the hybridization of "high" culture by so-called low culture, the permeation of the political by the economic and the over-determination of both by "cultural" icons and ideologies that have been products as much of colonial traditions, as of neocolonialism, nationalism, and the striving after democratic self-determination. It is true that many Latin American countries have and continue to deal with the promise and crisis of modernity, but this is no less true of the United States than of Germany and England. In tandem, if (Post)modernity is the awareness of this tension, then Latin America is no less exempt than, let us say, Italy and France. It is true: revolutions have failed, many violently suppressed and defeated, Marxism seems dead, labor is decimated, nationalism has become a perverse and defunct ideology, many Latin American countries sink further into poverty as their corrupt governments continue to squeeze the poor poorer by duly obliging the economic policies dictated by the World Bank, the IMF, and the multinationals, and prospects for transformation seem distant and demanding great utopian imagination. This same complaints can be heard in London, Chicago, México, Bogotá, Lima, and so on. What is clear is the imperative need to understand the specificity of the Latin American confrontation with the obsolescence of certain ideals and utopias of modernity, and the way this recognition has been registered in Latin America. Latin America must be allowed to offer its own diagnosis. Unless the postmodern permits the other to pronounce the nature of its own time, it will continue to perpetuate the colonial trust of modernity. Now, however, this perpetuation will exist in the mode of the negative, as a negation of any alternatives except that of the exhaustion of the West's own failed dreams. If freedom is insight into necessity, as Marx noted, then the others' emancipation is predicated in their naming of their present and their being able to paint their own future.

Eduardo Mendieta

THE ARTICLES FEATURED IN THIS ANTHOLOGY

Why Borges?

The reader of this anthology might wonder why we begin with Jorge Luis Borges's essay "A New Refutation of Time." Borges is not a theoretician or a philosopher, but a man of letters. His inquiry into philosophical matters is marked by an ironic gesture that ludically manipulates metaphysical and scientific certainties in order to make them fit into a fictional frame. By irreverently manipulating these discourses, Borges questions the claim that philosophical and scientific systems are the only disciplines that can properly enunciate what must be universally accepted as normative. Moreover, not only do Borges's fictions underscore the insufficiency of these purportedly universal systems, but his fictions also tend to flaunt the imaginative nature of these metaphysical projects, their literary texture. As John Sturrock eloquently put it, "Borges enjoys metaphysics for what it offers him as a writer of fiction. He appreciates speculative styles of philosophy for the very reasons that most practising philosophers in the West despair of them, as offering unfounded, contradictory and frequently incredible representations of the cosmos. Borges is not in the least skeptical of the human mind, only of its medium, language, whose co-ordination with reality, which is not verbal, he rightly finds unconvincing. Metaphysics to him is an art form, one way of producing what art produces which is 'visible unrealities'. He works the history of metaphysical thought, therefore, to his own great advantage and to the great disadvantage of the reputation of metaphysical thought."[1]

So, as the West comes to terms with the crisis of metaphysics, as it wrestles with the "visible unreality" of its *grand recits*, it also becomes enthralled with Borges's fictions. By opening this volume with Borges's hybrid texts, we cast suspicion on the discursive divisions established by modernity and by the opposition of the spheres of knowledge (philosophy and literature). Also we want to thematize through Borges's essay ("A New Refutation of Time"), "the refutation of time" implicit in the paradoxical signifier "Post-modern." In the process we want to reclaim Borges's writings as emerging from a Latin American crisis of representation, be this crisis postmodern or not.

Latin American "(Post)modernity": the Perennial Crisis of Hegemonic Perpectives

The section's title emblematizes the intellectual tension that results in bringing together (Post)modernity and Latin America. While the quotation marks that frame (Post)modernity in the title are meant to warn us against uncritically applying the term to the region, the adjective "perennial" conveys the sense that if (Post)modernity is indeed the crisis of modernity, such crisis has been an integral part of Latin America since 1492. If the crisis of modernity resonates today, at the twilight of the century, it is because contending and unheard voices have crept up in the midst of the center's habitat to challenge the hegemony of the center's epistemological claims. There is a thematic gradation in the arrangement of the articles in the second part: the section begins with Octavio Paz's and Leopoldo Zea's discussions on modernity; it moves to Enrique Dussel's challenge of Eurocentric notions of centrality and periphery, notions seminal for the elaboration of the idea of modernity and (Post)modernity; then, through the articles of Santiago Castro-Gómez and Ofelia Schutte, the section concretely faces the historical and epistemological nuances of the postmodern in Latin America. Finally, the section unveils (Post)modernity as a Eurocentric disguise in Walter Mignolo's inscription of the postmodern within the postcolonial situation as this last is exemplified in the border.

Octavio Paz (Mexican), is one of Latin America's foremost poets, essayists, and public intellectuals. "In Search of the Present" was Paz's 1990 Nobel Lecture. This is a significant essay insofar as Paz speaks about a modernity as a quest for our present, which is our contemporary social reality. Paz suggests that thus far Latin America has been living its modernity by proxy. The task is to realize that modernity is within Latin America, something that will be easier to accomplish given that ours is the "first age to live without a meta-historical doctrine." This already anticipates Paz's view of (Post)modernity. For him, (Post)modernity is a more modern modernity.

Leopoldo Zea is unquestionably one of the most important Latin American philosophers of the twentieth century. Zea explores how "America" has been defined in Spanish America as well as its role in world history. Zea's approach is centered on intellectual history and the reconstruction of world views with their respective ethos. In *Discurso desde la marginación y la barbarie* (1988), Zea argues that the modernity of central Europe has been predicated on the barbarization of both Spain and Russia, and thus of Latin America and other "Third World" countries. Essentially, however, for Zea modernity is political, cultural, economic, and social modernization, a modernization that nevertheless always threatens to turn into the nemesis of humanity. In the same vein as Paz, Zea sees (Post)modernity as the modernity of modernity, or neomodernity.

Enrique Dussel is one the most significant philosophers, theologians, and historians from Latin America. Dussel calls for an economic, political, and historical reading of modernity that sees its inception with the inauguration of a world system in which Europe's centrality was based on the subordination of the New World. Unless this is recognized, argues Dussel, we will be unable to rescue and utilize the "normative" contents of modernity. (Post)modernity, on the other hand, needs to be criticized insofar as certain currents within it reject reason *in toto*. As a total and totalizing critique of reason, (Post)modernity can only aid in the furthering of the adverse and dark aspects of modernity. As a critique of reason that points to the false universality of European modernity, however, (Post)modernity can be and must be seen as an ally, argues Dussel.

In "The Challenge of Postmodernity to Latin American Philosophy," Santiago Castro-Gómez begins with a discussion of the opponents of (Post)modernity, Hinkelammert and Vázquez being the most noteworthy, proceeds with a discussion of the development of cultural studies (Canclini, Brunner, Richard, et al.), and concludes with the exorcising of four major misunderstandings and clichés about (Post)modernity. These four "clichés" are: the claim that modernity has come to an end, the end of history, the death of the subject, and the end of utopia. For instance, Castro-Gómez discerns in the postmodern celebration of the decentered subject the possibility of new moral attitudes. Finally, with respect to the claim that postmodernism signals the demise of utopian thinking, the Colombian philosopher notes that postmodernism in fact allows for a new type of sober utopian criticism that is predicated neither on the impossible eradication of difference nor on the dogmatic affirmation of absolute Otherness. The issue is which differences are tolerable and how are they to be brought into discussion in such a way that their respective claims may be voiced and respected.

Ofelia Schutte's essay registers two ways in which (Post)modernity may be interpreted in the Latin America context. Schutte differentiates between a metaphysical and a political reading of (Post)modernity, noting that the two do not have to converge. Like one's aesthetics is not guarantee of one's politics, one's metaphysics—or critique thereof—is not a warrant for one's politics. One of the major aspects of (Post)modernity is its devastating onslaught on all stable categories, be they reason, history, teleology, nation, or identity. Yet, Schutte notes that certain provisional and qualified notions of identity are important when moving at the level of the political. It is these 'strategic' political identity constructs that certain Latin American philosophers have appealed to when formulating agendas of transformation and liberation. Using José Martí's seminal "Our America" essays as a critical foil, Schutte turns to the political continuities and epistemic ruptures in the discourses of counterhegemony and anti-imperialism that have been formulated from Latin America.

This section closes with Walter Mignolo's article. In a similar fashion to Dussel's, Mignolo calls for a reassessment of the ways in which we have thought about modernity. For Mignolo, modernity is the period in the history of the West in which its domination of other people reached its zenith. To consider modernity without being attentive to its colonial and neocolonial traditions is not only an eschewed approach, but also one detrimental to our ability to understand our present. Considering the colonial and neocolonial traditions still operative in contemporary societies requires new methods, new ways of understanding the codetermination of cultures. Such new techniques of analysis were exhibited masterfully in his *The Darker Side of the Renaissance: Literacy, Territoriality, and Colonization* (1995). In this work Mignolo offers a devastating critique of discourse of modernity in terms of a dismantling of the civilizing, evangelical, and literacy projects of the Renaissance. Looking at the "colonization of language, memory, and space," brought on by the Renaissance, Mignolo detects the "denial of the denial of coevalness," in which temporal narratives take primacy and displace locality and spatiality. To counter this hegemonic strategy, Mignolo offers the method of a "plurotopic hermeneutics." In his essay written for this volume, Mignolo expands this method into his proposal for a "borderland gnosis," which is attentive to local histories and imperial designs. Mignolo argues that localized narratives, always at odds with teleologically and chronologically organized ones, can offer a standpoint for critique but also for reconstruction and promise.

Postmodern Apertures and Latin American Alterity: Politics, Spirituality, the Politics of Literature, and Identity Politics

The articles in this section register the global reach of Latin American otherness produced by the postmodern debate. Much in the spirit of Nelly Richard's strategic ambivalence towards (Post)modernity, the articles grouped in this session are critical of hegemonic (Post)modernity while simultaneously taking advantage of the space this debate provides for bringing to surface Latin American alterity, be this alterity spiritual, political, aesthetic, ethnic, or feminist.

   In "Tiresias's Paradox in the Third Millennium," Iris M. Zavala reaccents the problem of Latin American identity by resorting to the classical paradox of Tiresias (the androgynous blind seer). The challenge is not to think identity from the universal (exclusionary) notions inherited by Modernity, but to think of identity precisely from the particular and the unfinished; the "not-all" that, according to Lacan, characterizes feminine subjectivity. But, far from inciting the reader to stop at thinking identity as difference and fall thereafter to the vapid celebration of difference that characterizes current attitudes about multiculturalism, she challenges the reader to think of difference as a constantly conflictual relationship with the other's claim to *jouissance*. A difference thought dialogically is conflictive because it is always subjected to the response of the other. It also prevents the subject from surrendering his/her *jouissance* to tutelary powers (the big Other) which emerge as sole surveyors of a community's *jouissance*.

Zavala moves on to identify literary texts which have functioned as spaces of fantasy for much of Latin America's colonized history. In these spaces (e.g., Baroque, Romantic, Modernista, Magical-Realist, and neobaroque) what becomes evident is a *plus de jouir* which subverts the tutelage of the big Other in its many guises: the conqueror, the caudillo, and the American imperialist). In a retroactive gesture, Zavala unearths the significations of these texts for present and future theorizations of Latin American identity. What is at stake is an understanding of such identity from a truly democratic ethos, one whose conflictual and dialogical nature ensures the constant presence of alterity. Because Zavala's retroactive reading of Latin America preempts the all-to-hasty deployment of postmodern theories to explain and put forward notions of Latin American identity, her essay is a necessary point of contention in this anthology.

In her analysis of Peninsular literary modernity and in her references to Latin American literature, Zavala points out that many of the textual aspects seen as postmodern by the center (decentering of the subject, dissolution of borders among literary genres, reader's participation, among others) are actually constitutive of the formal elements and the thematic preoccupations of Hispanic (literary) modernity. In this sense her stand resonates in Marcelo Paz's article who, as noted, argues that the (Post)modernity that the center sees in

Latin American literature is, conversely, for Latin America, its literary modernity.

Marcelo Paz discusses the nuances of (Post)modernity from a political stand. He evaluates the desirability of the postmodern as a theoretical construct that provides a helpful understanding of Latin American cultural products, namely, its literature. Paz's stand towards the postmodern is ambivalent; on the one hand, he undermines hegemonic (Post)modernity because it is totalizing; on the other hand he is willing to textualize (Post)modernity, as Richard would argue, not to opt out of a global debate, since doing so would amount to marginalizing Latin America. In what can be called his textualization of hegemonic (Post)modernity, Paz challenges the center's appropriation of Latin American cultural products, an appropriation which seeks to validate the center's theoretical claims with peripheral examples. This critic is deeply entrenched in a Latin American historiography; therefore, for him, Borges (a postmodern writer for the center) epitomizes Latin American literary modernity, (the so-called boom). Latin American (Post)modernity (the postboom) would be exemplified by writers such as Ricardo Piglia and Luisa Valenzuela, among others. These writers, for instance, have taken advantage of the laxity between discourses brought about by deconstruction and have penned a fiction whose parody of historical discourse serves as an account of the unspoken years of terror known, in Argentinean contemporary history, as the "Dirty War."

Pedro Lange-Churión deals with (Post)modernity as a crisis of representation. Like the rest of the authors featured in this section, his relation to (Post)modernity is ambivalent: while he recognizes the democratizing impetus the postmodern gives to Latin American alterity, he is also critical of the pernicious influence (Post)modernity might exert on the continent, above all when its theoretical and aesthetic sophistication can serve to veil and even further the concrete infirmities of of the continent. Lange-Churión reads (Post)modernity intertextually by comparing some of its premises with those of the Latin American baroque and neobaroque. In resorting to the Latin American neobaroque in order to explain Latin America's postmodern effects, Lange-Churión not only unearths the epistemological

potential of this aesthetic phenomenon (a potential that is quite frequent in Latin American literature; and which is, in itself, a challenge
to the primacy of philosophical discourse) but he is also advancing an
interpretive scheme of Latin America that is voiced by the "subaltern
subject" from his/her own cultural location.

In keeping with her rebuttal of an essentialist Latin American,
Richard sees (Post)modernity as one more theoretical construction
which can be capitalized on by Latin American theoreticians. Since
(Post)modernity amounts to a corrosive critique of modernity's epistemological categories (subject, power, authority, center, etc.), it, if
astutely rearticulated from the periphery, can offer an opening for
the voicing of peripheral realities. Richard resorts to Christine Buci-
Glucksmann's baroque image, the fold (*el pliegue*) "the unreasonable
reason," to account for the interstices of (Post)modernity where this
logic can be rescued from neoconservatism. Quoting Huyssen, she
argues that "if the postmodern is a historical and cultural condition
(no matter how incipient), then the oppositional and strategic practices should be located *in the interior* of (Post)modernity, not of
course in its shining facades." Alluding to Buci-Glucksmann's work is
a strategic move, because she argues that the archeology of the
modern has been characterized by an obsession with the feminine;
whenever the rationality of culture is in crisis, we hear talk of the
feminization of culture. Since (Post)modernity is precisely one of
these crises, the crossroads between (Post)modernity and feminism
becomes evident for Richard. After developing a matrix that displays
the diverse types of feminisms that interact in the postmodern
moment and that have become a classic debate among feminists (feminism of equality versus feminism of difference), Richard advises critical flexibility in dealing with these categories. Such flexibility is even
more pertinent for Latin Americans, since the continent's context is
riddled with multiple mechanisms of oppression whose patriarchal
underpinning runs through subjects, discourses and institutions. In
order to disentangle the patriarchal thrust beneath this oppresive
labyrinth, the Latin American feminist must feel at ease with diverse
critical perspectives, for no one particular perspective will suffice to
deter the multiple manifestations of Latin American phallogocen-

trism. She welcomes a revision of fixed feminist positions that would in turn allow "dimensions of creativity, phantasy and pleasure, taste and style, to mix *aesthetic* pulsation with *will to change.*"

Guillermo Gómez-Peña, in his artwork, writing, and solo acts, embodies the problems of the border as they pertain to the the ideological mapping of the world (the geopolitical borders) as well as to the mapping of our identities (internal borders). His humor, just like Borges's, is corrosive; unlike Borges, whose fictions seek to undermine all temporal notions, the cultural and political urgency of the questions Gómez-Peña raises are immediate and present in an almost physical sense. Thus, we deemed it appropriate to begin with the vast and playful questions of one and close with the specific and playful questions of the other. His healthy mockery of physical borders allows us to close this anthology with a text that induces laughter. After the laughter comes a reflection quite fitting for an anthology about Latin America written in English: Where exactly is the United States located? Where exactly is Latin America located? Where is Latin America in the United States and so on, and so forth.

Eduardo Mendieta and Pedro Lange-Churión

NOTE

1. John Sturrock, *Paper Tigers: The Ideal Fictions of Jorge Luis Borges* (Oxford: Clarendon Press, 1977), p. 277.

PART I

Jorge Luis Borges

Jorge Luis Borges

NEW REFUTATION OF TIME

Vor mir war keine Zeit, nach mir wird keine seyn,
Mit mir gebiert sie sich, mit mir geht sie auch ein.
—Daniel von Czepko: *Sexcenta monodisticha*
sapientum (1655) III, ii

PROLOGUE

If published at the middle of the eighteenth century, this refutation
(or its name) would endure in the bibliographies of Hume and perhaps would have been mentioned by Huxley or Kemp Smith. Published in 1947—after Bergson—it is the anachronous reductio ad
absurdum of an obsolete system or, what is worse, the feeble machi-
nation of an Argentine adrift on the sea of metaphysics. Both conjec-
tures are verisimilar and perhaps true; to correct them I cannot
promise a startling conclusion in exchange for my rudimentary
dialectic. The thesis I shall expound is as ancient as Zeno's arrow of
the chariot of the Greek king in the *Milinda Pañha*; whatever novelty
it possesses consists in the application of Berkeley's classic instrument to that end. Berkeley and his successor, David Hume, abound
in paragraphs that contradict or exclude my thesis; nevertheless, I
believe I have deduced the inevitable consequence of their doctrine.

From Jorge Luis Borges, *Other Inquisitions, 1937–1952*, trans. Ruth L. C. Simms
(Austin: University of Texas Press, 1965). Reprinted with permission.

The first article (A) is from 1944 and appeared in No. 115 of *Sur*; the second article (B), from 1946, is a revision of the first. I deliberately did not combine the two into one article, because I knew that the reading of the two similar texts could facilitate the understanding of an indocile subject.

A word about the title. I am not unaware that it is an example of the monster which logicians have called *contradictio in adjecto*, because to say that a refutation of time is new (or old) is to attribute to it a predicate of a temporal nature, which restores the notion that the subject attempts to destroy. But I shall let it stand, so that this very subtle joke may prove that I do not exaggerate the importance of these word games. Apart from that, our language is so saturated and animated with time that it is very possible that not one line in [these pages] does not somehow demand or invoke it.

I dedicate these studies to my ancestor, Juan Crisóstomo Lafunur (1797–1824), who has left Argentine letters some memorable poetry, and who tried to reform the teaching of philosophy by purifying it from theological shadows and exposing the principles of Locke and Condillac. He died in exile; like all men, he was born at the wrong time.

J.L.B.
Buenos Aires, December 23, 1946

A

I

In the course of a life dedicated to literature and, occasionally, to metaphysical perplexity, I have perceived or sensed a refutation of time, which I myself disbelieve, but which comes to visit me at night and in the weary dawn with the illusory force of an axiom. That refutation is in all my books in one way or another: there is a prefiguring of it in the poems "Inscripción en cualquier sepulcro" and "El truco," from my volume of poetry *Fervor de Buenos Aires* (1923); it is declared in two articles in my book *Inquisiciones* (1925), on page 46 of *Evaristo Carriego* (1930), in the story "Sentirse en muerte" from my *Historia de la eternidad* (1936), and in the note on page 24 of my *El jardin de senderos que se bifurcan* (1942). None of the texts I have enumerated satisfies me, not even "Sentirse en muerte," which is less demonstrative and reasoned than divinatory and pathetic. I shall try to consolidate them all with this article.

Two arguments led me to this refutation: Berkeley's idealism and Leibniz's principle of indiscernibles.

Berkeley (*The Principles of Human Knowledge*, 3) observed:

> That neither our thoughts, nor passions, nor ideas formed by the imagination, exist without the mind, is what everybody will allow.— And to me it is no less evident that the various *Sensations*, or *ideas imprinted on the sense*, however blended or combined together (that is, whatever *objects* they compose), cannot exist otherwise than in a mind perceiving them. . . . The table I write on I say exists, that is, I see and feel it; and if I were out of my study I should say it existed—meaning thereby that if I was in my study I might perceive it, or that some other spirit actually does perceive it. . . . For as to what is said of the absolute existence of unthinking things without any relation to their being perceived, that is to me perfectly unintelligible. Their *esse* is *percipi*, nor is it possible they should have any existence out of the minds or thinking things which perceive them.

Foreseeing objections, he added in paragraph 23:

> But, say you, surely there is nothing easier than for me to imagine trees, for instance, in a park, or books existing in a closet, and nobody by to perceive them. I answer, you may so, there is no difficulty in it; but what is all this, I beseech you, more than framing in *your* mind certain ideas which you call books and trees, and at the same time omitting to frame the idea of any one that may perceive them? But do not you yourself perceive or think of them all the while? purpose: it only shews you have the power of imagining or forming ideas in your mind; but it does not shew that can conceive it possible the objects of your thought may exist without the mind.

In paragraph 6, he had already stated:

> Some truths there are so near and obvious to the mind that a man need only open his eyes to see them. Such I take this important one

to be, viz., that all the choir of heaven and furniture of the earth, in a word all those bodies which compose the mighty frame of the world, have not any subsistence without a mind—that their *being* is *to be perceived or known*; that consequently so long as they are not actually perceived by me, or do not exist in my mind or that of any other created spirit, they must either have no existence at all, or else subsist in the mind of some Eternal Spirit.

That, in the words of its inventor, is the idealist doctrine. Understanding it is easy; the difficult thing is to think within its limits. Schopenhauer himself, when he explains it, commits culpable negligences. In the first lines of the first book of his *Welt als Wille und Vorstellung*—in 1819—he makes the following statement, which entitles him to the imperishable bewilderment of all men: "The world is my representation. The man who confesses this truth is well aware that he does not know a sun or an earth, but only some eyes that see a sun and a hand that feels the contact of an earth." That is to say, for the idealist Schopenhauer man's eyes and hand are less illusory or apparential than the earth and the sun. In 1844 he published a supplementary volume. In the first chapter he rediscovers and exaggerates the old error: he defines the universe as a cerebral phenomenon and distinguishes "the world in the head" from "the world outside of the head." But in 1713 Berkeley had made Philonous say: "The brain therefore you speak of, being a sensible thing, exists only in the mind. Now, I would fain know whether you think it reasonable to suppose, that one idea or thing existing in the mind, occasions all other ideas. And if you think so, pray how do you account for the origin of the primary idea or brain itself?"

The dualism or cerebralism of Schopenhauer can be opposed effectively to the monism of Spiller. The latter (*The Mind of Man*, 1902, Chapter 8) argues that the retina and the cutaneous surface invoked to explain the visual and the tactile are, in turn, two tactile and visual systems; and that the room we see (the "objective") is no larger than the imagined one (the "cerebral") and does not contain it, since they are two independent visual systems. Berkeley (*The Principles of Human Knowledge*, pages 10 and 116) also denied the primary qualities—the solidity and the extension of things—and absolute space.

Berkeley affirmed the continuous existence of objects, since even if some individual did not perceive them, God perceived them. More logically, Hume denied it (*A Treatise of Human Nature*, I, 4, 2). Berkeley affirmed personal identity, because "I myself am not my ideas, but somewhat else, a thinking, active principle" (*Dialogues*, 3). Hume, the skeptic, refuted it and made each man "a bundle or collection of different perceptions, which succeed each other with an inconceivable rapidity" (*A treatise*, I, 4, 6). They both affirm time: for Berkeley it is "the succession of ideas in my mind, which flow uniformly and is participated by all beings" (*The Principles of Human Knowledge*, 98); for Hume time "must be composed of indivisible moments" (*A treatise*, I, 2, 2).

I have amassed some quotations from the apologists of idealism, I have offered their canonical passages, I have been iterative and explicit, I have censured Schopenhauer (not without ingratitude), to help my reader penetrate that unstable mental world. A world of evanescent impressions; a world without matter or spirit, neither objective nor subjective; a world without the ideal architecture of space; a would made of time, of the absolute uniform time of the *Principia*; and indefatigable labyrinth, a chaos, a dream—the almost complete disintegration to which David Hume came.

Once the idealist argument is admitted, I believe that it is possible—perhaps inevitable—to go further. For Hume it is not licit to speak of the shape of the moon or of its color; the shape and the color *are* the moon; nor can one speak of the perceptions of the mind, since the mind is nothing more than a series of perceptions. The Cartesian "I think, therefore I am" is invalidated. To say " I think" is to postulate the ego; it is a *petitio principii*. In the eighteenth century Lichtenberg proposed that instead of "I think," we should say impersonally "it thinks," as we say "it thunders" or "it rains." I repeat: there is not a secret ego behind faces that governs actions and receives impressions; we are only the series of those imaginary actions and those errant impressions. The series? If we deny spirit and matter, which are continuities, and if we deny space also, I do not know what right we have to the continuity that is time.

Imagine any present. On a Mississippi night Huckleberry Finn awakens. The raft, lost in the partial darkness, is floating down the river. Perhaps the weather is cool. Huckleberry Finn recognizes the quiet relentless sound of water; he opens his eyes lazily. He sees a vague number of stars, he sees an indistinct streak of trees; then he sinks into an immemorial sleep that envelopes him like murky water.[1] The metaphysics of idealism declare that it is risky and futile to add a material substance (the object) and a spiritual substance (the subject) to those perceptions. I maintain that it is no less illogical to think that they are terms of a series whose beginning is as inconceivable as its end. To add to the river and the shore perceived by Huck the notion of another substantive river and another shore, to add another perception to that immediate network of perceptions is, for idealism, unjustifiable. For me, it is no less unjustifiable to add chronological precision: the fact, for example, that the event occurred on June 7, 1849, between 4:10 and 4:11 A.M. Or in other words: I deny, with the arguments of idealism, the vast temporal series that idealism admits. Hume has denied the existence of absolute space, in which each thing has its place; I deny the existence of one time, in which all events are linked together. To deny coexistence is no less difficult than to deny succession.

I deny the successive, in a large number of cases; I deny the contemporaneous also, in a large number of cases. The lover who thinks, "While I was so happy thinking of my loved one's fidelity, she was deceiving me," deceives himself: if each state we live is absolute, that happiness was not contemporaneous with that deceit; the discovery of that deceit is one more state, incapable of modifying the "previous" ones, but not the remembrance of them. The misfortune of today is no more real than past happiness. I shall give a more concrete example. At the beginning of August 1824 Captain Isidoro Suárez, leading a squadron of Peruvian Hussars, achieved the victory of Junin; at the beginning of August 1824 De Quincey published a diatribe against *Wilhelm Meisters Lehrjahre*. Those events were not contemporaneous (they are now), for the two men died, Suárez in the city of Montevideo, De Quincey in Edinburgh, each without knowing of the other. Every instant is autonomous. Neither revenge nor pardon nor prisons nor even oblivion can modify the invulnerable past. No less vain to me are hope and fear, which always relate to future events: that is, to events that will not happen to us, who are the minutiae of the present. I am told that the present, the "specious present" of the psychologists, lasts between several seconds and a tiny fraction of a second; that is how long the history of the universe lasts. Or rather, there is no such history, as there is no life of a man, nor even one of his nights; each moment we live exists, not its imaginary aggregate. The universe, the sum of all the events, is a collection that is no less ideal than that of all the horses Shakespeare dreamed—one, many, none?—between 1592 and 1594. I might add that if time is a mental process, how can it be shared by thousands, or even two different men?

Interrupted and burdened by examples, the argument of the foregoing paragraphs may seem intricate. I shall try a more direct method. Let us consider a life in which repetitions are abundant; mine, for example. I never pass Recoleta cemetery without remembering that my father, my grandparents, and my great grandparents are buried there, as I shall be; then I remember that I have already remembered that, many times before. I cannot walk down my neighborhood streets in the solitude of night without thinking that night is pleasing to us because, like memory, it erases idle details. I cannot mourn the loss of a love or a friendship without reflection that one can lose only what one has never really had. Each time I come to a certain place in the South, I think of you, Helen; each time the air brings me a scent of eucalyptus, I think of Adrogué, in my childhood; each time I remember Fragment 91 of Heraclitus: "You will not go down twice the same river," I admire his dialectic skill, because the facility with which we accept the first meaning ("The river is different") clandestinely imposes the second one ("I am different") and gives us the illusion of having invented it. Each time I hear a Germanophile vituperating Yiddish, I pause and think that Yiddish is, after all, a German dialect, barely maculated by language of the Holy Spirit. Those tautologies (and others I shall not disclose) are my whole life. Naturally, they are repeated without precision; there are differences of emphasis, temperature, light, general physiological state. But I suspect that the number of circumstantial variations is not infinite: we can postulate, in the mind of an individual (or of two individuals who do not know

each other, but on whom the same process is acting), two identical
moments. Having postulated that identity, we must ask: Are those
identical moments the same? Is a *single repeated term* enough to disrupt and confound the series of time? Are the enthusiasts who devote
a lifetime to a line by Shakespeare not literally Shakespeare?

I am still not certain of the ethics of the system I have outlined. I do
not know whether it exists. The fifth paragraph of chapter 4 in the *San-
hedrin* of the Mishnah declares that, for the Justice of God, he who kills
a single man destroys the world; if there is no plurality, he who annihilated all men would be no more guilty than the primitive and solitary
Cain, which is orthodox, nor more universal in his destruction, which
can be magic. I believe that is true. The tumultuous general catastro-
phes—fires, wars, epidemics—are but a single sorrow, illusorily multiplied in many mirrors. That is Bernard Shaw's judgement when he states
(*Guide to Socialism, 86*) that what one person can suffer is the maximum
that can be suffered on earth. If one person dies of inanition, he will
suffer all the inanition that has been or will be. If 10,000 persons die with
him, he will not be 10,000 hungrier nor will he suffer 10,000 longer.
There is no point in being overwhelmed by the appalling total of human
suffering; such a total does not exist. Neither poverty nor pain is accu-
mulable. Compare also *The Problem of Pain* (VII) by C. S. Lewis.

Lucretius (*De rerum natura*, I, 830) attributes to Anaxagoras the
doctrine that gold consists of particles of gold; fire, of sparks; bone, of
imperceptible little bones. Josiah Royce, perhaps influenced by St.
Augustine, believes that time consists of time and that "Every now within
which something happens is therefore *also* a succession" (*The World and
the Individual*, II, 139) That proposition is compatible with my own.

II

All language is of a successive nature; it is not an effective tool for reasoning the eternal, the intemporal. Those who were displeased with the
foregoing argumentation might prefer this piece from 1928, which is
part of the story "Sentirse en Muerte," mentioned earlier in this article.

And here I should like to record an experience I had several nights ago: too evanescent and ecstatic a trifle to be called an adventure; too unreasonable and sentimental to be a thought. There is a scene and a word: a word I had said before but never lived with complete dedication until that night. I shall relate it now, with the accidents of time and place that brought about its revelation.

I remember it this way. I had spent the afternoon in Barracas, a place rarely visited, a place whose very distance from the scene of my later wanderings gave an aura of strangeness to that day. As I had nothing to do in the evening and the weather was fair, I went out after dinner to walk and remember. I did not wish to have a set destination. I followed a random course, as much as possible; I accepted, with no conscious prejudice other than avoiding the avenues or wide streets, the most obscure invitations of chance. But a kind of familiar gravitation drew me toward certain sections I shall always remember, for they arouse in me a kind of reverence. I am not speaking of the precise environment of my childhood, my own neighborhood, but of the still mysterious fringe area beyond it, which I have possessed completely in words and but little in reality, an area that is familiar and mythological at the same time. The opposite of the known —its wrong side, so to speak—are those streets to me, almost as completely hidden as the buried foundation of our house or our invisible skeleton.

The walk brought me to a corner. I breathed the night, feeling the peaceful respite from thought. The sight that greeted my eyes, uncomplicated to be sure, seemed simplified by my fatigue. Its very typicality made it unreal. The street was lined with low houses, and, although the first impression was poverty, the second was surely happiness. The street was very poor and very pretty. None of the houses stood out from the rest; the fig tree cast a shadow; the doors—higher than the elongated lines of the walls—seemed to be made of the same infinite substance as the night. The footpath ran along steeply above the street, which was of elemental clay, clay of a still unconquered America. To the rear the alley was already the pampa, descending toward the Maldonado. On the muddy and chaotic ground a rose-colored adobe wall seemed not to harbor moonglow but to shed a light of its own. I suspect that there can be no better way of denoting tenderness than by means of that rose color.

I stood there looking at that simplicity. I thought, no doubt aloud, "This is the same as it was thirty years ago." I guessed at the date: a recent time in other countries, but already remote in this changing part of the world. Perhaps a bird was singing and I felt for him a small, bird-sized affection. What stands out most clearly: in the already vertiginous silence the only noise was the intemporal sound of the crickets. The easy thought, "I am in the 1800s," ceased to be a few careless words and deepened into reality. I felt dead—that I was an abstract perceiver of the world; I felt an undefined fear imbued with knowledge, the supreme clarity of metaphysics. No, I did not believe I had traveled across the presumptive waters of time; rather I suspected I was the possessor of the reticent or absent meaning of the inconceivable word "eternity." Only later was I able to define that imagining.

And now I shall write it like this: that pure representation of homogeneous facts—clear night, limpid wall, rural scent of honeysuckle, elemental clay—is not merely identical to the scene on that corner so many years ago; it is, without similarities or repetitions, the same. If we can perceive that identity, time is a delusion: the indifference and inseparability of one moment of time's apparent yesterday and another of its apparent today are enough to disintegrate it.

It is evident that the number of these human moments is not infinite. The basic ones are still more impersonal—moments of physical suffering and physical joy, of the approach of sleep, of the hearing of a single piece of music, of much intensity or much dejection. This is the conclusion I derive: life is too poor not to be immortal. But we do not even possess the certainty of our poverty, since time, easily refutable in the area of the senses, is not so easily refutable in the intellectual sphere, from whose essence the concept of succession seems inseparable. So then, let my intimation of an idea remain as an emotional anecdote. The real moment of ecstasy and the possible insinuation of eternity which that night so generously bestowed on me will be crystallized in the avowed irresolution of these pages.

B

Of the many doctrines recorded by the history of philosophy, idealism is perhaps the most ancient and the most widely divulged. The observation is Carlyle's (*Novalis*, 1829). Without any hope of completing the infinite census, I should like to add to the philosophers he mentioned the Platonists, for whom prototypes are the only reality (Norris, Judah Abrabanel, Gemistus, Plotinus); the theologians, for whom everything that is not the divinity is contingent (Malebranche, Johannes Eckhart); the monists, who make of the universe a vain adjective of the Absolute (Bradley, Hegel, Parmenides). Idealism is as old as metaphysical inquietude. Its most clever apologist, George Berkeley, flourished in the eighteenth century. Contrary to Schopenhauer's statement (*Welt als Wille und Vorstellung, II, I*), Berkeley's merit could not have consisted in the intuitive perception of that doctrine, but in the arguments he conceived to reason it. Berkeley utilized those arguments against the notion of matter; Hume applied them to consciousness. My purpose is to apply them to time. But first I shall summarize briefly the various stages of that dialectic.

Berkeley denied matter. That does not mean, it should be understood, that he denied colors, odors, flavors, sounds, and contacts. What he denied was that, outside of those perceptions or components of the eternal world, there was an invisible, intangible something called matter. He denied that there were pains that no one feels, colors that no one sees, forms that no one touches. He reasoned that to add matter to perceptions is to add to the world an inconceivable superfluous world. He believed in the apparential world fabricated by the senses, but he considered that the material world (Toland's, say) was an illusory duplication. He observed (*The Principles of Human Knowledge*, 3):

> That neither our thoughts, nor passions, nor ideas formed by the imagination, exist without the mind, is what everybody will allow.—
> And to me it is no less evident that the various *Sensations*, or *ideas imprinted on the sense*, however blended or combined together (that is, whatever objects they compose), cannot exist otherwise than in a mind perceiving them. . . . The table I write on I say exists, that is, I see and feel it; and if I were out of my study I should

say it existed—meaning thereby that if I was in my study I might perceive it, or that some other spirit actually does perceive it. . . . For as to what is said of the absolute existence of unthinking things without any relation to their being perceived, that is to me perfectly unintelligible. Their *esse* is *percipi*, nor is it possible they should have any existence out of the minds or thinking things which perceive them.

Foreseeing objections, he added in paragraph 23:

But, say you, surely there is nothing easier than for me to imagine trees, for instance, in a park, or books existing in a closet, and nobody by to perceive them. I answer, you may so, there is no difficulty in it; but what is all this, I beseech you, more than framing in *your* mind certain ideas which you call books and trees, and at the same time omitting to frame the idea of any one that may perceive them? But do not you yourself perceive or think of them all the while? This therefore is nothing to the purpose; it only shews you have the power of imagining or forming ideas in you mind; but it does not shew that you can conceive it possible the objects of your thought may exist without the mind.

In paragraph 6 he had already stated:

Some truths are so near and obvious to the mind that a man need only open his eyes to see them. Such I take this important one to be, viz., that all the choir of heaven and furniture of the earth, in a word all those bodies which compose the mighty frame of the world, have not any subsistence without a mind— that their *being* is *to be perveived or known*; that consequently so long as they are not actually perceived by me, or do not exist in my mind or that of any other created spirit, they must either have no existence at all, or else subsist in the mind of some Eternal Spirit.

(Berkeley's God is a ubiquitous spectator whose purpose is to give coherence to the world.)

The doctrine I have just expounded has been misinterpreted. Herbert Spencer believes he refutes it (*Principles of Psychology,* VIII, 6) by reasoning that if there is nothing but consciousness, then it must be infinite in time and space. It is true that consciousness is infinite in time if we understand that all time is time perceived by someone, and false if we infer that that time must, necessarily, span an infinite number of centuries. That consciousness must be infinite in space is illicit, since Berkeley (*The Principles of Human Knowlege*, 116; *Siris*, 266) repeatedly denied absolute space. Even more indecipherable is the error Schopenhauer makes (*Welt als Wille und Vorstellung*, II, I) when he teaches that for the idealists the world is a cerebral phenomenon. However, Berkeley had written (*Dialogues Between Hylas and Philonous*, II): "The brain . . . being a sensible thing, exists only in the mind. Now, I would fain know whether you think it reasonable to suppose, that one idea or thing existing in the mind, occasions all other ideas. And if you think so, pray how do you account for the origin of that primary idea or brain itself?" The brain, in fact, is no less a part of the external world than the constellation Centaurus.

Berkeley denied that there was an object behind sense impressions. David Hume denied that there was a subject behind the perception of changes. Berkeley denied matter; Hume denied the spirit. Berkeley did not wish us to add the mataphysical notion of matter to the succession of impressions, while Hume did not wish us to add the metaphysical notion of a self to the succession of mental states. This amplification of Berkeley's arguments is so logical that Berkeley had alreeady foreseen it, as Alexander Campbell Fraser points out, and had even tried to confute it by means of the Cartesian *ergo sum*. Hylas, foreshadowing David Hume, had said in the third and last of the *Dialogues*: "in consequence of your own principles, it should follow that you are only a system of floating ideas, without any substance to support them. . . . And there is no more meaning in spiritual substance than in material substance, the one is to be exploded as well as the other." Hume corroborates this:

> I may venture to affirm of the rest of mandkind, that they are nothing but a bundle or collection of different perceptions, which succeed each other with an inconceivable rapidity. . . . The mind is a kind of theatre, where several perceptions successively make their appearance; pass, repass, glide away, and mingle in an infinite variety of postures and situations. . . . The comparison of the theatre must not mislead us. They are the successive perceptions only, that constitute the mind; nor have we the most distant notion of the

place where these scenes are represented, or of the materials of which it is composed. (*A Treatise of Human Nature*, I, 4, 6)

Having admitted the idealist argument, I believe it is possible—perhaps inevitable—to go further. For Berkeley, time is "the succession of ideas . . . which flows uniformly and is participated by all beings" (*The Principles of Human Knowledge*, 98); for Hume, it is "composed of indivisible moments" (*A Treatise of Human Nature*, I, 2, 2). Nevertheless, having denied matter and spirit, which are continuities, and having denied space also, I do not know with what right we shall retain the continuity that is time. Outside of each perception (actual or conjectural) matter does not exist; outside of each mental state the spirit does not exist; nor will time exist ouside of each present instant. Let us select a moment of the greatest simplicity, that of the dream of Chuang Tzu (Herbert Allen Giles, *Chuang Tzu*, 1889). Around 2,400 years ago Chuang Tzu dreamed that he was a butterfly and when he awakened he did not know if he was a man who had dreamed he was a butterfly, or a butterfly dreaming it was a man. Let us not consider the awakening; let us consider the moment of the dream; or one of the moments. "I dreamed that I was a butterfly flying through the air and that I knew nothing of Chuang Tzu," says the ancient text. We shall never know if Chuang Tzu saw a garden over which he seemed to be flying, or a moving yellow triangle, which was undoubtedly he himself, but we know that the image was subjective, although it was supplied by the memory. The doctrine of psychophysical parallelism will avow that this image must have been caused by some change in the dreamer's nervous system; according to Berkeley, at that moment neither Chuang Tzu's body nor the black bedroom in which he dreamed existed, except as a perception in the divine mind. Hume simplifies it even more: at that moment Chuang Tzu's spirit did not exist; only the colors of the dream and the certainty of being a butterfly existed. It existed as a momentary term of the "bundle or collection of different perceptions" which was, some four centuries before Christ, the mind of Chuang Tzu; they existed as term n of an infinite temporal series, between n − 1 and n + 1. There is no other reality for idealism than that of the mental processes; to add to the butterfly that is percieved an objective butterfly seems to be a vain duplication; to add an ego to the processes seems no less excessive. It acknowledges that there was a dreaming, a perceiving, but not a dreamer or even a dream; and that to speak of objects and of subjects is to gravitate toward an impure mythology. Now then, if each psychic state is self sufficient, if to connect it to a circumstance or to an ego is an illicit and vain addition, what right have we to impose on it, later, a place in time? Chuang Tzu dreamed that he was a butterfly and during that dream he was not Chuang Tzu—he was a butterfly. How, having abolished space and the ego, shall we connect those instants to the instants of awakening and to the feudal age of Chinese history? That does not mean that we shall never know, even approximately, the date of the dream; it means that the chronological determination of an event, of any event on earth, is alien and exterior to the event. In China, Chuang Tzu's dream is proverbial; imagine that one of its almost infinite readers dreams he is a butterfly and then that he is Chuang Tzu. Imagine that, by a not impossible chance, this dream is an exact repetition of the master's dream. Having postulated that identity, we must ask: Those instants that coincide—are they not the same? Is not *one single repeated term* enough to disrupt and confound the history of the world, to tell us that there is no such history?

To deny time is really two denials: the denial of the succession of the terms of a series, the denial of the synchronism of the terms of two series. In fact, if each term is absolute, its relations are reduced to the consciousness that those relations exist. One state precedes another if it is known to be anterior to it; State G is contemporaneous with State H if it is known to be contemporaneous with it. Contrary to Schopenhauer's declaration[2] in his table of fundamental truths (*Welt als Wille und Vorstellung*, II, 4), each fraction of time does not fill all space simultaneously, time is not ubiquitous. (Naturally, at this stage of the argument, space no longer exists.)

Meinong, in his theory of apprehension, admits the apprehension of imaginary objects: the fourth dimension, say, or the sensible statue of Condillac, or the hypothetical animal of Lotze, or the square root of minus one. If the reasons I have indicated are valid, then matter, the ego, the external world, universal history, our lives also belong to that nebulous orb.

Furthermore, the phrase *negation of time* is ambigous. It can mean the eternity of Plato or Boethius and also the dilemmas of Sextus Empiricus. The latter (*Adversus mathematicos*, XI, 197) denies the past, which already was, and the future, which has not yet been, and argues that the present is divisible or indivisible. It is not indivisible, because in that case it would have no beginning that would connect it to the past nor end that would connect it to the future, nor even a middle, because a thing that has no beginning and end cannot have a middle; neither is it divisible, because in that case it would consist of a part that was and another part that is not. *Ergo*, the present does not exist, and since the past and future do not exist either, time does not exist. F. H. Bradley rediscovers and improves that perplexity. He observes (*Appearance and Reality*, IV) that if the now is divisible into other nows it is less complicated than time, and if it is indivisible, time is a mere relation between intemporal things. As you see, those reasonings deny the parts in order to deny the whole; I reject the whole to exalt each one of the parts. By the dialectic of Berkeley and Hume I have arrived at Schopenhauer's statement:

> The form of the appearance of the will is only the present, not the past or the future; the latter do not exist except in the concept and by the linking of the consciousness, submitted to the principle of reason. No one has lived in the past, no one will live in the future; the present is the form of all life, it is a possession that no misfortune can take away. . . . Time is like an infinitely rotating circle: the descending arc is the past, the ascending one is the future; above, there is an indivisible point that touches the tangent and is the now. . . . Motionless like the tangent, that extensionless point marks the contact of the object, whose form is time, with the subject, which is formless, because it does not belong to the knowable and is a preliminary condition of knowledge. (*Welt als Wille und Vorstellung*, I, 54)

A Buddist tract from the fifth century, the *Visuddhimagga* (Way of Purity), illustrates the same doctrine with the same figure: "Strictly speaking, the life of a being has the duration of an idea. As a carriage wheel touches the ground in only one place when it turns, life lasts as long as a single idea" (Radhakrishnan, *Indian philosophy*, I, 373). Other Buddhist texts say that the world is annihilated and resurges again 6,500,000,000 times a day and that every man is an illusion, vertiginously made of a series of momentary and lone men. "The man of a past moment," says the *Way of Purity*, "has lived, but he does not live nor will he live; the man of a future moment will live, but he has not lived nor does he live; the man of the present moment lives, but he has not lived nor will he live" (*Indian Philosophy*, I, 407). We can compare this with the words of Plutarch: "The man of yesterday has died in the man of today, the man of today dies in the man of tomorrow" (*De E apud Delphos*, 18).

And yet, and yet—to deny temporal succession, to deny the ego, to deny the astronomical universe, are apparent desperations and secret assuagements. Our destiny (unlike the hell of Swedenborg and the hell of Tibetan mythology) is not horrible because of its unreality; it is horrible because it is irreversible and ironbound. Time is the substance I am made of. Time is a river that carries me away, but I am the river; it is a tiger that mangles me, but I am the tiger; it is a fire that consumes me, but I am the fire. The world, alas, is real; I, alas, am Borges.

NOTE TO THE PROLOGUE

All expositions of Buddhism mention the *Milinda Pañha*, an apologetic work from the second century, which relates a discussion between the King of the Bactrians, Menander, and the monk Nagasena. The latter reasons that as the King's Chariot is not the wheels, nor the body, nor the axis, nor the pole, nor the yoke, neither is man matter, form, impressions, ideas, instincts, or consciousness. He is not the combination of those parts nor does he exists apart from them. After a controversy that lasts for many days, Menander (Milinda) is converted to the faith of the Buddha.

The *Milinda Pañha* has been translated into English by Rhys Davids (Oxford, 1890–94).

NOTES

1. For the facility of the reader, I have selected an instant between two dreams, a literary instant, not a historical one. If anyone suspects a fallacy, he can insert another example; from his own life, if he wishes.

2. And previously by Newton, who affirmed: "Each particle of space is eternal, each indivisible moment of duration is everywhere" (*Principia*, III, 42).

PART 2

Latin American "Postmodernity" as the Perennial Crisis of Hegemonic Perspectives

Octavio Paz

IN SEARCH OF THE PRESENT

I begin with two words that men have uttered since the dawn of humanity: Thank you. The word *gratitude* has equivalents in every language, and in each tongue its range of meanings is abundant. In the Romance languages this breadth spans the spiritual and the physical, from the divine grace conceded to men to deliver them from error and death, to the bodily grace of the dancing girl or of the cat leaping through the underbrush. Grace means pardon, forgiveness, favor, benefice, inspiration. It is a form of address, a pleasing style of speaking or painting, a gesture expressing politeness, and—in short—an act that reveals spiritual goodness. Grace is a gift. The person who receives it, the favored one, is grateful; and if he is not base, he expresses his gratitude. That is what I am doing at this very moment with these weightless words. I hope my emotion compensates for their weightlessness. If each of my words were a drop of water, you would see through them and glimpse what I feel. Gratitude, acknowledgment. Also an indefinable mixture of fear and surprise at finding myself here before you, in this place which is the home of both Swedish learning and world literature.

Languages are vast realities that transcend those political entities we call nations. The European languages we speak in the Americas

Octavio Paz, *In Search of the Present*, 1990 Nobel Lecture—Bilingual Education, translated by Anthony Stanton (New York: Harcurt Brace Jovanovich, 1990). Copyright © 1990 The Nobel Foundation. Reprinted with permission of The Nobel Foundation.

illustrate this. The special position of our literatures, when compared to those of England, Spain, Portugal, and France, derives precisely from this fundamental fact: they are literatures written in transplanted tongues. Languages are born and grow in the native soil, nourished by a common history. The European languages were uprooted and taken to an unknown and unnamed world: in the new soil of the societies of America, they grew and were transformed. The same plant, yet a different plant. Our literatures did not passively accept the changing fortunes of their transplanted languages: they participated in the process and even accelerated it. Soon they ceased to be mere transatlantic reflections. At times they have been the negation of the literatures of Europe; more often, they have been a reply.

In spite of these oscillations, the link has never been broken. My classics are those of my language, and I consider myself to be a descendant of Lope and Quevedo, as any Spanish writer would . . . yet I am not a Spaniard. I think that most writers of Spanish America as well as those from the United States, Brazil, and Canada would say the same as regards the English, Portuguese, and French traditions. To understand more clearly the special position of writers in the Americas, we should compare it to the dialogue maintained by Japanese, Chinese, or Arabic writers with the different literatures of Europe: a dialogue that cuts across multiple languages and civilizations. Our dialogue, on the other hand, takes place within the same language. We are Europeans, yet we are not Europeans. What are we, then? It is difficult to define what we are, but our works speak for us.

In the field of literature, the great novelty of the present century has been the appearance of the American literatures. The first to appear was that of the English-speaking part, and then, in the second half of the twentieth century, that of Latin America in its two great branches, Spanish America and Brazil. Although they are very different, these three literatures have one common feature: the conflict, which is more ideological than literary, between cosmopolitan and nativist tendencies, between Europeanism and Americanism. What is the legacy of this dispute? The polemics have disappeared; what remain are the works. Apart from this general resemblance, the dif-

ferences between the three literatures are multiple and profound.
One of them belongs more to history than to literature. The development of Anglo-American literature coincides with the rise of the
United States as a world power, whereas the rise of our literature
coincides with the political and social misfortunes —and upheavals—
of our nations. Which demonstrates once again the limitations of historical determinism: social disturbances and the decline of empires
sometimes coincide with moments of artistic and literary splendor. Li-
Po and Tu Fu witnessed the fall of the Tang dynasty; Velázquez
painted for Felipe IV; Seneca and Lucan were contemporaries, and
victims, of Nero. Other differences are of a literary nature and pertain more to individual works than to the character of each literature. But can we say that a literature has a *character*? Does it possess
a set of features that distinguishes it from other literatures? I doubt
it. A literature is not defined by some fanciful, intangible character;
it is, rather, a society of unique works united by relations of both
opposition and affinity.

The first basic difference between Latin-American and Anglo-
American literature lies in the diversity of their origins. Both began
as projections of Europe. In the case of North America, the projection of an island; in our case, of a peninsula. Two regions that are geographically, historically, and culturally eccentric. The origins of
North America are in England and the Reformation; ours are in
Spain, Portugal, and the Counter-Reformation. For the case of
Spanish America, I should briefly mention what separates Spain's
identity from those of other European countries. Spain is no less
eccentric than England, but its eccentricity is of a different kind. The
eccentricity of the English is insular and is characterized by isolation:
an eccentricity that excludes. Hispanic eccentricity is peninsular,
consisting of the coexistence of different civilizations and different
pasts: an eccentricity that includes. In what would later be Catholic
Spain, the Visigoths professed the heresy of Arianism, and we could
speak also about the centuries of the dominance of Arabic civilization, the influence of Jewish thought, and the Reconquest, among
other peculiarities.

Hispanic eccentricity is reproduced and multiplied in America, especially in countries such as Mexico and Peru, where ancient and splendid civilizations once existed. In Mexico the Spaniards encountered history as well as geography. And that history still lives: it is a present rather than a past. The temples and gods of pre-Columbian Mexico may be a pile of ruins, but the spirit that breathed life into that world has not disappeared; it speaks to us in the hermetic language of myth and legend, in forms of social coexistence, in popular art, in customs. Being a Mexican writer means listening to the voice of that present—that presence. Listening to it, speaking with it, deciphering it, expressing it. . . . After this brief digression we may be able to perceive the peculiar relation that simultaneously binds us to and separates us from the European tradition.

The consciousness of being separate is a constant feature of our spiritual history. This separation is sometimes experienced as a wound that marks an internal division, and anguished awareness that invites introspection; at other times it appears as a challenge, a spur to action, to go forth into the outside world and encounter others. It is true that the feeling of separation is universal and not peculiar to Spanish Americans. It is born at the very moment of our birth: as we are wrenched from the Whole, we fall into a foreign land. This never-healing wound is the unfathomable depth of every man. All our ventures and exploits, all our acts and dreams, are bridges designed to overcome the separation and reunite us with the world and our fellow beings. Each man's life and the collective history of humanity can thus be seen as an attempt to reconstruct the original situation. An unfinished and endless cure for our divided condition. But it is not my intention to provide yet another description of this feeling. I am simply stressing the fact that for us this existential need expresses itself in historical terms. It thus becomes an awareness of our history. How and when does this feeling appear and how is it transformed into consciousness? The reply to this double-edged question can be given in the form of a theory or a personal testimony. I prefer the latter, for there are many theories and none is entirely convincing.

The feeling of separation is bound up with the oldest and vaguest of my memories: the first cry, the first scare. Like every child, I built emotional bridges in the imagination to link me to the world and to other people. I lived in a town on the outskirts of Mexico City, in an old dilapidated house that had a junglelike garden an a great room full of books. First games and first lessons. The garden soon became the center of my world; the library, an enchanted cave. I read alone but played with my cousins and schoolmates. There was fig tree, temple of vegetation, four pine trees, three ash trees, and prickly plants that produced purple grazes. Adobe walls. Time was elastic; space was a spinning wheel. All time, past or future, real or imaginary, was pure presence, and space transformed itself ceaselessly. The beyond was here, all was here: a valley, a mountain, a distant country, the neighbors' patio. Books with pictures, especially history books, eagerly leafed through, supplied images of deserts and jungles, palaces and hovels, warriors and princesses, beggars and kings. We were shipwrecked with Sinbad and with Robinson Crusoe, we fought with D'Artagnan, we took Valencia with the Cid. How I would have liked to stay forever on the Isle of Calypso! In summer the green branches of the fig tree would sway like the sails of a caravel or a pirate ship. High up on the mast, swept by the wind, I could make out islands and continents, lands that vanished as soon as they became tangible. The world was limitless yet always within reach, and time, pliable, weaved a seamless present.

When was the spell broken? Gradually rather than suddenly. It is hard to accept betrayal by a friend, deception by the woman we love, or learn that freedom is the mask of a tyrant. This discovery is a slow and tricky process, because we ourselves are the accomplices of the betrayals and deceptions. Nevertheless, I can remember fairly clearly an incident that was the first sign, although it was quickly forgotten. I must have been about six. One of my cousins, who was a little older, showed me a North American magazine with a photograph of soldiers marching down a wide avenue, probably in New York. "They've returned from the war," she said. These few words disturbed me, as if they foreshadowed the end of the world or the Second Coming. I vaguely knew that somewhere far away a war had ended and that the soldiers were marching to celebrate their victory. But for me, that war had taken place in another time, not here and now. The photograph refuted me. I felt dislodged from the present.

After that, time began to fracture more and more. And space, to multiply. The experience was repeated with increasing frequency. Any piece of information, a harmless phrase, the headline in a newspaper, proved the outside world's existence and my own unreality. I felt that my world was disintegrating, that the real present was somewhere else. My time—the time of the garden, the games with friends, the drowsiness in the grass at three in the afternoon, under the sun, a fig torn open (black and red like a live coal, yet sweet and fresh)— was a fictitious time. In spite of what my senses told me, the time from over there, belonging to the others, was the real one. I accepted the inevitable. That was how my expulsion from the present began.

It may seem paradoxical to say that we have been expelled from the present, and it is a feeling we have all had at some moment. Some of us experienced it first as a condemnation, later transformed into consciousness and action. The search for the present is not the pursuit of an earthly paradise or of a timeless eternity; it is the search for reality. For us Spanish Americans this present was not in our own countries: it was the time lived by others—by the English, the French, the Germans. It was the time of New York, Paris, London. We had to go and look for it and bring it back home. These years were also the years of my discovery of literature. I began writing poems. I did not know what made me write them; I was moved by an inner need that is difficult to define. Only now have I understood that there was a secret relationship between what I have called my expulsion from the present and the writing of poetry. Poetry, in love with the instant, seeks to relive it in the poem, thus separating it from sequential time and turning it into a fixed present. But at that time I wrote without wondering why I was doing it. I was searching for the gateway to the present: I wanted to belong to my time and to my century. Later, this desire became an obsession: I wanted to be a modern poet. My search for modernity had begun.

What is modernity? It is, first of all, an ambiguous term: there are as many types of modernity as there are societies. Each society has its own. The word's meaning is as uncertain and arbitrary as the name of the period that precedes it, the Middle Ages. If we are modern when compared to medieval times, are we perhaps the Middle

Ages of a future modernity? Is a name that changes with time a real name? Modernity is a word in search of its meaning. Is it an idea, a mirage or a moment of history? Are we the children of modernity or are we its creators? Nobody knows for sure. Nor does it matter much: we follow it, we pursue it. For me at that time modernity was fused with the present or, rather, produced it: the present was modernity's final and supreme flower. My case is not unique, not exceptional: from the Symbolist period, all modern poets have chased after that magnetic and elusive figure. Baudelaire was the first. He was also the first to touch her and discover that she is nothing but time that crumbles in one's hands. I am not going to relate my adventures in pursuit of modernity; they are not very different from those of other twentieth-century poets. Modernity has been a universal passion. Since 1850 she has been our goddess and our demoness. In recent years there has been an attempt to exorcise her, and there has been much talk of "postmodernism." But what is postmodernism if not an even more modern modernity?

For us Latin Americans the search for poetic modernity runs historically parallel to the repeated attempts to modernize our countries. This movement begins at the end of the eighteenth century and includes Spain herself. While the United States was born into modernity and, as de Tocqeville observed, by 1830 was already the womb of the future, we were born at the moment when Spain and Portugal were moving away from modernity. This is why there was frequent talk of "Europeanizing" our countries: the modern was outside and had to be imported. In Mexico this precess began just before the War of Independence. Later, it became a great ideological and political debate that divided Mexican society throughout the nineteenth century. One event was to call into question not the legitimacy of the reform movement but the way in which it had been implemented: the Mexican Revolution. The Mexican Revolution, unlike its twentieth-century counterparts, was not the expression of a vaguely utopian ideology but rather the explosion of a reality that had been historically and psychologically repressed. It was not the work of a group of ideologists intent on introducing principles derived from a political theory; it was a popular uprising that unmasked what had been hidden. For this reason it was more of a revelation than a revolution. Mexico was searching for the present outside only to find it within, buried but alive. The search for modernity led us to discover our antiquity, the hidden face of the nation. I am not sure whether this unexpected historic lesson has been learned by all: that between tradition and modernity there is a bridge. When they are mutually isolated, tradition stagnates and modernity vaporizes; when joined, modernity breaths life into tradition, and tradition responds by providing depth and gravity.

The search for poetic modernity was a quest, in the allegorical and chivalric sense this word had in the twelfth century. Crossing several wastelands, visiting castles of mirrors, and camping among ghostly tribes, I found no grail. But I did discover the modern tradition. Because modernity is not a poetic school but a lineage, a family dispersed over several continents and which for two centuries has survived many sudden changes and misfortunes: public indifference, isolation, and tribunals in the name of religious, political, academic, and sexual orthodoxy. Being a tradition and not a doctrine, it has been able to persist and to change at the same time. This is also why it is so diverse. Each poetic adventure is distinct, and each poet has sown a different plant in the miraculous forest of speaking trees. Yet if the poems are different and each path distinct, what is it that unites these poets? Not an aesthetic but a search. My search was not fanciful, even though the idea of modernity is a mirage, a maze of reflections. One day I found myself back at the starting point: the search for modernity was a return to the origins. Modernity had led me to the source of my beginning, to my antiquity. Separation now became reconciliation. And so I learned that the poet is a pulse in the rhythmic flow of generations.

The idea of modernity is a by-product of our conception of history as a unique and linear process of succession. Although its origins are in Judeo-Christianity, it breaks with Christian doctrine. In Christianity, the cyclical time of pagan cultures is supplanted by unrepeatable history, something that has a beginning and will have an end. Sequential time was the profane time of history, an arena for the actions of fallen men, yet still governed by a sacred time which had neither beginning nor end. After Judgement Day there will be no future either in heaven or in hell. In the realm of eternity there is no succession, because everything *is*. Being triumphs over becoming. The new time, our modern conception of time, is linear like that of Christianity, but open to infinity and with no reference to eternity. Ours is the time of preface history, an irreversible and perpetually unfinished time that marches toward the future and not toward its end. History's sun is the future, and Progress is the name of this movement toward the future.

Christians see the world, or what used to be the *siécle* or worldly life, as a place of trial: souls can be either lost or saved in this world. In the new conception, the historical subject is not the individual soul but the human race, sometimes viewed as a whole and sometimes through a chosen group that represents it: the developed nations of the West, the proletariat, the white race, or some other entity. Both the pagan and Christian philosophical traditions had exalted Being as changeless perfection overflowing with plenitude; but we adore Change, the motor of progress and the model for our societies. Change articulates itself in two privileged ways: as evolution and as revolution. The trot and the leap. Modernity is the spearhead of historical movement, the incarnation of evolution or revolution, those two faces of progress. Finally, progress takes place thanks to the dual application of science and technology to the realm of nature and to the use of her immense resources.

Modern man has defined himself as a historical being. But earlier societies chose to define themselves in terms of other values and ideas. The Greeks, venerating the *polis* and the circle, were unaware of progress. Seneca, like the Stoics, was much concerned about the eternal return; Saint Augustine believed that the end of the world was imminent; and Saint Thomas constructed a scale of the degree of being, linking the smallest creatures to the Creator, and so on. One after the other, these ideas and beliefs were abandoned. It seems to me that the same decline is beginning to affect our idea of progress and , as a result, our vision of time, history, and ourselves. We are witnessing the twilight of the future. The decline of the idea of modernity and the popularity of the dubious notion of "postmodernism" are phenomena that affect not only literature and the arts. We are experiencing the crisis of the essential ideas and beliefs that have guided mankind for over two centuries. I have dealt with this matter at length elsewhere. Here I can only offer a brief summary.

In the first place, the concept of a process that is infinite and synonymous with endless progress has been called into question. I need hardly mention what everybody knows: our natural resources are finite and will one day be exhausted. In addition, we have inflicted what may be irreparable damage on the natural environment. And our own species is endangered. Science and technology, the instruments of progress, have shown with alarming clarity that they can easily become destructive forces. The existence of nuclear weapons is a refutation of the idea that progress in inherent in history. This refutation, I add, can only be called devastating.

In the second place, we have the fate of the historical subject, mankind, in the twentieth century. Seldom have nations or individuals suffered so much. Two world wars, tyrannies spread over five continents, the atomic bomb, and the proliferation of one of the cruelest and most lethal institutions known to man: the concentration camp. Modern technology has provided countless benefits, but it is impossible to close our eyes to the technologically assisted slaughter, torture, humiliation, and degradation inflicted on millions of innocent people in our century.

In the third place, the belief in the necessity of progress has been shaken. For our grandparents and our parents, the ruins of history (corpses, desolate battlefields, devastated cities) did not invalidate the underlying goodness of the historical process. The scaffolds and tyrannies, the conflicts and savage civil wars were the price to be paid for progress, the blood money to be offered to the god of history. A god? Yes, reason itself was deified, according to Hegel, and prodigal in cruel acts of cunning. The alleged rationality of history has vanished. Even in the very stronghold of order, regularity, and coherence—the pure science of mathematics—the old notions of accident and catastrophe have reappeared. This disturbing resurrection reminds me of the terrors that marked the advent of the millennium, and the anguish of the Aztecs at the end of each cosmic cycle.

The last element in this hasty enumeration is the collapse of all the philosophical and historical hypotheses that claimed to reveal the laws governing the course of history. The believers, confident that they held the keys to history, erected powerful states over pyramids of corpses. These arrogant constructions, destined in theory to liberate men, were very quickly transformed into gigantic prisons. Today we have seen them fall, overthrown not by their ideological enemies but by the impatience and the desire for freedom of the new generations. Is this the end of all utopias? It is the end, rather, of the idea of history as a phenomenon that can be predicted. Historical determinism has been shown to be a costly and bloodstained fantasy. History is unpredictable because its agent, mankind, is the personification of indeterminism.

This short review indicates that we are very probably at the end of a historical period and at the beginning of another. The end of the Modern Age, or merely a mutation of it? It is difficult to tell. In any case, the collapse of utopian schemes has left a great void—not in the countries where this ideology has been proved a failure, but in those where many embraced it with enthusiasm and hope. For the first time in history mankind lives in a sort of spiritual wilderness and not, as before, in the shadow of those religious and political systems that consoled us at the same time as they oppressed us. Although all societies are historical, each one has lived under the guidance and inspiration of a set of metahistorical beliefs and ideas. Ours is the first age that is ready to live without a metahistorical doctrine. Our absolutes, whether they be religious or philosophical, moral or aesthetic, are not collective and private. A dangerous experience, because it is impossible to know whether or not the tensions and conflicts unleashed in this privatization of ideas and beliefs that belonged traditionally to the public domain will end up by destroying the social fabric. Men could then become possessed once more by ancient religious fury or by fanatical nationalism. It would be terrible if the fall of the abstract idol of ideology were to foreshadow the resurrection of the buried passions of tribes, sects, and churches. The signs, unfortunately, are disturbing.

The decline of the ideologies I have called metahistorical, by which I mean those that assign to history a goal and a direction, implies the tacit abandonment of global solutions. With good sense, we tend more and more toward limited remedies to solve concrete problems. It is prudent to abstain from legislating about the future. Yet the present requires much more than attention to immediate needs; it demands global soul-searching. For a long time I have firmly believed that the twilight of the future heralds the advent of the now. To think about the now means first of all to recover the critical vision. For example, the triumph of the market economy (a triumph due to the adversary's default) cannot be simply a cause for joy. As a mechanism the market is efficient, but like all mechanisms it lacks both conscience and compassion. We must find a way of integrating it into society so that it expresses the social contract and becomes and instrument of justice and fairness. The advanced democratic societies have reached an enviable level of prosperity; at the same time they are island of abundance in an ocean of universal misery. And the market is inextricably connected to the deterioration of the environment. Pollution affects not only the air, the rivers, and the forests, but also our souls. A society possessed by the frantic need to produce more in order to consume more tends to reduce ideas, feelings, art, love, friendship, and people themselves to consumer goods. Everything becomes an item to be bought, used, and then thrown on the rubbish dump. No other society has produced so much waste as ours has. Material and moral waste.

Reflecting on the now does not mean relinquishing the future or forgetting about the past. The present is the meeting place for the two directions of time. It should not be confused with facile hedonism. True, the tree of pleasure does not grow in the past or in the future but only at this very moment; yet death, too, is a fruit of the present. It cannot be rejected, for it is part of life. Living well means dying well. We must learn how to look death in the face. The present is alternately luminous and somber, like a sphere that unites the two halves of action and contemplation. Thus, just as we have had philosophies of the past and of the future, of eternity and of the void, tomorrow we shall have a philosophy of the present. The poetic experience could be one of its foundations. What do we know about the present? Nothing or almost nothing. Yet the poets do know one thing; the present is the source of presences.

In this pilgrimage in search of modernity I lost my way at many points, only to find myself again. I returned to the source and discovered that modernity is not outside but within us. It is today and the most ancient antiquity; it is tomorrow and the beginning of the world; it is a thousand years old and yet newborn. It speaks in Nahuatl, draws Chinese ideograms from the ninth century, and appears on the television screen. This intact present, recently unearthed, shakes off the dust of centuries, smiles, and suddenly takes wing and flies out through the window. A simultaneous plurality of time and presence: modernity breaks with the immediate past only to recover and age-old past. It transforms a tiny fertility figure from the neolithic into our contemporary. We pursue modernity in her incessant metamorphoses yet we never catch her. Each encounter ends in flight. We embrace her, but she escapes, disappears immediately, and we clutch the air. The instant is the bird that is everywhere and nowhere. We want to trap it alive, but it flaps its wings and is gone in a spray of syllables. We are left empty handed. Then the door of perception opens slightly and the *other time* appears, the real time we had been seeking without knowing it: the present, the presence.

Leopoldo Zea

3

LATIN AMERICA AND THE PROBLEM OF MODERNITY

I. WALLS COLLAPSE

Nineteen eighty-nine was the beginning of a new history, the end of the century and end of the millennium. This was a key year in a history that will change in its totality. That very same year was celebrated the bicentennial of the French revolution. Michel Rocard, of France, recalls with euphoria the words of Victor Hugo: "In the twentieth century there will be a magnificent nation. It will not be called France, it will be called Europe, and the next century will be called humanity." This is the point of departure for a globalization that will encompass the whole of humanity. Mikhael Gorbachev, the man of *perestroika* in the Soviet Union, the artifice, without perhaps so intending, of the changes that will follow the euphoria, attended the festivities of the bicentennial of the French revolution that is related with the Russian socialist revolution of 1917, which he saw as an extension and amplification of the French. One sole and great revolution which will make of the twenty-first century that nation that will be called humanity. "The new epoch—said Gorbachev—demands that we interpret through a new optic the renowned slogans of the French revolution: liberty, equality, fraternity. As they preserve their historical vitality, these slogans acquire a different content;

From *Cuadernos Americanos: Nueva época* 4, no. 46 (July–August 1994): 11–28. Translated by Eduardo Mendieta.

namely: humanity will have a future if it is recognized that the freedom and the well being of all determines the well being and freedom of each people and each human being." It does not suffice to declare oneself free in order to be so fully free. The well being of other human beings has to be made possible as something proper to humanity. In this way, the revolution that was began in the eighteenth century is only the anticipation of the socialist revolution of the twentieth century. This already implies an equal distribution of efforts, sacrifices, and benefits.

Thus began the collapse of walls, fortifications, and of everything that divides Europe from the rest of the world. Only one great ideology at the service of humanity, its freedoms and necessities, is profiled. The countries within the socialist bloc emancipate themselves from the Soviet Union, justified by *perestroika* and without resistance from its directors. Thus opened for these peoples the possibility to enter the so-called free world that so much attempted to seduce them to shake off communism. There is no resistance within the Soviet Union. Within it, the peoples that formed it make similar demands for self-determination, what is proper to peoples who discover themselves different among themselves. The walls are brought down, the cold war ends and with it the arsenals of this war become obsolete. Similarly, there ends the ideological struggle. However, demons until now hidden are also unleashed. It will be these demons that will put an end to the euphoria of 1989.

2. NEW WALLS ARE ERECTED

The euphoria with respect to the possibility of a nation that in the twenty-first century will be called humanity, common European house, that could be a common house of humanity, will encounter obstacles. Gorbachev will encounter immediately such as that of Mitterrand who asks: Common house? Its dwellers can always chose their possible neighbors! In this very same year of 1989, there appears the essay by the philosopher from the United States Francis Fukayama: *The End of History*. Here there is talk neither of a

common house of humanity, nor even of the common European
house, but instead of the liberal world of the nineteenth century that
truncated the First World War of the twentieth century, then the
second and with it two revolutions: the socialist of 1917 and the
nationalist of the peoples that will be called third-worldist. Francis
Fukayama writes: "It is possible that what we are witnessing is not
simply the end of the cold war or the twilight of a determined period
of post-war history, but the end of history itself; that is to say, the last
stage of the ideological evolution of humanity and the universalization of Western liberal democracy as the ultimate form of human government." A homogenous state "with liberal democracy in the political sphere combined with easy access to VCRs and stereos in the
economy." The economy of free market, which being so excludes
those that are not prepared for competition that this implies. Outside
remain, thus, the so-called Third World and with it the countries that
have broken with the integration that had been imposed upon them
by real socialism. It is obvious that the philosopher from the United
States thinks that it is the United States who is most capable of guar-
anteeing this new, although rather old, history that was halted in the
twentieth century. A little later, at the beginning of 1991, the president of the United States, George Bush, when declaring war against
Iraq, says before the House of Representatives: "The United States
assumes in great measure a leadership position in this initiative.
Among the nations of the world, only the United States has both the
moral stature and the means to sustain it." It is not the triumph of
humanity as such, but rather of a group of men who are not in disposition to live together and share their achievements with people
who have not demonstrated to be at its level. The Third World, and
with it Latin America, will have to loose all hope of entering the
neoliberal world if they are not before in condition to do so. A difficult condition for these peoples because in a society of competition
the winners are not inclined to form competitors. The United States,
at the end of the 1989 itself, when the last bastion of real communism
falls in Rumania, bombs and occupies Panama in order to punish a
thief who had been at its service and who had stopped being so. Later,
in the Gulf of the Persian Gulf, another people was punished whose

leader had been brought to power in order to confront a dangerous obstacle to Western hegemony, Iran.

If for Eastern Europe the end of the Cold War meant its emancipation from Soviet hegemony, for Western Europe it will mean the possibility of making real a dream that had been put in march in 1959, the integration of Europe itself and with it the possibility of the common house of Europe. In this dream was not contemplated the entrance of Eastern Europe, free from Soviet domination. For Western Europe, this was the opportunity to break the dependance that its protector, the United States, imposed as a guarantee of its integrity before the Soviet Union, an integrity that had to be paid by submitting to the interests of the powerful protector. As a result of the unilateral withdrawal of the leader of the Soviet Union, Gorbachev, from the arms race, which prevented its people from entering a world that was not embittered by the capitalist way of life, the United States found itself forced to withdraw from Western Europe. Its powerful arsenal thus became obsolete. Europe not only could be part of the world of which Fukayama spoke, but also could be its own leader. Something similar took place in the Pacific, where peoples like the Japanese could enter the market economy, who, like the Europeans, were better prepared than the United States because they were not forced to build arms. Instead, they produced domestic commodities, as was demanded by the market economy. The war against Iraq, headed by the United States, was but a warning to Europe that there still remained enemies to be vanquished: the people of the Third World could threaten the development of the West. But this was useless; Europe knew that it could follow its own path without any dependence.

3. THE DEMONS ARE UNLEASHED

Western Europe soon began to see as a burden the other Europe, the one that had formed within real socialism. In this, Fukayama had reason. With respect to the America discovered by Europe five hundred years before, one could already dispense with it. But not only of Latin America, but also of the United States, backward as they were in that market economy. The two great losers of the Second World War, Germany in Europe and Japan in the Pacific, became the leaders in the making of domestic commodities at the reach of the common people that could pay for them.

Before Eastern Europe, new walls had to be erected, this time to not let in anyone, and thus similarly to make front against the countries of the so-called Third World. It repels and expels from its markets the military power itself, the United States, who had stopped being necessary in a world without cold war. The demons began to emerge. At first, the United States and Western Europe were in agreement about dismantling the Soviet Union, thus stimulating the nationalism that were erupting. The acknowledgment of the independence of the Baltic countries by the United States will be the beginning of the end of the Soviet Union and of the detonator of the order that was emergent, Mikhael Gorbachev. The ambitions of Western Germany lead it to assimilate the other Germany in order to later on recognize the independence of Slovania and Croatia, and with that to dismantle, also, Yugoslavia. The hidden demons were let loose, present in the tragedies of the division of the Soviet Union and Yugoslavia.

4. THE UNITED STATES NEEDS LATIN AMERICA

In 1992, the United States, the power that emerged in the world discovered by Colon five hundred years ago, had grown enough in order to impose its presence in Europe, but now Europe became aware that, as with the rest of that America, it became dispensable. The problems that face Europe and the Pacific are with respect to the new economy. President Bush sees how the universal leadership of the United States is in the balance. This country has been displaced from the great markets of Europe and Asia. What is to be done?

To the south of its frontiers there is a great set of countries until now seen as mere backyards to its interests. Peoples to which it would like to send to nothingness in the Western world in order to rescue the goals that were frustrated in the twentieth century. But to the south of the frontiers of the United States, in Latin America, there is more than cheap raw materials, that the new technology makes dispensable, more than cheap labor that automatization makes less necessary. There reside five hundred million people that instead of being a ballast can be a great market for the nation that has been displaced from the great world markets, five hundred million potential buyers. But for that it will be necessary that this region, Latin America, overcomes its ancestral misery, the material and political backwardness that was imposed upon it by five hundred years of colonial and neocolonial history. These people can become a great consumer; but poor, miserable people will never be able to be good consumers. It will be necessary that this region incorporate itself to modernity, that it participate in the development of the power that considers itself to be the great winner of the end of the cold war. George Bush makes the proposal that first Mexico, and later the rest of Latin America, be integrated with the United States to a great market that would be capable of confronting and superseding those that are already formed in Europe and Asia. First with Mexico, with the treaty of free commerce of North America, continuing with the rest of the countries of Latin America according to the initiative for the Americas by President Bush himself.

For Latin America this can be the possibility of the realization of an old dream, namely of its incorporation to Modernity, of which Western Europe and the United States are the motor. The United States knows that for its own good this must be made possible. For this reason the defeat of President Bush in the elections of 1992, far from annulling this possibility, made it possible that it would be picked up by the triumphant candidate, Bill Clinton. His crushing triumph was the triumph of the minorities that together formed a majority that struggle against the margination that had been object of the powerful country. There also begin to be unleashed the demons, made explicit in the events like Los Angeles, California, in 1992. Clinton understood the message and for that reason his main preoccupation will be the internal problems of the United States, that is, those of the people of the United States that include those millions of marginalized. The supposed imperial domination that Bush still tried to retain, will be abandoned because the social cost that has to be paid is too high for the poorest of the United States and its weak neighbors to the south of its borders. The treaty of free commerce and the economic integration of the rest of Latin America continue being a priority to the United States in a broader context.

5. RESISTANCE TO THE INTEGRATION OF THE AMERICAS

The first step will not be easy, the treaty with Mexico, which encounters great internal and external obstacles. Internal because they imply for Mexico economic and political changes that will affect interest created in the system that emerged in the revolution of 1910. External because there are many interest groups that consider that such a treaty will affect them, regardless whether it will benefit the United States as a nation. It is this latter group that lament the hegemonic relinquishment of the United States over the world. This resistance is made patent in the question: how can be integrated economically to the United States an economically inferior people like the Mexican? This was formulated by Ross Perot, who thinks that this ought to be done with Europe and Japan instead. But it is precisely Europe and Japan who represent for the United States an economic problem. Resistances are vanquished in all sides. The treaty is approved by the United State's Congress in November of 1993. It becomes immediately apparent the importance that NAFTA has for the United States. President Clinton meets in Seattle with the countries of the Pacific Area in order to overcome the differences between the United States and the countries in the Pacific Rim. Immediately, Clinton travels to Europe in order to put an end to differences that exist between GATT and Europe. The United States strengthens itself economically, which represents for Mexico and Latin America a great hope with respect to their inclusion into modernity. The first of January of 1994 is set in march the treatise that, notwithstanding the obstacles, shows itself as a great opportunity for the realization of the Latin American dreams of modernization.

However, that first of January, the Mexicans awaken surprised when seen on television a man without a face that from the Lacandona jungle declares war to "the Mexican Federal Army, fundamental pillar of the dictatorship that we suffer, which is monopolized by the party in power and which is headed by the federal executive which is today held by its maximum and illegitimate chief Carlos Salina de Gortari." It is asked of the other power that they depose the dictator and they say that they will march on the capital, "defeating the federal army." This is a declaration of war by people without faces, powerfully armed, but followed by a troop of indigenous youths insufficiently armed, who even carry rifles of painted wood.

6. THE DREAM OF THE LATIN AMERICAN MODERNITY

Alfonso Reyes spoke before the European intelligence of the American or Latin American intelligence and of the misfortunes that prevented it from entering into the modernity that is embodied in Western Europe and the United States. Among them, "the specific one of being American," that is, born and rooted in a soil that was not the focus of civilization. Another, that of "its latin cultural and not saxon formation." In turn, another fatality, that of "belonging to the hispanic orbis," to the people who had lost the race of history in 1588 against England and in 1898 against the United States, defeated in the Gulf of Mexico and in the Pacific by the descendants of the same men that had defeated it in 1588. Another misfortune, that of being part of a world loaded with indigenous peoples and the mestizaje with indians and people of other races, such as the African. Diversity of races that when integrated formed what José Vasconcelos dignified as the "Cosmic Race" [La Raza Cósmica]. The Iberian domination was expelled from America through the insurrection of its colonies and the defeat that was imposed upon it by the Saxon America, leaving a "power vacuum" which was immediately tried to be filled by countries from Western Europe and the United States. Facing this situation, the long struggle of the peoples who had entered history under the sign of dependence and who tried to depart from it in order to be able to form an active and not passive part in modernity; a modernity that, throughout the span of the nineteenth and twentieth centuries, had reached a development never before imagined.

To enter modernity, in the nineteenth century, the Latin American intelligentsia tried to erase the only history that it had, that which was formed by three long centuries of colonization. One had to change the skin and to cleanse one's brain. One had to renounce an identity imposed by colonization and to appropriate the identity of the peoples who were the motor of the progress and civilization of modernity. One had to be like the Europeans or the yanquis of the south. "Let us be like the United States," cried the civilizers of Latin America. The reformers and educators of the region clamored for mental emancipation; for that it is necessary to use philosophies and doctrines that it was supposed had made of Western Europe and the United States the most forward of modernity.

This was a vain undertaking because it implied confronting and defeating habits and customs imposed throughout three centuries of colonization, and also defeating internal and external interests that opposed modernity, given that this implied a great danger to modernity's interests. This also implied confronting modernity's leaders themselves, a modernity that presupposed a competition in which the best ones imposed themselves in a struggle such as that described by Darwin in the *Origin of the Species*. The lords of modernity, the Western world, were not going to allow the free emergence of people that could contradict the already attained successes. Latin Americans had to struggle, within and without, in order to enter modernity.

But, what is modernity? The point of departure is the idea that man is not only part of nature but also that he dominates it and places it at his service. It was in this way that it was carried out in Europe and in the same way it was continued in North America. In order to accomplish this, it was necessary to be in the capacity to make nature instrumental to their interests. And within nature there are other men, those that the expansion initiated in 1492 subjugates not only in America, but also in Asia, Africa, and Oceania. It is the indigenous people, of which Arnold Toynbee speaks when he said: "When we westerners called certain people 'indigenous' is because we see them as trees that walk or as savage animals that infest the country, which can only be treated as vermin to be exterminated or as domesticable animals to be used." This is the necessitated relationship that is established between colonizers and colonized: the indigenous seen as part of the flora and fauna to be utilized and destroyed. It will be a long and almost useless struggle that these so-called indigenous peoples will have to undertake so that they be recognized as humans, that is, as equals to their colonizers and as such to be able to participate in the use of nature, which implied putting an end to the submittal of man as if he were part of nature.

These efforts have been answered with different forms of violence, such as the dirty war that makes of the misfortune of this region an adequate instrument to maintain domination over them. The Mexican revolution of 1910 will be expression of this struggle to brake the chains that prevent entry into modernity. This revolution was able to attain some achievements departing from the situations that the Western world itself has to face, which has been the waste brought about by the two great world wars, the nationalist revolution began in 1910 in Mexico and the socialist in 1917 in Russia. The first revolutions that tried in Latin America to follow the footsteps of the Mexican failed because of the dirty war to which they were submitted, with the triumph of the interests of the Latin American oligarchies, propelled as the instrument of repression at the service of the developed world, as were the military dictatorships that emerged in the south cone and those that scourged Central America. The Mexican revolution, through the political organization that it gave itself, was able to confront the internal interests that easily place themselves at the service of foreign interests. Frank Tannenbaum spoke with emphasis of "Mexico as anvil of United States's foreign policy." He considered that what took place in Mexico because of its resistance, will also take place in the rest of Latin America and in the world in process of development. This is, precisely, what is becoming very clear right now.

7. INTERRUPTED HOPE

The problems of the United States at the end of the cold war, annulling its relationship with the people under its armed protection in Europe and the pacific rim, made of America to the south of its frontiers something necessary in order to extricate itself from the marginalization of which it was object. However, the possibility that Latin America could enter modernity in another relation that was not already that of a simple instrument will face many expressed difficulties, precisely in the pronouncements that the prosperous Western world made of itself. Now it is announced, not the end of history, but the end of the possible development of the peoples who did not attain it.

The exploitation of nature upon which modernity had raised itself could no longer be continued. Nature already presented the bill to its prosperous exploiters. The president of the United States, George Bush, in the conference on Ecology that took place in Rio de Janeiro in 1992, announced the end of this exploitation. Development could no longer follow this path. For that the Western World promised to halt an exploitation that nature was longer to admit. At the same time it was asked of the peoples that did not achieved development, to abstain from doing so; that they had to renounce development through this path. Everything must be stopped. The underdeveloped nations ought to renounce development. But, in addition, the developed world, while being so, cannot share what has been achieved because misery then would be generalized.

Luis Donaldo Colosio, in June of 1993, as director of the National Institute of Solidarity, organized an international seminar on "Freedom and Justice in Modern Societies," which many experts from Europe, the United States, Mexico and many Latin American countries attended. There the problem of modernity itself was formulated as the expression of the development that societies can attain. Experts from Europe and the United States maintained that development itself had come to an end. We cannot go any further, but neither can anything be done for the peoples that have not attained development. Everything that was reached by the Western world, everything that was accumulated by it, could not be shared, because this then would

only originate misery for those who by their own effort had attained
development. We could only think of small compensations, that is,
alms that either little or no help to a world condemned to underdevelopment, or, in other words, a world condemned to remain outside of a
modernity that had exhausted its possibilities.

It was within this context or hope originated in the problems that
faced the United States and the premonitions that portend that development was possible, that the Mexicans awakened the first of January to the news of the armed uprising that if it were to be successful
could put an end, or at least postpone even further its dreams of modernization. The executive branch of the government, overcoming the
bewilderment of this surprising declaration of war, confronted the
insubordinated, easily expelling them from the towns in Chiapas,
which had been taken by them in surprise. They were rounded up in
order to be given the final blow. However, the president of the
republic, Carlos Salinas, declared an unilateral cease fire, offering
total amnesty, made changes in his cabinet and suggested dialogue.
The path of repression that was followed in other countries of South
America and which expanded the dirty war that has caused so much
damage in the region was not to be taken.

Obviously, and arranged by the insurgents without face, this was
an action to prevent the treaty of free commerce from getting off the
ground. The same voices that in Mexico had opposed its signing justified the uprising and condemned the counteroffensive of the military.
But also, as much in the United States as in Europe, the rebellion—
launched by those whose miseries throughout five hundred years
have not been resolved—was defended and magnified. The armed
response to the declaration of war and the violence initiated was condemned. Some spoke of people armed with sticks and make-believe
arms of wood that was precisely what the leaders of the uprising had
given them. The internal and external media as well as nonstate
agents condemned Mexico for having responded to the declaration of
war with the offensive that the president himself had halted immediately. In the United States, the same opposers of the treaty with
Mexico that will be posteriorly extended to the whole of Latin
America demanded the annulment of the treaty because Mexico had

not respected the human rights of the indigenous peoples, nor had their government done anything to put an end to the misery of five hundred years of colonization. Some even spoke of the acknowledgment of an army led by people that hid their faces.

After this blow there followed the assassination of the PRI candidate for the presidency of the republic, Luis Donaldo Colosio. The killer declared that he would not speak or that he would speak only before the media and nonstate organizations. It was a matter of repeating the same situation as with the Chiapas uprising. Mario, the killer, like Marcos, the subversive, were patriots that when violating the laws of the nation and of coexistence were doing so for the benefit of the democracy and freedom in Mexico. For democracy, we had to make of the whole of Mexico a great Lacandona jungle. Some insisted on condemning Mexico and its government, and censuring the annulment of the treaty. The question: How could we integrate with a people that does not even respect the life of its presidential candidate? In Mexico the answer clamored: Look what happened with John and Robert Kennedy in the United States.

8. TO MARGINALIZE MISERY

The possibility of Mexico and Latin America's entry into modernity finds itself thus submitted to two fires that complement each other in maintaining the region in marginalization. The entry into modernity, it was once again replied, implies being prepared for it and to a demanded competition that has made possible a supposedly infinite development. A readiness for which the peoples like those from Latin America, the so-called Third World and the peoples until only recently under real socialism, are disqualified. For this reason, to make them capable has been and continues to be the central preoccupation, as is illustrated in the education that is to be offered for it. This making able has again and again clashed with the interests of the dominators who throughout the long colonization have become powers and oligarchies in order to maintain their privileges. To become capable for change is to become capable to put an end to the obstacles that prevent the development of the nation. Our universities and other educational and cultural institutions make great efforts to obtain academic excellence, the making capable for the good use of the ideas, science and technology that have made possible modernity.

The internal opposition stems from the forces that know that they will loose their privileges when ignorance, and the lack of preparation, disappear, and they thus are in opposition when they say: how can it be asked of peoples that can barely survive that they make an effort in the knowledge of ideas, science, and technology that will allow them to confront external domination? Absolutely free education is demanded, which is to be paid for by the government, which will be imposed upon a people with scarce resources to work for survival itself. This can only be superseded by people in some fashion privileged as instruments of dependency imposed internally and externally. Some will simply have to work while others will make it with the work of the others, in order to maintain intact the situation inherited by imposed dependency.

It is also spoken of the supposed losing of identity of the peoples under colonization, given that it is obvious that the peoples, when developed, will be different from what they were under undervelopment. This implies the loss of identity itself. Which identity? If identity is understood as a way of being concretely, proper to each human being, this cannot be lost if this benefits the extraordinary elements that modernity offers. To think in this fashion is to continue the absurd pretention of the Latin American civilizers and positivists of the nineteenth century, who attempted to stop being what they were in order to be like those in Europe and in the United States who had been the spring of modernity. The attempt to erase one's ineluctable history, even if it was colonial, to peel off one's skin, to wash one's brain in order to become the yanqui of the south, never worked. Japan, and with it the peoples of the Pacific Rim, are demonstrating that their peoples have not had to renounce their history, their identity, their peculiar mode of being in order to be able to assimilate the science and technology of modernity; rather, they had adapted it to their particular identity and thus have been able to compete with success with the nations themselves that originated modernity.

The peoples that began modernity, made so not only dominating nature, but also man and peoples over which they expanded, which obviously has given them advantage over the manipulated peoples. These, who with their riches and work made possible modernity, in order to break the yoke of domination, will have to show their capacity in an unequal struggle. How to break through the limitations, proper to misery, imposed by colonization, and to overcome and demonstrate their capacity for science and a technology that has never been to its reach? Improvising, and when improvising, failing, and when failing, learning again and again until triumphing. Thus was done by the peoples themselves of the Western World, Europe and the United States, but throughout many centuries. It will be more difficult for peoples like those from Latin America, formed under colonization, which is a great obstacle. They are required to do in years what the Western world did in centuries. In this sense, to learn, assimilate, adopt and transform what has already been made in order to create its own. This is what the Asian people are already doing. Why not the Latin Americans?

From the point of view of the Western world, this jump is impossible. To enter modernity, the peoples that with their wealth and their servile work has made it possible, can only wait. Now it is said that nature and development had arrived at their end, for which reason they will have to remain where they are. Some people above, others under or thrown to the vacuum of the super-marginalization. "But thy vile race, Though thou didst learn," said Prospero to Caliban in Shakespeare's *The Tempest*, "had that in't which good natures Could not abide to be with" [Act one, scene two]. With these people, it is insisted, no one can associate; so that this can be possible it will have to learned in years what the Western world learned in centuries.

Hence the obstacles to the North American Free Trade Agreement between Mexico, the United States and Canada; unequal economies that are only expressions of unequal people. We must deal with Europeans and now with the Asians, but not with people whose poverty, whose misery, can in turn destabilize a great nation like the United States. This inequality can tempt industries hungry for profits to relocate where labor is cheaper and when doing so leaving unemployed the workers from the United States and other developed regions of the world. No effort, it is maintained, can overcome misery and ignorance. To invest in this misery would only increase the misery of the peoples themselves who have reached development.

9. REQUIRED COEXISTENCE

This, more or less, was what Francis Fukayama meant when he spoke of the end of history. End of history for the people who have reached development and with it a free world where the best will always be rewarded. Outside of this world, in history, the peoples from the so-called Third World, among them Latin America and the peoples who formed themselves under communism. This is an absolute negative to the sharing of development, the fruits of a modernity that is considered to have arrived at its end. A negative made explicit by Western Europe in relation with their now free neighbors of Eastern Europe, now liberated from Soviet hegemony. This negative was also given expression in Western Germany's resistance to the assimilation of a Germany so different as was the communist one. An equal resistance is deployed against the people that under colonialism were displaced to the centers of modernity, to the very entrails of it, to do the work that the prosperous lords refused to do. In the United State there is an equal resistance against the multiple ethnicities that its expansion brought into its midst and that it now feels corrodes it. Europe, the United States, the Western world in general, dream of an autarky that reality now shows to be impossible. In some fashion, now they have to take into account the peoples on the other side of the borders and on the other side of the seas that it already has in its insides.

The United States, marginalized by Europe and Asia, capable of producing weapons, but no domestic wares demanded by peoples for whom the cold war has ended, has been left without the necessary market for a production that has to be accelerated and not halted. This required taking into account the peoples at the other side of its borders and those that already live in its midst, and thus required searching for a continental integration in which raw materials, production and consumption are linked. This, however, means integrating those peoples who before were not in a condition to participate in the consumption of markets. This was the way in which President Bush understood it, and in a broader sense by his successor, President Bill Clinton. It was necessary to establish a new relationship with Mexico and the rest of Latin America. This new relationship will depend on United State's relationship with the nations in Europe and Asia that already undertook a quest for something in common that overcomes mere competition.

The vice president of the United States, Al Gore, when speaking of NAFTA with Mexico, said: "The ratification of the treaty puts an end to the myth that is impossible to reach agreements of free commerce between countries of different economic levels." These inequalities will be overcome by the treaty itself, as it will also have to overcome the inequalities that the United States itself has with respect to other countries from Asia and Europe. The United States's imperialism has passed to the annals of history. The United States only gave beginning to the fabrication of persuasive armaments, too expensive for an economy whose feet of clay became evident at the end of the Second World War, something that is also becoming clear in Western Europe. The United States must now compete, but also negotiate with the people who yesterday were under its hegemony. For this reason, "on the relationship with Mexico"—adds Gore— "depends the future of our relations with the continent and our relations with the rest of the world." Everyone needs each other; for this reason what Frank Tannenbaum said is the more valid: "Mexico is the anvil in which the United State's foreign policy is forged." This is a great opportunity so that Modernity does not exhaust and limit itself thus halting the peoples who still want to form part of it.

10. THE FUTURE AS PANDEMONIUM?

Arnold Toynbee, in his *A Study of History*, spoke of the determinisms that were present at the beginning of modernity and in this last twentieth century. The determinism inspired by the Protestant reformation that divided the Christian church in the sixteenth century; from this there emerged the puritanism, from which in turn, in the opinion of various sociologist like Tawney and Weber, derived the determinism that made possible capitalist ideology. In the nineteenth century, it was the philosophy of Karl Marx which gave origin to another determinism, the communist, that throughout the face of the planet confronted the puritanical-capitalist determinism. "The addicts of predesterinarian creeds on whom their faith has had this fortifying and stimulating effect seem all of them to have made the bold assumption that their own will was coincident with the will of God or with the law of Nature or with the decrees of Necessity, and was therefore bound, *a priori*, to prevail. The Calvinist's Jehovah is a God who vindicates His Elect; The Marxian's Historical Necessity is an impersonal force that brings about the Dictatorship of the Proletariat. Such an assumption gives a confidence in victory which, as the history of war teaches, is one of the springs of *moral* and is therefore apt to justify itself by achieving the results which it has taken for granted in advance."[1] The appearance of Marxist determinism called into question the presuppositions of Calvinist determinism. The Calvinist determinist began to think that possibly God was not with them. Throughout the twentieth century, the new determinism challenged the prior one: "The disillusioned predestinarian who has been taught by harsh experience that his God is not, after all, on his side is condemned to arrive at the devastating conclusion that he and his fellow-homunculi are: But helpless pieces in the game He plays."[2]

The United States, a prolongation of Europe in America, departed from the puritan determinism expressed in *Manifest Destiny*, which it began to impose on its neighbors to the south of its borders, such as Mexico, and then later to the Gulf of Mexico and the Antilles, expanding throughout the length of the earth in order to occupy "power vacuums" in Latin America, Asia and Africa left by European colonialism. It displaced Spain, urged by the same Manifest Destiny that led it to not only expel Europe from its colonies, but also to take part in the destiny of Europe itself. It is thus that it entangles itself, against the warnings of the founding fathers, in two World Wars begun in Europe. In both wars the United States were the ones to benefit and they used this instrument to impose its protection over Europe itself.

This was a protection against evil par excellence, incarnated in the other determinism, the communist. Communism which with the Soviet Union had become a power capable of putting in check the capitalist puritanism. The long Cold War was the expression of the struggle between these two determinisms. The collapse of one, communism, showed the supposed predetermination of the other, capitalism.

Calvinist determinism was made evident in the United States's rhetoric during the Cold War, as was the case with the speeches from Presidents Ronald Reagan and George Bush. This rhetoric could have continued had not the leader of the Soviet Union, Mikhael Gorbachev, grown tired of being evil par excellence. Tired of playing the role of Satan, or of the good before the capitalist demon, which had prevented the Russian people from achieving the economic and social welfare that socialism itself offered. To put an end to this absurd situation was the proposal of Gorbachev in the Bicentennial of the French Revolution in 1989. The Soviet Union abandoned, unilaterally, the arms race, thus putting an end to the Cold War.

The United States, as the leader of the Western world, as much in the philosophy of Fukayama as in the speeches by President George Bush, declared the absolute winner the puritan determinism, capitalism. This world does not want to know anything of Gorbachev's call for help to make less difficult his people's entry to the capitalist form of life, without abandoning socialist solidarity. For the West this was the great opportunity to put an end to a power that would more dangerous were it to enter into the economy of market competition. This power had to be eliminated in a definitive fashion. For this reason the nationalisms that have now emerged were stimulated. The same will be done in Germany, in Yugoslavia, in order to impose its own regional hegemony. The demons of nationalism, the old ethnicities dominated by determinisms were thus awaken and liberated. These demons now extend through the whole of Europe and the United States, thus calling into question the idea of the supposed triumph of capitalist and liberal determinism. These demons now smash against the borders of Europe as they smash against the borders of the United States, demons that are already inside the entrails of the peoples who were brought inside when both expanded through the earth.

Summarizing, Mexico's problem to incorporate itself to modernity, as those of the rest of Latin America and other regions of the world, come from the resistance of people who have enter modernity to share its fruits with the people who have only been the object of manipulation solely in benefit of those who have enjoyed and enjoy its exclusive privileges. The hidden demons that the puritan and marxist determinism hid have now come out to the surface. These determinisms opened, after all, hopes; their end vitiates these hopes. We can no longer return to the nineteenth century, to the savage capitalism that only made of the peoples that suffered it its own tool. For this reason there now come to the surface the multiple resentments of the now growing marginalized of the earth. The old gods of the German, Slavic, Latin, indigenous mythologies are reappearing, surfacing like Wotan did at the end of the First World War, the German god exalted by Wagner and used to satisfy those marginalized by the defeat.

Something similar is taking place in Latin America: in the Lacondonian jungle in Mexico some already speak of Wotan-Zapata. The Mayan gods are resurrected and with that it is spoken of a race that, like the German, will impose itself over a continent that will be of pure indians. It is spoken of the Incan gods of the Shining Path in Peru. Outside this supposedly indian continent are left out the criollos and mestizos, the people is not of the race of the first inhabitants of the continent discovered five hundred years ago. All of this is a product of the froth of discontent of disappointed people due to the lack of solidarity that it has encountered and that now tries to claim for past sufferings. These are people marginalized for their ethnicity, skin, gender, sexual inclination, religion, nationality, social status. It is this ghost that haunts the entire world now, which is not that of communism, of which Marx spoke, but of the many marginalized of the earth.

NOTES

1. Arnold Toynbee, *A Study of History*, vol. 1 (New York & London: Oxford University Press, 1946), p. 450.

2. Ibid.

Enrique Dussel

THE "WORLD-SYSTEM"
Europe as "Center" and Its "Periphery," beyond Eurocentrism

In this lecture we will study the question of modernity. As a matter of fact there are two paradigms of modernity, and in the following we will characterize both of them.

a) The first, from an eurocentric horizon, formulates that the phenomena of modernity is *exclusively* European; that it develops from out of the Middle Ages and later on diffuses itself throughout the entire world. Weber situates the "problem of universal history" with the questions that is thus formulated:

> To what combination of circumstances the fact should be attributed
> that in *Western civilization*, and in Western civilization only, cul-
> tural phenomena have appeared which (as *we* like to think) lie in a
> line of development having *universal* significance and value.[1]

Europe had, according to this paradigm, exceptional *internal* characteristics that allowed it to supersede, through its rationality, all other cultures. Philosophically, no one else better than Hegel expresses this thesis of modernity:

> The German Spirit is the Spirit of the new World. Its aim is the real-
> ization of absolute Truth as the unlimited self-determination (*Selb-
> stbestimmung*) of Freedom—*that* Freedom which has its own
> absolute form itself as its purport.[2]

Paper presented at the Conference on Globalization and Culture, Duke University, November 1994. Translated by Eduardo Mendieta.

What demands attention here is that the Spirit of Europe (the German spirit) is the absolute Truth that determines or realizes itself through itself without owing anything to anyone. This thesis, which I will call the "Eurocentric paradigm" (in opposition to the "*world* paradigm"), is the one that has imposed itself not only in Europe and the United States, but also in the entire intellectual world of the world periphery. As we have said, the "pseudo-scientific" division of history into Antiquity (as antecedent), the Medieval Age (preparatory epoch), and the Modern Age (Europe) is an ideological and deforming organization of history. Philosophy and ethics need to break with this reductive horizon in order to open themselves to the "world," "planetary" sphere. This is already an ethical problem with respect to other cultures.

Chronology has its geopolitics. Modern subjectivity develops spatially, according to the "eurocentric paradigm" from the Italy of the Renaissance to the Germany of the Reformation and the Enlightenment, towards the France of the French Revolution.[3] This concerns central Europe.

b) The second paradigm, from a planetary horizon, conceptualizes Modernity as the culture of the *center* of the "world-system,"[4] of the first "world-system"—through the incorporation of Amerindia[5]—and as a result of the *management* of said "centrality." In other words, European Modernity is not an *independent*, autopoietic, self-referential system, but, instead, is "part" of a "world-system": its *center*. Modernity, then, is planetary. It begins with the *simultaneous* constitution of Spain with reference to its "periphery" (the first of all, properly speaking, Amerindia: the Caribbean, Mexico and Peru). *Simultaneously*, Europe (as a diachrony that has its premodern antecedents: the renaissance Italian cities and Portugal) will go on to *constitute* itself as "center" (as super-hegemonic power that from Spain passes to Holland, England and France. . .) over a growing "periphery" (Amerindia, Brazil, and slave supplying coasts of Africa, Poland in the sixteenth century,[6] consolidation of Latin Amerindia, North America, the Caribbean, Eastern Europe in the seventeenth century;[7] the Ottoman Empire, Russia, some Indian reigns, Sub-Asian, and the first penetration to continental Africa until the first half of the nineteenth century).[8] Modernity, then, would be for this planetary paradigm a phenomena proper to the "system" "center-periphery." Modernity is not a phenomena of Europe as *independent* system, but of Europe as "center." This simple hypothesis absolutely changes the concept of modernity, its origin, development and contemporary crisis; and thus, also the content of the belated modernity or postmodernity.

Furthermore, we sustain a thesis that qualifies the prior: the centrality of Europe in the "world-system" is not sole fruit of an internal superiority accumulated during the European Middle Age over against other cultures. Instead, it is also the effect of the simple fact of the discovery, conquest, colonization and integration (subsumption) of Amerindia (fundamentally). This simple fact will give Europe the determining *comparative advantage* over the Ottoman-Muslim world, India or China. Modernity is fruit of this happening, and not its cause. Subsequently, the *management* of the centrality of the "world-system" will allow Europe to transform itself in something like the "reflexive consciousness" (Modern Philosophy) of world history, and the many values, discoveries, inventions, technology, political institutions, etc. that are attributed to itself as its exclusive production, are in reality the effects of the *displacement* of the ancient center of the III stage of the inter-regional system towards Europe (following the diachronic way of the Renaissance to Portugal as antecedent, towards Spain, and later towards Flanders, England. . .). Even capitalism is fruit, and not cause, of this juncture of European planetarization and centralization within the "world-system." The human experience of 4,500 years of political, economic, technological, cultural relations of the "inter-regional system," will now be hegemonized by Europe—which had never been "center," and that during its best times only got to be a "periphery"—. The slipping takes place from central Asia towards the Eastern, and Italian, Mediterranean, more precisely towards Genoa, towards the Atlantic. With Portugal as an antecedent, it begins properly in Spain, and in the face of the impossibility of China even attempting to arrive through the Orient (the Pacific) to Europe, and thus to integrate Amerindia as its periphery. Let us look at the premises of the argument.

I. DEPLOYMENT OF THE "WORLD-SYSTEM"

Let us consider the deployment of world history departing from the rupture, due to the Ottoman-Muslim presence, of the III stage of the interregional system, which in its classic epoch had Baghdad as its center (from 762 to 1258 A.D.), and the transformation of the "inter-regional system" into the first "*world*-system," whose "center" would situate itself up to today in the North of the Atlantic. This change of "center" of the system will have its prehistory from the thirteenth through the fifteenth century A.D., and before the collapse of the III stage of the interregional system, but with the new IV stage of the "world-system" *originates* properly with 1492. Everything that had taken place in Europe was still a moment of *another* stage of the inter-regional system. Which state originated the deployment of the "world-system"? Our answer is: that it could annex Amerindia, and from it, as a springboard or "comparative advantage," it will go on to accumulate a priorly nonexisting superiority toward the end of the fifteenth century.

a) Why not China? The reason is very simple, and we would like to define it from the outset. For China[9] it was impossible to discover Amerindia (nontechnological impossibility, that is to say, empirically factual, but historical or geopolitical), for it had no interest in attempting to arrive at Europe because the "center" of the interregional system (in its III stage) was in the East, either in Central Asia or in India. To go towards completely "peripheral" Europe? This could not be an objective of Chinese foreign commerce.

In fact, Cheng Ho, between 1405 and 1433, was able to make seven successful voyages to the "center" of the system (he arrived at Sri Lanka, India and even to Eastern Africa). In 1479 Wang Chin attempted the same, but the archives of his predecessor were denied to him. China closed upon itself, and did not attempt to do what, precisely at that very same moment, Portugal was undertaking. Its internal politics—perhaps the rivalry of the mandarins against the new power of the merchant eunocos[10]—prevented its exit into foreign commerce. Had China undertaken it, however, it would have had to depart *toward the West* in order to reach the "center" of the system. The Chinese went towards the East, and they arrived at Alaska, and it appears that even as far as California, and even still more to the South, but when they did not find anything that would be of interest to its merchants, and as they went further away from the "center" of the "inter-regional system," the most probably abandoned the enterprise. China was not Spain for geopolitical reasons.

However, we still need to ask ourselves in order to refute the old "evidence," but which has been reinforced since Weber: Was China culturally *inferior* to Europe in the fifteenth century? According to those who have studied the question,[11] China was neither technologically[12] nor politically,[13] nor commercially, not even because of its humanism,[14] inferior. There is a certain mirage in this question. The histories of Western science and technology do not take strictly into account that the European "jump," the technological *boom* begins to take place in the sixteenth century, but that it is only in the seventeenth century that it shows its multiplying effects. The *formulation* of the modern technological paradigm (seventeenth century) is confused with the origin of modernity, without leaving time for the crisis of the Medieval model. No notice is taken that the scientific revolution—to talk with Kuhn—departs from a modernity which has already began, antecedent, as fruit of a "modern paradigm."[15] It is for that reason that in the fifteenth century (if we do not consider the posterior European inventions) Europe does not have any superiority over China. Needham himself allows himself to be bewitched by this mirage, when he writes:

> The fact is that in the spontaneous autochthonous development of chinese society did not produce any drastic change paralleling the *Renaissance and the scientific revolution* of the West.[16]

To place the Renaissance and the scientific revolution[17] as being *one and the same event* (one from the fourteenth century and the other from the seventeenth century) demonstrates the distortion of which we have spoken. The Renaissance is still an European event of a peripheral culture of the III stage of the inter-regional system. The "scientific revolution" is fruit of the formulation of the modern paradigm which needed more than a century of modernity in order to attain its maturity. Pierre Chaunu writes:

> Towards the end of the fifteenth century, to the extent to which his-
> torical literature allows us to understand it, the far East as an entity
> comparable to the Mediterranean . . . does not result under any
> inferior aspect, at least superficially, to the far West of the Euro-
> Asiatic continent.[18]

Let us repeat: Why not China? Because China found itself in the farthest East of the "inter-regional system," because it looked to the
"center": to India in the West.

b) Why not Portugal? For the same reason. That is, because it
found itself in the farthest point of the West of the same "inter-
regional system," and because *it also looked, and always, toward the
"center"*: toward the India of the East. Colon's proposal (the attempt
to reach the "center" through the West) to the king of Portugal was
as insane as it was for Colon to pretend to discover a new continent
(since he *only and always* attempted, and could not conceive another
hypothesis, to reach the "center" of the stage of III of the inter-
regional system[19]).

As we have seen, it is the Italian renaissance cities that are the
farthest point of the West (peripheral) of the inter-regional system,
that articulated anew, after the Crusades (which failed in 1291), continental Europe with the Mediterranean. The Crusades ought to be
considered as a frustrated attempt to connect with the "center" of the
system, the link which the Turks ruptured. The Italian cities, especially Genoa (which rivaled with Venice that had a presence in the
Eastern Mediterranean), attempted to open the Western Mediterranean towards the Atlantic, in order to reach once again through the
south of Africa the "center" of the system. The Genovese placed all
their experience in navigation and the economic power of their wealth
at the service of opening for themselves this path. It was the Genovese
who occupied the Canaries in 1312,[20] and it was they who invested in
Portugal and helped them to develop their navigational power.

Once the Crusades had failed, they could not count on the expansion of Russia through the steppes (who advancing through the frozen
woods of the North reached in the seventeenth century the Pacific
and Alaska[21]) that the Atlantic would be the only European door *to
the "center" of the system*. Portugal, the first European nation

already unified in the eleventh century, would transform the recon-quest[22] against the Muslims into the beginning of a process of Atlantic mercantile expansion. In 1419, the Portuguese discover the Madeiras Islands, in 1431 the Azores, in 1482 Zaire, in 1498 Vasco de Gama reaches India (the "center" of the inter-regional system). In 1415, Portugal occupies the African-Muslim Ceuta, in 1448 El-Ksar-es-Seghir, in 1471 Arzila. But all of this is the *continuation* of the inter-regional system whose connection was the Italian cities:

> In the twelfth century when Genoese and the Pisans first appeared in Catalonia, in the thirteen century when they first reach Portugal, this is part of the efforts of the Italians to draw the Iberian peoples into the international trade of the time. . . . As of 1317, according to Virginia Raus, "the city and the part of Lisbon would be the great centre of Genoese trade."[23]

A Portugal with contacts in the Islamic world, with numerous sailors (farmers expelled from an intensive agriculture), with a money economy, in "connection" with Italy, opened once again peripheral Europe to the inter-regional system. But because of this it did not stop being a "periphery." Not even the Portuguese could pretend to have abandoned this situation, since Portugal could have attempted to dominate the commercial exchange in the sea of the Arabs (the Indian sea[24]), but never pretend to produce the commodities of the East (silk fabrics, tropical products, the Sub-Sahara gold, etc.). In other words, it was an intermediary and always peripheral power of India, China or the Muslim world.

With Portugal we are in the anteroom, but still neither in moder-nity, nor in the "world-system" (the IV stage of the system which orig-inated, at least, between Egypt and Mesopotamia).

c) Why does Spain begin the "world-system," and with it, moder-nity? For the same reason that it was prevented in China and Por-tugal. Since Spain could not reach the "center" of the "inter-regional system" that was in Central Asia or India, could not go toward the East (since the Portuguese had already anticipated them, and thus has exclusivity rights) through the South of the Atlantic (around the Coasts of Western Africa, until the cape of Buena Esperanza discov-

ered in 1487), Spain only had left one opportunity: to go toward the
"center," to India, through *the Occident*, through the West, by
crossing the Atlantic ocean.[25] Because of this Spain "bumps" into,
"finds without looking," Amerindia, and with it the entire European
"Medieval paradigm" enters into crisis (which is the "paradigm" of a
peripheral culture, the Western farthest point of the stage III of the
"inter-regional system"), and thus inaugurates, slowly but irre-
versibly, the first *world* hegemony. This is the only "world-system"
that has existed in planetary history, and this is the modern system,
European in its "center," capitalist in its economy. This *Ethics of Liberation* pretends to situate itself explicitly (is it perhaps the first practical philosophy that attempts to do so "explicitly"?) within the
horizon of this modern "world-system," taking into consideration not
only the "center" (as has been done *exclusively* by modern philosophy from Descartes to Habermas, thus resulting in a *partial*,
provincial, regional view of the historical ethical event), *but also* its
"periphery" (and with this one obtains a *planetary* vision of the
human experience). This historical question is not informative or
anecdotal. It has a philosophical sense that is *strictu sensu*! I have
already treated the theme in another work.[26] In this work I showed
Colon's existential impossibility, a renaissance Genoese, of convincing himself that what he had discovered was not India. He navi-
gated, according to his own imagination, close to the coasts of the
fourth Asiatic peninsula (which Heinrich Hammer had already
drawn cartographically in Rome in 1489[27]), always close to the "Sinus
Magnus" (the great gulf of the Greeks, territorial sea of the Chinese)
when he transversed the Caribbean. Colon died in 1506 without
having superseded the horizon of stage III of the "inter-regional
system."[28] He was not able to supersede subjectively the "inter-
regional system"—with a history of 4500 years of transformations,
beginning with Egypt and Mesopotamia—and to open himself to the
new stage of the "world-system." The first one who suspected a *new*
(the *last* new) continent was Americo Vespucci, in 1503, and therefore, he was existentially and subjectively, the first "modern," the
first to unfold the horizon of the "Asian-Afro-Mediterranean system"
as "world-system," which incorporated for the first time Amerin-

dia.[29] This revolution in the *Weltanschaung*, of the cultural, scientific, religious, technological, political, ecological and economic horizon is the *origin* of modernity, seen from the perspective of a "world paradigm" and not solely from an eurocentric perspective. In the "world system" the accumulation in the "center" is for the first time accumulation in a world scale.[30] Within the new system everything changes qualitatively or radically. The very Medieval European "peripheral subsystem" changes internally as well. The founding event was the discovery of Amerindia in 1492.[31] Spain is ready to become the first modern state; through the discovery it begins to become the "center" of its first "periphery" (Amerindia), thus organizing the beginning of the slow shifting of the "center" of the older III stage of the "inter-regional system" (Baghdad of the thirteenth century), which had from peripheral Genoa (but western part of the "system") began a process of reconnection first with Portugal, and now with Spain, with Seville to be precise. Genoese, Italian wealth suddenly flows into Seville. The "experience" of the Eastern renaissance Mediterranean (and through it, of the Muslim world, of India and even China) are thus articulated with the imperial Spain of Carlos the V (who reaches to the central Europe of the bankers of Augsburg, to the Flanders of Amberes, and later, to Amsterdam, with Bohemia, Hungary, Austria and Milan, and especially the kingdom of the Two Sicilies, of the south of Italy, namely Sicily, Cerdeña, the Balareares and the numerous islands of the Mediterranean). But because of the economic failure of the political project of the "world-empire," the emperor Carlos the V abdicates in 1557: the path is left open for the "world system" of mercantile, industrial, and, today, transnational capitalism.

As an example let us take a level of analysis, amongst the many that may be analyzed—we would not want to be criticized as being a reductive economicist, because of the example that we have adopted. It is not a coincidence that twenty-five years after the discovery of the silver mines of Potosí in the high Peru and the mines in Zacateca in Mexico (1546)—from which a total of 18 thousand tons of silver arrived to in Spain between the years of 1503 and 1660—and thanks to the first shipments of this precious metal, Spain was able to pay, among the many campaigns of the Empire, the great armada which defeated the Turks in 1571 in Lepanto. This lead to the dominion of the Mediterranean as a connection with the "center" of the older stage of the system. However, the Mediterranean had died as the road of the "center" towards the "periphery" on the West, because now the Atlantic was structuring itself as the "center" of the new world-system![32]

Wallerstein writes:

> Bullion was desired as a preciosity, for consumption in Europe and even more for trade with Asia, but it was also a necessity for the expansion of the European economy.[33]

I have read, amongst the many unpublished letters of the General Indian Archive of Seville, the following text of July 1, 1550, signed in Bolivia by Domingo de Santo Tomás:

> It was four years ago, to conclude the perdition of this land, that a mouth of hell was discovered through which every year a great many people are immolated, which the greed of the Spaniards sacrifice to their god that is gold, and it is a mine of silver which is named Potosí.[34]

The rest is well known. The Spanish colony in Flanders will replace Spain as a hegemonic power in the "center" of the recently established "world-system"—it liberates itself from Spain in 1610. Seville, the first modern port (in relations with Amberes), after more than a century of splendor, will cede its place to Amsterdam[35] (city where Descartes will write in 1636 *Le Discours de la Méthode*, and where Spinoza will live[36]), naval, fishing, crafts power, where the agricultural export flows, the great expertise in all the branches of production; city which will, among many aspects, bankrupt Venice. After more than a century, modernity already showed in this city a metropolis with its definitive physiognomy: its port, the channels that as commercial ways reached to the houses of the bourgeoisie, the merchants (who used their fourth and fifth floor as cellars, from which boats where directly loaded with cranes); a thousand details of a capitalist metropolis. From 1689 on, England will challenge, and will end up imposing itself over Holland's hegemony —which however will always have to share with France, at least until 1763.

Amerindia, meanwhile, constitutes the fundamental structure of the first modernity. From 1492 to 1500 are colonized about 50 thousand Km2 (in the Caribbean, and firm land: from Venezuela to Panama).[37] In 1515 this number will reach 300 thousand km2 with about 3 million dominated Amerindians. Until 1550 more than two million km2 (which is greater area than the whole of Europe of the "center"), and up to more than 25 million (a low figure) of indigenous peoples,[38] many of which are integrated to a system of work which produces value (in Marx's strict sense) for the Europe of the "center" (in the "encomienda," "mita," haciendas, etc.). We would have to add, from 1520 onwards, the plantation slaves of African provenance (about 14 millions until the final stage of slavery in the fourteenth century, including Brazil, Cuba, and the United States). This enormous space and population will give to Europe, "center" of the "world-system," the *definitive comparative advantage* with respect to the Muslim, Indian, and Chinese worlds. It is for this reason that in the sixteenth century:

> The periphery (eastern Europe and Hispanic America) used forced labor (slavery and coerced cash-crop labor [of the Amerindian]). The core, as we shall see, increasingly used free labor.[39]

For the goals of this philosophical work, it is of interest to indicate solely that with the birth of the "world-system," the *"peripheral social formations"*[40] were also born:

> The form of *peripheral* formation will depend, finally, at the same time on the nature of the accumulated pre-capitalist formations and the forms of external aggression.[41]

These will be, at the end of the twentieth century, the Latin American peripheral formations, those of the African bantu, the Muslim world, India, the Asian South-East,[42] and China; to which one must also add part of Eastern Europe before the fall of existing socialism:

Schema I

AN EXAMPLE OF THE CENTER-PERIPHERY STRUCTURE IN THE "CENTER" AND COLONIAL "PERIPHERY" OF THE XVIII CENTURY

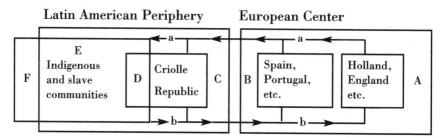

Annotations on the Schema: arrow a: domination and export of manufactured goods; arrow b: transfer of value and exploitation of labor; A: Power of the "center"; B: semi-peripheral nations; C: peripheral formations; D: exploitation of Amerindian labor or slaves; E: Indigenous communities; F: Ethnic communities who retained a certain exteriority to the "world-system."[43]

2. MODERNITY AS "MANAGEMENT" OF THE PLANETARY "CENTRALITY" AND ITS CONTEMPORARY CRISIS

We have thus arrived at the central thesis of this essay. If modernity were, and this is our hypothesis, fruit of the "management" of the "centrality" of the first "world-system," we now have to reflect on what this implies.

One must be conscious that there are at least, in its origin, two Modernities: (a) in first place, Hispanic, humanist, renaissance modernity, still linked to the old inter-regional system of Mediterranean and Muslim Christianity.[44] In this the "management" of the new system will be conceived from out of the older paradigm of the old inter-regional system. That is, Spain "manages" "centrality" as domination through the hegemony of an integral culture, a language, a religion (and thus, the evangelization process that Amerindia will suffer);

as military occupation, bureaucratic-political organization, economic expropriation, demographic presence (with hundreds of thousands of Spaniards or Portuguese who will inhabit for ever Amerindia), ecological transformation (through the modification of the fauna and flora), etc. This is the matter of the "Empire-World" project, and which as Wallerstein notes, failed with Carlos the V.[45] (b) In second place, there is the modernity of Anglo-Germanic Europe, which begins with the Amsterdam of Flanders, and which frequently passes as the *only* modernity (this is the interpretation of Sombart, Weber, Habermas or even the postmoderns, which will produce a "reductionist fallacy" which occludes the meaning of modernity, and, thus, the sense of its contemporary crisis). This second modernity, in order to be able to "manage" the immense "world-system," which suddenly opens itself to the small Holland,[46] which from being a Spanish colony now places itself as the "center" of the world-system, must accomplish or increase its efficacy through *simplification*. It is necessary to carry out an abstraction (favoring the *quantum* to the detriment of *qualitas*) which *leaves out* many valid variables (cultural, anthropological, ethical, political, and religious variables; aspects which are valuable even for the European of the sixteenth century) that will not allow an adequate, "factual"[47] or technologically possible "management" of the world-system. This *simplification* of complexity encompasses the totality of the "lifeworld" (*Lebenswelt*), of the relationship with nature (new technological and ecological position, that is no longer teleological), of subjectivity itself (new self-understanding of subjectivity), of community (new intersubjective and political relation), and, as synthesis, a new economic attitude will establish itself (practico-productive).

The first Hispanic renaissance and humanist modernity produced a theoretical or philosophical reflection of the highest importance, and which has gone unnoticed by the so-called modern philosophy (which is only the philosophy of the "second modernity"). The theoretical-philosophical thought of the sixteenth century has contemporary relevance because it is the first, and only, which lived and expressed the originary experience during the period of the constitution of the first "world-system." Thus, out of the theoretical "recourses" that were available (the scholastic-Muslim-Christian and renaissance philosophy), the central philosophical ethical question that resulted was the following: "What right has the European to occupy, dominate, and 'manage' the recently discovered, military conquered and in the process of being colonized, cultures?" From the seventeenth century on, the "second modernity" did not have to question the conscience (*Gewissen*) with these questions which had already been answered in fact: from Amsterdam, London or Paris (in the seventeenth century and from the eighteenth century onwards), "eurocentrism" (super-ideology which will establish the valid legitimacy, without falsification, of the domination of the world-system) will *no longer* be questioned, until the end of the twentieth century— and this, among other movements, by liberation philosophy.

In another work we have touched on the question.[48] Today we will only remind ourselves of the theme in general. Bartolomé de las Casas demonstrates in his numerous works, using an extraordinary bibliographical apparatus, grounding rationally and carefully his arguments, that the constitution of the world-system as European expansion in Amerindia (anticipation of the expansion in Africa and Asia) does not have any right; it is an unjust violence, and cannot have any ethical validity:

> The common ways mainly employed by the Spaniards who call themselves Christian and who have gone there to extirpate those pitiful nations and wipe them off the earth is by unjustly waging cruel and bloody wars. Then, when they have slain all those who fought for their lives or to escape the tortures they would have to endure, that is to say, when they have slain all the native rulers and young men (since the Spaniards usually spare only the women and children, who are subjected to the hardest and bitterest servitude ever suffered by man or beast), they enslave any survivors. . . . Their reason for killing and destroying such an infinite number of souls is that the Christians have an ultimate aim, which is to acquire gold, and to swell themselves with riches in a very brief time and thus rise to a high estate disproportionate to their merits. It should be kept in mind that their insatiable greed and ambition, the greatest ever seen in the world, is the cause of their villanies.[49]

Posteriorly, philosophy will no longer formulate this problematic, which showed itself unavoidable at the origin of the establishment of the world-system. For the ethics of liberation, this question is today still fundamental.

In the sixteenth century, then, is established the world-system in Seville, and philosophy questions, from out of the old philosophical paradigm, the praxis of domination, but it does not reach the formulation of the *new paradigm*. However, the origin of the new paradigm ought not to be confused with the origin of modernity. Modernity begins more than a century before (1492) the moment in which the paradigm, adequate to its very own new experience is formalized — to speak again with Kuhn. If we note the dates of the formulation of the new modern paradigm, we can conclude that it takes place in the first half of the seventeenth century.[50] This new paradigm corresponds to the exigencies of *efficacy*, technological "factibility" or control of the "management" of an enormous world-system in expansion; it is the expression of a necessary process of *simplification* through "rationalization" of the lifeworld, of the subsystems (economic, political, cultural, religious, etc.). "Rationalization" indicated by Werner Sombart,[51] Ernst Troeltsch,[52] or Max Weber,[53] is *effect* and not cause. On the other hand, the effects of that *simplifying rationalization* in order to *manage* the world-system are perhaps more profound and negative than Habermas or the post-moderns imagine.[54]

The corporeal Muslim-Medieval subjectivity is *simplified*: subjectivity is postulated as an *ego*, an I, about which Descartes writes:

Accordingly this 'I'—that is, the soul by which I am what I am—is *entirely* distinct from the body, and indeed is easier to know than the body, and would not fail to be whatever it is, even if the body did not exit.[55]

The body is a mere machine, *res extensa* entirely foreign to the soul.[56] Kant himself writes:

The human soul should be seen as being linked in the present life to two worlds at the same time: of these worlds, inasmuch as it forms with the body a personal unity, it feels but only the material world; on the contrary, as a member of world of the spirit [mind] (*als ein Glied der Geisterwelt* [without body] it receives and propagates the pure influences of immaterial natures.[57]

This dualism—which Kant will apply to its ethics, inasmuch as the "maxims" ought not to have any empirical or "pathological" motives—is posteriorly articulated through the negation of practical intelligence, which is replaced by instrumental reason, the one that will deal with technical, technological "management" (ethics disappears before an *more geometric* intelligence) in the *Critique of Judgment*. It is here that the conservative tradition (such as that of Heidegger) continues to perceive the *simplifying* suppression of the organic complexity of life, now replaced by a technique of the "will to power" (critiques elaborated by Nietzsche and Foucault. Galileo, with all the naive enthusiasm of a great discovery, writes:

> Philosophy is written in this grand book, the universe, which stands continually open to our gaze. But the book cannot be understood unless one first learns to comprehend the language and read the letters in which it is composed. It is written in the *language of mathematics*, and its characters are triangles, circles and other geometric figures, without which it is humanly impossible to understand a single word of it; without these, one wanders about in a dark labyrinth.[58]

Heidegger already said that the "*mathematical* position"[59] before entities is to have them already known "ready-to-hand" (in the axioms of science, for example) and to approach them only in order to use them. One does not "learn" a weapon, for instance, but instead one learns to make "use" of it, because one already knows what it is:

> The *mathemata* are the things insofar as we take cognizance of them as what we already know them to be in advance, the body as the bodily, the plant-like of the plant, the animal-like of the animal, the thingness of the thing, and so on.[60]

The "rationalization" of political life (bureaucratization), of the capitalist enterprise (administration), of daily life (calvinist asceticism or puritanism), the de-corporalization of subjectivity (with its alienating effects on living labor—criticized by Marx—as well as on its drives—analyzed by Freud—), the non-ethicalness of every economic or political gestation (understood only as technical engineering, etc.), the suppression of practical-communicative reason, now replaced by instrumental reason, the solipsistic individuality which negates the community, etc., are all examples of the diverse moments which are negated by the indicated *simplification*, apparently necessary for the "management" of the "centrality" of a world-system that Europe found itself in the need of perpetually carrying out. Capitalism, liberalism, dualism (without valorizing corporeality), etc., are *effects* of the management of this function which corresponded to Europe as "center" of the world-system. Effects that are constituted through mediations in systems that end up totalizing themselves. Capitalism, mediation of exploitation and accumulation (effect of the world-system), is later on transformed into an *independent system* that from out of its own self-referential and autopoietic logic can destroy Europe and its periphery, and even the entire planet. And this is what Weber observes, but reductively. That is to say, Weber notes part of the phenomena but not the horizon of the world-system. In fact, the formal procedure of *simplification* that turns *manageable* the world-system produces formal rationalized subsystems that later on do not have internal standards of self-regulation within its own limits of modernity, which could be redirected at the service of humanity. It is in this moment that there emerge critique from within the "center" (and from out of the "periphery," such as is mine) against modernity itself. Now one attributes to *ratio* all culpable causality (as object 'understanding' which is set through disintegration), from Nietzsche to Heidegger, or with the postmoderns—this culpability will be traced back as far as Socrates (Nietzsche), or even Parmenides himself (Heidegger). In fact, the modern *simplifications* (the dualism of an *ego-alma* without a body, teleological instrumental reason, the racism of the superiority of one's own culture, etc.) have many similarities with the *simplification* that Greek slavery produced in the II inter-regional system. The Greek *Weltanschaung* was advantageous to the modern man—not without complicity does he resuscitate the Greeks, as was done through the German romantics.[61] The subsumptive superseding (*Aufhebung*) of modernity will mean the critical consideration of *all* these simplifying reductions produced since its origin—and not only a few, like Habermas imagines. The most important of said reductions, next to the one of the solipsistic subjectivity, without community, is the negation of the corporeality of said subjectivity—to which are related the critiques of modernity by Marx, Nietzsche, Freud, Foucault, Levinas, and the ethics of liberation, as we will see throughout the length of this work.

Because of all of this, the concept that one has of modernity determines, as is evident, the pretention to its realization (such as is Habermas), or the type of critiques one may formulate against it (such as that of the postmoderns). In general, every debate between rationalists and postmoderns does not overcome the eurocentric horizon. The crisis of modernity (already noted by, as we have remarked frequently, Nietzsche and Heidegger) refers to internal aspects of Europe. The "peripheral world" would appear to be a passive spectator of a thematic that does not touch it, because it is a "barbarian," a "premodern," or simply, still in need of being "modernized." In other words, the eurocentric view reflects on the problem of the crisis of modernity solely with the European-North American moments (or even now Japanese), but it minimizes the periphery. To break through this "reductivist fallacy" is not easy. We will attempt to "indicate" the path towards its surmounting.

If modernity begins at the end of the fifteenth century, with a renaissance premodern process, and from there a transition is made to the properly modern in Spain, Amerindia forms part of "modernity" since the moment of the conquest and colonization (the mestizo world in Latin America is the only one that has as a much age as modernity[62]), since it was the first "barbarian" that modernity needed in its definition. If modernity enters into crisis at the end of the twentieth century, after five centuries of development, it is not a matter only of the moments detected by Weber and Habermas, or by Lyotard or Welsch,[63] but we will have to add the very ones of a "planetary" description of the phenomena of modernity.

To conclude, if we situate ourselves, instead, within the planetary horizon, one can distinguish at least the following positions in the face of the formulated problematic: (a) in first place, on the one hand, the "substantialist" developmentalist[64] (quasi-metaphysical) position that conceptualizes modernity as an *exclusively European* phenomena which had *expanded from the seventeenth century on* throughout all the "backward" cultures (eurocentric position in the "center" or modernizing in the "periphery"); modernity is a phenomena that must be concluded. Some of the ones who assume this first position (for example, Habermas and Apel), defenders of reason, do so critically, since they think that European superiority is not material, but formal: thanks to a new structure of critical questions.[65] On the other hand, there is the conservative "nihilist" position, which rejects modernity's positive qualities (of a Nietzsche or Heidegger, for instance), and that propose practically an annihilation without exit. The postmoderns take this second position (in their frontal attack on "reason" *as such*; with differences in the case of Levinas[66]), although, paradoxically, they also defend parts of the first position, from the perspective of a developmentalist eurocentrism.[67] The postmodern philosophers are admirers of postmodern art, of the *Media*, and although they affirm theoretically *difference*, they do not reflect on the origins of these systems that are fruit of a rationalization proper to the "management" of the European "centrality" in the world-system, before which they are profoundly uncritical, and, because of this, do not have possibilities of attempting to contribute valid alternatives (cultural, economic, political, etc.) for the peripheral nations, or the peoples or great majorities who are dominated by the center and/or the periphery.

b) In second place, we defend another position, from outside the periphery, one which considers the process of modernity as the already indicated rational "management" of the world-system. This position intends to recuperate the redeemable of modernity, and to negate the domination and exclusion in the world-system. It is then a project of liberation of a periphery negated from the very beginning of modernity. The problem is not the mere superseding of instrumental reason (as is for Habermas) or of the reason of *terror* of the postmoderns; instead, it is the question of the overcoming of the world-system itself, such as it has developed until today for the last 500 years. The problem is exhaustion of a civilizing system that has come to its end.[68] The overcoming of *cynical-managerial reason* (planetary administrative) of capitalism (as economic system), of liberalism (as political system), of eurocentrism (as ideology), of machismo (in erotics), of the reign of the white race (in racism), of the destruction of nature (in ecology), etc., presuppose the liberation of diverse types of oppressed and/or excluded. It is in this sense that the ethics of liberation defines itself as transmodern (since the postmoderns are still eurocentric). The end of the present stage of civilization shows itself some limits of the "system of 500 years"—as Noam Chomsky calls it.

These limits are: (a) in first place, the ecological destruction of the planet. From the very moment of its inception, Modernity has constituted nature as an "exploitable" object, with the increase in the rate of profit of capital[69] as its goal:

> For the first time, nature becomes purely an object for humankind, purely a matter of utility; ceases to be recognized as a power for itself.[70]

Once the earth is seen constituted as an "exploitable object" in favor of *quantum*, of capital, that can defeat all limits, all boundaries, there manifests the "great civilizing influence of capital," it now reaches finally its unsurmountable limit, where itself is its own limit, the impassable barrier for ethical-human progress, and we have arrived at this moment:

> The universality towards which it irresistibly strives encounters barriers in its own nature, which will, at a certain state of its development, allow it to be recognized as being itself the greatest barrier to this tendency, and hence will drive towards its own suspension.[71]

Given that nature is for modernity only a medium of production, it plays out its fate of being consumed, destroyed, and, in addition, accumulating geometrically upon the earth its debris, until it jeopardizes the reproduction or survival of life itself. Life is the absolute condition of capital; its destruction destroys capital. We have arrived at this state of affairs. The "system of 500 years" (modernity or capitalism) confronts its first absolute limit: the death of life in its totality, through the indiscriminate use of an antiecological technology constituted progressively through the sole criteria of the *quan-*

titative "management" of the world-system in modernity: the increase in the rate of profit. But capital cannot limit itself. There thus comes about the utmost danger for humanity.

b) The second limit of modernity is the destruction of humanity itself. "Living labor" is the other essential mediation of capital as such; the human subject is the only one that can "create" new value (surplus value, profit). Capital that defeats all barriers requires incrementally more absolute time of work, when it cannot supersede this limit, then it augments productivity through technology; but said increase decreases the importance of human labor. It is thus that there is *superfluous humanity* (displaced). The unemployed does not earn a salary, money; but money is the only mediation in the market through which one can acquire commodities in order to satisfy needs. In any event, work that is not employable by capital increases (increase in unemployment). It is thus that the proportion of needing subjects who are not solvent, clients, consumers, buyers—as much in the periphery as in the center.[72] It is poverty, poverty as the absolute limit of capital. Today we know how misery grows in the entire planet. It is a matter of a "law of modernity":

> Accumulation of wealth at one pole is, therefore, at the same time accumulation of misery, the torment of labour, slavery, ignorance, brutalization and moral degradation at the opposite pole. . . .[73]

The modern world-system cannot overcome this essential contradiction. The ethics of liberation reflects philosophically from out of this planetary horizon of the world-system; from out of this double limit which configures a terminal crisis of a civilizing process: The ecological destruction of the planet and the extinguishing in misery and hunger of the great majority of humanity. Before these two coimplicating phenomena of such planetary magnitude, the project of many philosophical schools would seem naïve and even ridiculous, irresponsible, irrelevant, cynical and even complicitous (as much in the center, but even worse yet in the periphery, in Latin America, Africa, and Asia), which are closed in their "ivory towers" of sterile eurocentric academicism. Already in 1968 Marcuse had written, referring to the opulent counties of late capitalism:

Why do we need liberation from such a society if it is capable—perhaps in the distant future, but apparently capable—of conquering poverty to a greater degreee than ever before, or reducing the toil of labour and the time of labour, and of raising the standard of living? If the price for all goods delivered, the price for this comfortable servitude, for all these achievements, is exacted from people far away from the metropolis and far way from its affluence? If the affluent society itself hardly notices what it is doing, how it is spreading terror and enslavement, how it is fighting liberation in all corners of the globe?[74]

c) The third limit of modernity is the impossibility of the subsumption of the populations, economies, nations, and cultures which it has been attacking since its origin and excluded from its horizon and cornered into poverty. This is the whole theme of the exclusion of African, Asian, Latin American altarity and the their indomitable will to survive. I will return to the theme, but for now I want to indicate that the globalizing "world-system" reaches a limit where the exteriority of the Alterity of the Other, locus of "resistance" and from whose analectical affirmation there departs the process of the negation of negation of liberation.

NOTES

1. Max Weber, *The Protestant Ethic and the Spirit of Capitalism*, trans. Talcott Parsons (New York: Charles Scribner's Sons, 1958), p. 13 (emphasis added). Later on Weber asks: "Why did not the scientific, the artistic, the political, or the economic development there [China, and India] enter upon that path of *rationalization* which is peculiar to the Occident?" (Ibid., p. 25). In order to argue this, Weber juxtaposes the Babylonians that did not know mathematized astronomy and the Greeks, who did (but Weber does not know that the Greeks learned it from the Egyptians); Or, as he also argues, that science emerged in the West, but not in India or China, etc., but he forgets to mention the Muslim world, from whom the Latin West learned Aristotelian "experiential," empirical exactitude (such as the Oxford Franciscans, or the Marcilios de Padua, etc.), and so on. Every Hellenistic, or eurocentric argument, such as Weber's, can be falsified if we take 1492 as the ultimate date of comparison between the supposed superiority of the West and other cultures.

2. Georg Wilhelm Friedrich Hegel, *The Philosophy of History*, trans. J. Sibree (New York: Dover Publications, Inc. 1956), p. 341.

3. Following Hegel, Habermas in 1988, p. 27.

4. The "world-system" or planetary system of the IV stage of the same inter-regional system of the Asiatic-African-Mediterranean continent, but now—correcting Frank's conceptualization—factially "planetary." See Frank, 1990. On the "world-system" problematic see: Abu-Lughod, 1989; Brenner, 1983; Hodgson, 1974; Kennedy, 1987; McNeill, 1964; Modelski, 1987; Mann, 1986; Stavarianos, 1970; Thompson, 1989; Tilly, 1984; Wallerstein, 1974 and 1984.

5. On this point, as I already mentioned, I am not in agreement with Frank on calling "world-system" the prior moments of the system, which I therefore call them "inter-regional systems."

6. Wallerstein, 1974, I, cap.6.

7. Ibid., II, caps.4 y 5.

8. Ibid., III, cap.3.

9. See Lattimore, 1962; Rossabi, 1982. For a description of the situation of the world in 1400, see Wolf, 1982, pp. 24 ff.

10. There are other reasons for this nonexternal expansion: the existence of "space" in the neighboring territories to the empire, which took all its power in order to "conquer the south" through the cultivation of rice and its defense from the barbarian "North." See Wallerstein, 1974, I, ed.cast. pp.80 ff, which has many good arguments against Weber's eurocentrism.

11. For example, Joseph Needham, 1961, 1963, and 1965. All of these with respect to the control of ships, which the Chinese already dominated since the first century after Christ. The Chinese use of the compass, paper, and gunpowder and other discoveries is well known.

12. Perhaps the only disadvantage was the Portugese caravel (invented in 1441), used to navigate the Atlantic (which was not needed in the Indian sea), and the cannon. This last one, although spectacular, outside naval wars never had any real effect in Asia until the nineteenth century. Carlo Cipolla, 1965, on pp. 106–107, writes: "Chinese fire-arms were at least as good as the Western, if not better."

13. The first bureaucracy (as the Weberian high stage of political rationalization) is the state mandarin structure of political exercise. The mandarin are not nobles, nor warriors, nor aristocratic or commercial plutocracy; they are *strictly* a bureaucratic elite whose exams are *exclusively* based in the dominion of culture and the laws of the Chinese empire.

14. William de Bary indicates that the individualism of Wang Yangming, in the fifteenth century, which expressed the ideology of the bureacratic class, was as advanced as that of the Renaissance (Bary, 1970).

15. Through many examples, Thomas Kuhn (Kuhn, 1962), situates the modern scientific revolution, fruit of the expression of the new paradigm, practically with Newton (seventeenth century). He does not study with care the impact that events such as the discovery of America, the roundness of the earth, empirically proved since 1520, etc., could have had on the science,

the "scientific community," of the sixteenth century, since the structuration of the first "world-system."

16. Needham, 1963, p. 139.

17. A. R. Hall place the scientific revolution beginning with the 1500s (see Hall, 1954).

18. Pierre Chaunu, 1955, vol. 8/1, p. 50.

19. *Factically*, Colon will be the first Modern, but not *existentially* (since his *interpretation of the world* remained always that of a renaissance Genovese: a member of a peripheral Italy of the III "inter-regional system"). See Taviani, 1982; O'Gorman, 1957.

20. See Zunzunegui, 1941.

21. Russia was not yet integrated as "periphery" in the III stage of the inter-regional system (nor in the modern world-system, except until the eighteenth century with Peter the Great and the founding of St. Petersburg on the Baltic).

22. Portugal, already in 1095 has the rank of empire. In Algarve, 1249, the reconquest concludes with this empire. Enrique the Navigator (1394–1460), as patron gathers the sciences of cartography, astronomy and the techniques of navigation and construction of ships, which originated in the Muslim world (since he had contact with the Moroccans) and the Italian renaissance (via Genoa).

23. Wallerstein, 1974, I, pp. 49–50. See Verlinden, 1953; Rau, 1957.

24. See Chaudhuri, 1985.

25. My argument would seem to be the same as Blaut's (1992), pp. 28ff, but in fact it is different. It is not that Spain was "geographically" closer to Amerindia. No. It is not a question of distances. It is that and much more. It is a matter that Spain had to go through Amerindia not only because it was closer (which in fact took place, especially with respect to Asiatic cultures, although this was not the case with the Turk-Muslim empire that had arrived at Morocco), but because this was the demanded path to the "center" of the "system"—question which is not dealt with by Blaut. Furthermore, and on the other hand, is just as different from that of André Gunder Frank (Blaut, 1992, pp. 65-80), because for him 1492 is only a secondary internal change of the same world-system. However, if it is understood that the "inter-regional system," in its stage prior to 1492, is the "same" system but not yet as a "world" system, then 1492 assumes a greater importance than Frank grants it. Even if the system *is the same*, there exists a qualitative jump (which, under other aspects, is the origin capitalism proper, to which Frank denies importance because of his prior denial of relevance to concepts such as "value," "surplus value," and, therefore, attributes "capital" to the "wealth" [use-value with a virtual possibility of transforming itself into exchange-value, but not capital] accumulated in the stages I–III of the inter-regional system). This is a grave theoretical question.

26. Dussel, 1995.

27. See Dussel, 1993a, Appendix 4, where the map of the fourth Asiatic peninsula is reproduced (after the Arabian, Indian and Malacan), certainly product of Genovese navigations, where South America is a peninsula attached to the south of China. This explains why the Genovese Colon would hold the opinion Asia would not be so far from Europe (South America=Fourth peninsula of China).

28. This is what I called, philosophically, the "invention" of Amerindia seen as India, in all of its details. Colon, existentially, neither "discovered" nor reached Amerindia. He "invented" something which was non-existent: India in the place of Amerindia, which prevented him from "discovering" what he had before his own eyes. See Dussel, 1993a, cap.2.

29. This is the meaning of the title of chapter two of my already cited work: "From the *Invention* to the *Discovery* of America."

30. See Amin, 1970. This work is not yet developed on the "world-system" hypothesis. It would appear as though the colonial world were a *rear or subsequent* and *outside* space to European Medieval capitalism which is transformed "in" Europe as modern. My hypothesis is more radical: the fact of the discovery of Amerindia, of its integration as "periphery" is a *simultaneous* and *co-constitutive* fact of the restructuration of Europe *from within* as "center" of the only new world-system that is, only now and *not before*, capitalism (first mercantile and later industrial).

31. We have spoken of "Amerindia" and not of America, because it is a question, during the entire sixteenth century, of a continent inhabited by "Indians" (wrongly called because of the mirage that the "inter-regional system" of the third stage still produced in the still being born "world-system." They were called Indians because of India, "center" of the inter-regional system that was begining to fade). Anglo-Saxon North-America will be born slowly in the seventeenth century, but it will be an event "internal" to a growing modernity in Amerindia. This is the *originating* "periphery" of modernity, constitutive of its first definition. It is the "other face" of the very same phenomena of modernity.

32. All of the subsequent hegemonic power will remain until the present on their shores: Spain, Holland, England, (and France partly), until 1945, and the United States in the present. Thanks to Japan, China and the California of the United States, the Pacific appears for the first time as a counterweight. This is perhaps a novelty of the next century, the twenty-first.

33. Wallerstein, 1974, I, p. 45.

34. *Archivo General de Indias* (Sevilla), Charcas 313 (see Dussel, 1970, p. I; which was part of my doctoral thesis at the Sorbonne in 1967).

35. Wallerstein, 1974, I, 165 ff: "From Seville to Amsterdam: The Failure of Empire."

36. It should be remembered that Spinoza (Espinosa), who lived in

Amsterdam (1632–1677), descended from a "azquenazí" family from the Muslim world of Granada, expelled from Spain and that was exiled in the Spanish colony of Flanders.

37. See Chaunu, 1969, pp.119–76.

38. Europe had approximately 56 million inhabitants in 1500, and 82 million in 1600 (See Cardoso, 1979, t.I, p.114).

39. Wallerstein, 1974, I, p.103.

40. See Samir Amin, 1974, pp. 309 ff.

41. Ibid., p.312.

42. The colonial process of these formations ends, for the most part, after the so-called World War II (1945), given that the North-American super-power requires neither military occupation, nor political-bureacratic domination (proper only to the old European powers, such as France and England); but rather the management of the dominion of economic-financial dependence in its transnational stage.

43. See Dussel, 1983, t.I/1, pp. 223–41.

44. "Muslim" means here the most "cultured" and civilized of the fifteenth century.

45. I think that, exactly, to *manage* the new world-system according to old practices had to fail because it operated with variable that made it unmanageable. Modernity *had began* but it had not given itself the new way to "manage" the system.

46. Later on, it will also have to "manage" the system of the English Island. Both nations had very exiguous territories, with little population at their begining, without any other capacity than their creative "bourgeois attitude" before existence. Because of their weakness, they had to perform a great reform of "management" of the planetary metropolitan enterprise.

47. The technical "factibility" will become a criteria of truth, of possibility, of existence; Vico's "verum et *factum* conventuntur."

48. See Dussel, 1993a, chap. 5: "Critique of the myth of Modernity." During the sixteenth century there were three theoretical positions before the fact of the constitution of the world-system: (1) that of Ginés de Sepúlveda, the *modern* renaissance and humanist scholar, who rereads Aristotle and demonstrates the natural slavery of the Amerindian, and thus concludes on the legitimacy of the conquest; (2) that of the Franciscans, such as Mendieta, who attempts an utopian Amerindian Christinaity (a "republic of Indians" under the hegemony of Catholic religion), proper to the III Christian-Muslim inter-regional system; and (3) Bartolomé de las Casas's position, *the beginning of a critical "counter-discourse" in the interior of Modernity* (which in his work of 1536, a century before *Le Discours de la Méthode*, he titles *De unico modo* [The only way], shows that "argumentation" is the rational means through which to attract the Amerindian to the new civilization). Habermas, as we will see later on, speaks of "counter-dis-

course," and suggests that said counter-discourse is only two centuries old (beginning with Kant). Liberation Philosophy suggests, instead, that this counter-discourse begins in the sixteenth century (In 1511 in Santo Domingo with Antón de Montesinos?!), decidely with Bartolomé de las Casas in 1514 (see Dussel, 1983, I/1, pp.17–27).

49. Bartolomé de las Casas, *The Devastation of the Indies: A Brief Account*, trans. by Herma Briffault (Baltimore and London: The Johns Hopkins University Press, 1992), p. 31. I have placed this text at the beginning of volume I of my work *Para una ética de la liberación latinoamericana* (Dussel, 1973), since it synthesizes the general hypothesis of the ethics of liberation.

50. Frequently, in the contemporary histories of philosophy, and of course of ethics, a "jump" is made from the Greeks (from Plato and Aristotles) to Descartes (1596–1650), who takes up residence in Amsterdam in 1629 and writes *Le Discours de la Méthode*, as we indicated above. That is, there is a jump from Greece to Amsterdam. In the interim, 21 centuries have gone by without any other content of importance. Studies are began with Bacon (1561–1626), Kepler (1571–1630), Galileo (1571–1630) or Newton (1643–1727). Campanella writes *Civitas Solis* in 1602. Everything would seem to be situated at the begining of the seventeenth century, the moment I have called the second moment of Modernity.

51. See Sombart, 1902 and 1920.

52. See Troeltsch, 1923.

53. See Habermas, 1981, t.I, II. Habermas insists on the Weberian discovery of "rationalization," but he forgets to ask after its cause. I believe that my hypothesis goes deeper and further back: Weberian rationalization (accepted by Habermas, Apel, Lyotard, etc.) is the apparently necessary mediation of a deforming simplification (by instrumental reason) of practical reality, in order to transform it into something "manageable," governable, given the complexity of the inmense world-system. It is not only the internal "manageability" of Europe, but also, and above all, *planetary* (center-periphery) "management." Habermas's attempt to assimilate instrumental reason into communicative reason is not sufficient because the moments of his diagnosis on the *origin itself of the process of rationalization* are not sufficient.

54. The Postmoderns, as eurocentric, concur, more or less, with the Weberian diagnosis of Modernity. Rather, they underscore certain rationalizing aspects or mediums (means of communication, etc.) of Modernity, some they reject wrathfully as metaphysical dogmatisms, but others they accept as inevitable phenomena and frequently as positive transformations.

55. René Descartes, *The Philosophical Works of Descartes*, Vol 1, "Discourse on the Method," Part Four, p. 127.

56. See Dussel, 1974a (at the end) and 1974b, cap.2, § 4. Contemporary theories of the functions of the brain put in question definitively this dualistic mechanism.

57. Kant, *Träume eines Geistersehers* (1766), A 36; in Kant, 1968, II, p. 940.

58. Stillman Drake, *Discoveries and Opinions of Galileo* (New York: Doubleday, Anchor Books, 1957), pp. 237–38.

59. See Dussel, 1973b.

60. Martin Heidegger, *What is a Thing*, trans. by W.B. Barton, et. al, (Chicago: Henry Regnery Company, 1967), p. 73.

61. See Martin Bernal, 1989, I, cap.V, pp. 224ss.

62. Amerindia and Europe have a premodern history, just as Africa and Asia do. Only the hybrid world, the syncretic culture, the Latin American *mestiza* race that was born in the fifteenth century (the child of Malinche and Hernán Cortés can be considered as its symbol; see Octavio Paz, 1950), has 500 years.

63. See among others: Lyotard, 1979; Rorty, 1979; Derrida, 1964, 1967a y 1967b; Marquart, 1981; Vattimo, 1985; Welsch, 1993; etc.

64. This Spanish word (*desarrollismo*), which does not exist in other languages, points to the "fallacy" that pretends the same "development" (the word *Entwicklung* has a strictly Hegelian philosophical origin) for the "center" as for the "periphery," not taking note that the "periphery" is not *backward* (see Hinkelammert, 1970a and 1970b). In other words, it is not a temporal *prius* that awaits a development similar to that of Europe or the United States (like the child/adult), but that instead it is the asymmetrical position of the dominated, the *simultaneous* position of the exploited (like the free lord/slave). The "immature" (child) could follow the path of the "mature" (adult) and get to "develop" herself, while the "exploited" (slave) no matter how much she works will never be "free" (lord), because her own dominated subjectivity includes her "relationship" with the dominator. The "modernizers" of the "periphery" are developmentalists because they do not realize that the "relationship" of planetary domination has to be overcome as prerequisite for "*national* development." Globalizatin has not extinguished, not by the least, the "national" question.

65. See Habermas, 1981, t.I, I, 2, from sec. [B] to sec. [D], and especially the debate with P. Winch and A. MacIntyre.

66. We will see that Levinas, "father of French postmodernism" (from Derrida on), is neither postmodern nor negates reason. Instead, he is a critic of the *totalization* of reason (instrumental, strategic, cynical, ontological, etc.). Liberation Philosophy, since the end of the decade of the 60s, studied Levinas because of his radical critique of domination. In the preface to my work, *Philosophy of Liberation* (Dussel, 1985), I indicated that the philosophy of liberation is a "postmodern" philosophy, one which departed from the "second Heidegger," but also from the critique of"*totalized* reason" carried out by Marcuse and Levinas. It would seem as though we were "postmoderns" *avant la lettre*. In fact, however, we were critics of ontology and

Modernity from (*desde*) the periphery, which meant (and which still *means*) something entirely different, as we intend to explain.

67. Up to now, the postmoderns remain eurocentric. The dialogue with "different" cultures is, for now, an unfullfilled promised. They think that mass culture, the *media* (television, movies, etc.) will impact peripheral urban cultures to the extent that they will annihilate their "differences," in such a way that what Vattimo sees in Torino, or Lyotard in Paris, will be shortly the same in New Delhi and Nairobi; and they do not take the time to analyze the *hard* irreductibility of the hybrid cultural horizon (which is not *absolutely* an exteriority, but that will not be during centuries a univocal interiority to the globalized system) that receives those information impacts.

68. See Jameson's work, 1991, on the "cultural logic of late capitalism as postmodernism."

69. In Stalinist real socialism, the criteria was the "increase in the rate of production"—measured, in any event, by an approximate market value of commodities. It is a question of the same time of fetishism. See Hinkelammert, 1984, chap.4: "Marco categorial del pensamiento soviético" (pp. 123 ff).

70. Karl Mark, *Grundrisse*, trans. Martin Nicolaus (New York: Penguin Books, 1973), p. 410.

71. Ibid., p. 410.

72. Pure necessity without money is no market, it is only misery, growing and unavoidable misery.

73. Marx, *Capital*, vol. 1, p. 799. Here we must remember once more that *Human Development Report 1992*, 1992, already demostrated in an incontrivertible manner that the richer 20 percent of the planet consumes today (as never before in global history) the 82.7 percent of goods (incomes) of the planet, while the remaining 80 percent of humanity only consumes the 17.3 percent of said goods. Such concentration is product of the "world-system" we have been delineating.

74. Hebert Marcuse, "Liberation from the Affluent Society," in *To Free a Generation: The Dialectics of Liberation*, ed. David Cooper (New York: Collier Books, 1967), p. 181.

Santiago Castro-Gómez

THE CHALLENGE OF POSTMODERNITY
TO LATIN AMERICAN PHILOSOPHY

In 1979, at the Ninth Inter-American Congress of Philosophy, Horacio Cerutti presented a paper entitled "Possibilities and limits of a Latin American philosophy *after* the philosophy of liberation." Cerutti recognized liberation philosophy's wholehearted intention of dealing with Latin American reality as a philosophical problem. It had thus returned to an interest in the need for and the meaning of thought immersed in the reality of the Latin American peoples. Such an endeavor had already been outlined in the nineteenth century by Juan Bautista Alberdi and the other initiators of Latin America's "mental emancipation." Cerutti also recognized liberation philosophy's great effort philosophically to absorb the contributions of the two other intellectual currents that appeared respectively in the first and the second half of the 1960s: the "theory of dependence" and the "theology of liberation." Despite these gains, at that time (1979) the Argentine philosopher already thought that the three liberationist approaches had become sterile and unproductive.[1] Among the reasons mentioned by Cerutti as leading to this decline were (1) the distorted reception of the theory of dependence both by liberation philosophy and liberation theology, which separated it from the theoretical nucleus of reflection which sustained and constituted it, and (2) the outdatedness of a certain kind of "Christian" thought which

From Santiago Castro-Gómez, *Crítica de la Razón Latinoamericana* (Barcelona: Puvill Libros, 1996), chap. 1. Translated by Nancy E. Bedford de Stutz.

demanded faith as a prelude to philosophizing in a liberating fashion.[2]

Today, over fifteen years after Cerutti's reflections, it is worth reintroducing the matters he expounded, reformulating them in the following way: What kind of social-structural transformations have quickened the aging of the philosophical, sociological, and theological categories used by liberationist discourse in its various forms? Which contributions made by these discourses should we retain in order to carry out a contemporary diagnosis of Latin American societies? And what kind of readjustment in our categories do we need in order to consolidate a new kind of *critical discourse* in Latin America?

I very much doubt that any thinker in Latin America still linked to liberation philosophy or theology can help but asking him—or herself about the inevitable readjustment in ideas brought on by the collapse of the Eastern European socialist regimes. Even taking into account the differences that existed among them, almost all the liberationist approaches were strongly influenced by the rhetoric that served to consolidate Socialism ideologically. The liberation of the oppressed, the thesis that imperialism was the only culprit of the Latin American nations' poverty and misery, the moral and revolutionary reserves of the people, the establishment of a society in which there would be no class antagonisms, all of these were central motifs for philosophical and theological reflection in Latin America in the 1960s and 1970s. It was the time of the Cold War, which led to an ideological polarization of the entire continent; of fear of an atomic threat which menaced all of humanity; of the African emancipation processes; of the student movement and of the height of the national liberation guerrilla movements; of the Cuban revolution and of Fidel's valiant behavior in the Sierra Maestra and the Bay of Pigs; of the sacrifices of Che Guevara and Camilo Torres in South America; of Juan Domingo Perón's virtual apotheosis upon returning to Argentina; of Monseñor Romero's martyrdom and that of many other committed Christians in Central America; of the triumph of the Unidad Popular in Chile and of the Sandinista movement in Nicaragua; of the resistance to the brutal fascist dictatorships that bloodied the southern portion of the continent. In not a few sectors of society at that time an atmosphere of hope was breathed according to which it would soon be possible to achieve true revolution and finally to topple the power of the capitalist bourgeoisie, thus leading Latin America out of its poverty and underdevelopment.

However, the 1980s passed without the desired revolution taking shape anywhere. And in the places where its presence insinuated itself, it was crushed without pity by the powerful forces of the established order, which showed their immunity to structural "quantitative leaps." Quite on the contrary, poverty grew as did the foreign debts and the enormous cities, to the point that those years passed into history under the the inglorious title of "the lost decade." Yet what was lost in Latin America is not measurable only in quantitative terms (decrease of per capita income, of the gross national product, of exports); it also includes an ideological disenchantment which permeates the entire fabric of our societies.

How should we interpret phenomena such as the failure of socialism or the change of sensibility that can be observed at present in almost all Western countries, including Latin America, of course? We think that a dialogue with the theoreticians of postmodernity could throw some light on this matter. However, such a dialogue demands first of all that we confront the great critical avalanche stemming primarily certain philosophical sectors in Latin America that still resist the task of rethinking their discourse in accordance with the new demands of the time. Accordingly, we shall examine the content of these criticisms, then move to a dialogue with the new tendencies in the Latin American social sciences, and lastly examine some of the theoretical "postmodern" proposals, emphasizing those elements which can serve us in revitalizing a critical discourse in Latin America.

I. LATIN AMERICAN PHILOSOPHY'S CRITIQUE OF POSTMODERNITY

In the opinion of Mexican thinker Gabriel Vargas Lozano, the debate over postmodernism alludes to the new phenomena which are appearing in the present phase of capitalist development.[3] Following the analyses of Fredric Jameson, a North American Marxist, Vargas Lozano states that postmodernity is a name for the cultural logic of "late capitalism." The emergence of new features in industrialized societies, such as the popularization of mass culture, the rate and complexity of the automation of work, and the growing mechanization of daily life, lead the capitalist system to develop an "ideology" that allows it to compensate for the conflict between the new depersonalizing tendencies and the old ideas about individual or collective life. In order to face these adjustment conflicts, the capitalist system needs to rid itself of its own past (that is to say of the emancipation ideals characteristic of modernity) and to announce the advent of a postmodern period, in which reality is transformed into images, and time into the repetition of an eternal present. We are therefore faced with an ideological legitimization of the system, in accordance with a computerized capitalism's orientation toward consumerism.

Adolfo Sánchez Vázquez also cites Jameson and believes that postmodernity is an ideology proper to the "third phase of capitalist expansion," which began after the end of the Second World War.[4] In contradistinction to the two other phases, the third knows no boundaries of any kind, and is even able to penetrate areas such as nature, art and the collective unconscious. In order to achieve its objectives, "late capitalism" spawns an ideology able completely to immobilize any attempt to change society. Postmodern thought throws the very idea of a "foundation" overboard, and this leads to the failure of any attempt to give legitimacy to a project of social transformation. By denying the emancipating potential of modernity, postmodernity disqualifies political action and displaces attention toward the contemplative sphere of aesthetics. In addition, by means of announcing the "death of the subject" and the "end of history," postmodern philosophers liberate artists from the responsibity to protest given them by modern aesthetics. Likewise, the vindication of fragmentation and eclecticism eliminates any kind of political resistance and leads people to await the end resignedly.

Franz Hinkelammert, an economist and philosopher, sees in postmodernity a dangerous return to the sources of Nazism.[5] Nietzsche's influence on postmodern philosophers is no coincidence, for even as he did, they corrode the very foundations of rationality. As was the case with their master Nietzsche, postmodern authors identify God with the "master narrative" of universal ethics and persistently announce God's death. And just as Nietzsche legitimized the power of the strongest by arguing that a universal ethic is the ethic of the poor, of slaves and of the weak, postmodernism sides with the rich countries, undermining the foundations of a universalist ethic of human rights based on reason. In this way, postmodernism presents itself as the best ally of contemporary neoliberal tendencies, which are oriented toward the expulsion of ethical universalism from the economic realm.

Hinkelammert also states that postmodernism's "antirationalism" has an anarchist lineage stretching from the workers' movements of the nineteenth century to the student protests of the 1960s. In his opinion, their protests against tend to clash with any kind of institution. Their final objective is to construct an ideal stateless society. He warns, however, that the anti-institutionalism of anarchist movements prevents them from proposing a political project, and this always leads them to look for extremist solutions. Such is the case of terrorist and guerrilla groups, who, unable to find a way to abolish the state from the Left, moved in the direction indicated by Bakunin: destruction as creative passion.

According to Hinkelammert, today's neoliberalism offers all anarchists new possibilities for abolishing the state. It is therefore not surprising that a good number of hippies, Maoists and other members of former protest groups have landed in neoliberalism. This reunion gives birth to "anarcho-capitalism," the new market religion founded by Milton Friedman, among whose preachers are Nozick, Glucksmann, Hayek, Fukayama, Vargas Llosa, and Octavio Paz. They all pursue the ancient dream of the abolition of the state, this time upon the realistic basis of radical capitalism and no longer on the romantic basis imagined by Bakunin. Nevertheless, the final result is the same: to abolish the state by means of the totalization of the market, no matter how many human sacrifices this might take. The postmodern battle to eradicate modernity is in Hinkelammert's eyes a mechanism to eliminate the enemies of "totality": no more utopias, no theory able to reflect on totality as such, no universal ethic.[6]

The Cuban philosopher Pablo Guadarrama, in turn, warns us of the grave danger entailed by the negation of two fundamental concepts for Latin America: social progress and the linear sense of history.[7] The postmodern critique of teleologism consists in not recognizing an undeniable fact: there never has been an historical process that is not built on inferior or less advanced stages. Another thing is that some peoples "advance" at more accelerated rhythms than others, or that they reach greater or lesser levels of standards of living in the economic or cultural orders. What is certain, avers Guadarrama, is that there exist "moments of ascent in the humanization of humanity."[8] And Latin America does not constitute the exception, but confirms the rule. In some areas of the continent is observed a persistence of precapitalist forms of production, while in others there exist very advanced processes of industrialization. The existence of different "degrees of development" in the social structure of Latin American countries results, therefore, undeniable.

Precisely because of this reason, Guadarrama thinks that one cannot speak of a Latin American "entry" into postmodernity. As long as Latin American does not settle accounts with modernity, that is, as long as no complete experience of this historical process has been had, it is useless and futile to think of a postmodern living. "The Habermasian criteria that modernity is an incomplete project— writes Guadarrama—has encountered justified sympathizers in the Latin American compass, where the fragility of the greater part of the paradigms of equality, liberty, and fraternity, secularization, humanism, Enlightenment, etc., which so much inspired our thinkers and leaders in prior centuries, is made most evident. The idea that we have not yet become moderns and already is demanded that we become postmoderns has been made common."[9]

One of the most interesting criticisms is that of Argentine philosopher Arturo Andrés Roig, for whom postmodernism, besides being a discourse that is out of place in our social reality, is also an "alienating discourse," for it invalidates the most excellent achievements of Latin American thought and philosophy. To claim that modernity is worn out would imply sacrificing a powerful weapon which has been used by all the liberating tendencies in Latin America, namely, critical narratives. Roig states that modernity was not only made up of violence and irrationality, but also by openness to the critical functions of thought. The so-called philosophy of suspicion (Nietzsche, Marx, Freud) teaches us that "behind" our immediate comprehension of a text there lies hidden another level of meaning, the interpretation of which needs to be mediated by criticism. And it is precisely this idea of "unmasking," that has given meaning to Latin American philosophy, which has been interested in pointing out the ideological mechanisms of "opressive discourse." To give up suspicion, as postmodern thinkers propose, is to stop denouncing and to fall into the trap of a "justifying discourse" traceable to the great centers of world power.[10]

Roig points out that this "justifying discourse," which would have us believe that we have arrived to a state of "epistemological orphanhood," holds that all utopias have been definitively discredited and that history has reached its culmination. But in Roig's opinion, Latin American philosophy has been characterized by being a "morning" thought, whose symbol is not the Hegelian owl but rather the Argentine lark. In other words, it is not a discourse that looks backwards in order to justify the past, as Hegel's did, but rather one that always looks forward, firmly embedded in the utopian function of thought. For this reason, to give up this "future-oriented discourse," would mean giving up hope for the better life desired by oppressed groups in Latin America. To fall into postmodern nihilism means renouncing participation in favor of "laissez faire" economics and fostering a weak political will kept satiated by cassette-players and stereos.[11]

2. POSTMODERNITY AS THE "STATE OF THE CULTURE" IN LATIN AMERICA

Perhaps the best way to begin to respond to these criticisms is to show that what has been called "postmodernity" is not a purely *ideological* phenomenon, that is to say, it is not a conceptual game thought up by depressed, nihilistic "First-World" intellectuals. Rather, it is above all a change in sensibility at the *lifeworld level*. It has appeared in the last 30 years not only in the "central" regions of the West, but also in its "peripheral" regions. Purely conceptual elaborations in sociology, architecture, philosophy and literary theory would thus constitute "reflective" moments that point to this change in sensibility. I therefore propose to show that postmodernity is not a simple "trap" fallen into by certain intellectuals who insist on interpreting Latin American reality using the ideological models of another reality, but rather that it is present in contemporary Western civilization as a whole, including Latin America.[12]

In order to carry out this objective I will refer to some of the most recent studies carried out by Latin American social scientists, among whose names I could mention José Joaquín Brunner, Roberto Follari, Beatriz Sarlo, Norbert Lechner, Orlando Fals Borda, Nelly Richard, and Daniel García Delgado, among many others. These new approaches go beyond what we might call the "open veins syndrome,"[13] in that they are not focussed on investigating the structural causes of underdevelopment at the level of international economic relations, i.e., on exogenous factors, but concentrate rather on the way in which the processes of modernization have been assimilated into the culture.[14]

I would like to begin by responding to the question about the necessity and/or pertinence of the discussion on postmodernity in Latin America. Almost all the authors discussed above agree in pointing out that a Latin American debate on postmodernity either responds to the foreignism of alienated elites that try to follow whatever international discussion is "in vogue"; or that it is the ideological expression of "late capitalism" in its present phase of global expansion. In both cases, criticism is based on the same presupposition: the socioeconomic inequality between postindustrial societies with their hyperconsumerism and Latin American societies, marked by poverty, illiteracy and violence, would make a transfer of the discussion's theoretical-critical contents impossible or questionable. However, Nelly Richard, a Chilean philosopher, has indicated that this argument remains entrapped within the thought structures of the Enlightenment, whereby cultural processes are seen as subordinate to sociopolitical development. If, on the other hand, we use structures of analysis according to which the spheres of culture and society relate to each other assymetrically, in a nonresolved dialectic of contradiction and imbalance, what will result is that the structural fulfillment of First World societies would not have to be reproduced in Latin America in order to find postmodern *cultural registers* there. These cultural manifestations have entered into the Latin American scene for very different reasons and circumstances to those observed in the "central" countries, for they result from a "peripheral" experience of modernity.[15] For this reason, to take a First World model of economic-social development as the guaranteed point of departure on the basis of which a discussion on postmodernity in Latin America would be meaningful or not, means to continue to be trapped in the very conceptual Eurocentrism of which many of the authors mentioned above are trying to liberate themselves. It is not a matter of imitating or transcribing a debate on the crisis of modernity in European societies, but rather of thinking about the way in which Latin America has *taken on* that modernity (and that crisis), living them out in a *different* way.

Nelly Richard stresses two factors which, in her opinion, explain the reticence of one sector of Latin American intellectuals to enter into the debate about postmodernity. The first is the trauma of colonization, which leads to many intellectuals looking askance at everything that comes from "the outside," marking a boundary between what is imported and what is "one's own," what is foreign and what is national. The second factor has to do with the criticism implicit in postmodern discourse of the heroic ideals of the generation that proclaimed its Latin American faith in revolution and in the "hombre nuevo."[16] It is therefore not surprising that instead of taking advantage of postmodern criticism of the dominating system of modernity, *redirecting its meaning from a Latin American perspective*, a good many of our intellectuals have chosen to look at this criticism as a new "imperialistic ideology." Luckily, not a few authors have argued for a Latin American perspective to the debate over postmodernity, knowing that in it problems are being treated that are of great interest for diagnosing the *ambiguity* with which Latin America always lived out modernity.

Let us first examine the diagnosis carried out by Argentine political scientist Daniel García Delgado, for whom Latin America is experimenting a transition from "holistic culture" in force from the 1940s to the 1980s to the "neoindividualistic culture" of the 1990s.[17] Holistic culture was characterized by defining "extended identities" based on a sense of belonging to collectives and on "class" solidarities in the bosom of a political community that emphasized the integrative function of the "nation," the revolutionary role of popular culture and the working class, and redistributive justice guaranteed by the state. Neoindividualistic culture, on the other hand, is characterized by a global tendency toward the formation of "restricted identities" marked by the retreat toward small groups and the private sphere. The identification with "national" elements that formerly acted as an integrating, orientating element is dissolving in the face of a transnational culture impelled by the media. This loss of traditional certainties forces the individual to retrench to a reduced, manageable sphere that allows control over the formation of one's own identity.

García Delgado tells us that this loss of traditional certainties is not only produced as a result of the bankruptcy of the national state in the face of transnational "economic imperialism." It is also a consequence of, among other factors, the dissolution of the ideological antagonisms that resulted from Latin American civil wars in the nineteenth century and which were later reinforced in the twentieth century by the Cold War. The traditional processes of social integration once faced individuals and groups with "enemies" such as conservatives, liberals, the oligarchy, imperialists or communists, thus fusing and giving meaning to mass politics. Now, however, they are losing momentum to the extent that, with the disappearance of well-defined ideological blocs, political power is becoming increasingly complex and difficult to pinpoint. "Heavy ideologies" cease to function as integrative elements, opening the door to a culture that is skeptical in the face of "master narratives." Social integration is displaced to the sphere of "light ideologies," which offer the individual the opportunity of being the protagonist at least of his or her own life. The cult of the body, the relaxation of sexual mores, the intense enjoyment of a moment through rock music and drugs, the ecological culture, the acquisition of faddish products, and the private religiosity of certain Protestant groups are examples of the new inwardness of culture.

Looking for the causes of this change of sensibility in Latin America, Argentine sociologist Roberto Follari points to two main factors: in the first place, the remarkable brutality with which dictatorships in the South Cone eliminated or weakened political organizations, sowing fear.[18] In consequence, a strong disbelief in the possibility of structural changes in society has emerged, for it is evident before even beginning how high the social cost of such an attempt would be. Seen from this perspective, both the "softening" of political opinions and the lack of adherence to any project of "holistic integration" are inevitable. The second factor mentioned by Follari is the lack of social alternatives.[19] The poverty of wide sectors of the population, the shrinking income of the middle class, the corruption of the political class—all of these elements lead into a culture of immediacy, in which what is most important is surviving today; tomorrow can be worried about when it comes. Wide segments of the population have been forced in the last few years to survive by means of the informal economy, bereft of protection and social representation, turned entirely over to their luck. Given the lack of a project for the future, the present becomes the only meaningful horizon.

It is not surprising that in such conditions a pessimistic sensibility has spread through Latin America which, as opposed to what some believe, has not come to it from the "outside," as a product imported by intellectual elites, but rather has developed inside as the result of a long historical process: of the experience of having lived for 500 years in socioeconomic backwardness, with authoritarianism and inequality present at all levels of daily life, without any political project having been able to remedy the situation. The promises of economic reform and social justice made by all political parties have failed roundly in Latin America, and this failure has come to be a part of collective memory, to the point that the great majority of the population is indifferent to any political offer promising a new order. We are experiencing a growing lack of confidence in political institutions and in the efficacy of participation in the public sphere which, as mentioned above, leads to a search for personal realization in the private domain.

An example of this disenchantment is the strong opposition to the exacerbated messianism introduced by the revolutionary movements of previous decades. While the revolutionary left tended to identify the utopia of an egalitarian society with a possible future, the tendency at this time, as is shown clearly by sociologist Norbert Lechner, is to "unload" politics of all reductionist elements, ridding it of any ethical-religious motivations.[20] That is to say, in the face of a heroic vision of politics and a messianic vision of the future, politics is now restated as "the art of the possible." The result is, therefore, a sense of political disenchantment, in that a series of illusions created by the so-called ideological inflation of the 1960s have provoked a reaction. What is now important is not to "break away from the system" but rather to reform it from within by reestablishing politics as a space in which to negotiate.

Such a *deheroization* also implies that institutionalized politics is no longer understood as an activity oriented by rational ideals, but rather that it has become a performance produced by the *mass media*. The decisive factor for a candidate or a party to have access to power is no longer the rationality of their political ideals, but rather their ability to create a fictitious reality, and passsing it off for genuine. Style, gestures, voice modulation, in a word: a presidential candidate's "charisma" is "produced" in accordance with the criteria of aesthetics and publicity, so that it can be "sold" successfully in the image market. Argentine thinker Beatriz Sarlo mentions the case of the presidential elections in Peru, in which both Fujimori and Vargas Llosa presented themselves to the public using carefully crafted images.[21] Fujimori appears dressed as a karate champion, with a white kimono tightened at the waist, dividing a brick in two with the side of his right hand. Vargas Llosa appears visiting a slum, emotionally greeting poorly dressed persons with indian features. In both cases there is a substitution of political discourse with stage scenery built for contemplation by the mass media, through which the candidates try to seem what they are not. Fujimori does not want to be associated with the Peruvian political class, so in order not to seem like a politician he dresses up as a karate champion. Vargas Llosa, for his part, wants to seem like an intellectual whose moral principles lead him to identify with the suffering of the poor. The political statement is thus integrated into a *symbolic hyperrealism* in which the image does not refer to a given reality, but is rather a saleable product that refers only to itself. Politics becomes a *simulacrum*, made in the image of images whose only reality is that of a world occupied by a sole discourse unified by the rhetoric of the electronic media.

The influence exerted on the Latin American collective imagination by the media has been one of the topics most frequently treated by the social sciences in the last few years. This is certainly not gratuitous: while up to the 1950s, personal and collective identities in Latin America were still formed according to traditional models of socialization, with the popularization of the mass media this situation has changed radically. Television, movies, radio, and videos are leading to the discovery of other social realities and of numerous language games, which tend to relativize a person's own culture. Chilean sociologist José Joaquín Brunner is of the opinion that the mass media have given shape to a symbolic hyperreality in Latin America, in which the signified no longer derive from their signifiers, but rather from decontextualized signifieds.[22] This implies that people's socialization is due in large part to transnational behavioral criteria and guidelines, which produces an ambiguous distancing from their own cultural traditions. Mass culture promotes the dissolution of traditional certainties that used to guarantee social integration, thus shaping a complex scene in which national and transnational factors coexist.

Probing further into the phenomenon of disenchantment with tradition, Brunner points out a consequence of modernization that was not even considered by the thinkers who developed the theory of dependence: the massive schooling process in Latin America. Due to the modernization of the school system, the disadvantaged sectors of society are submitted to a new process: they are uprooted from their traditional cultural milieu and exposed to an intensive, systematic socialization carried out by the school. The primary agent of socialization is no longer the family but rather the school, which is now in charge of implementing the physical and mental discipline that equips the individual to take on a specific role in society. School transmits a modern worldview, which is based on Western humanist traditions and on the scientific model for understanding natural processes. All of this implies, as Brunner says, that the distinction between "high" and "popular" culture is tending to disappear in Latin America. Popular culture, understood as a symbolic universe that transmits a people's religious, moral, and cognitive heritage, can no longer resist the advances of the schooling process, the cultural industry, and the mass media. The forms of popular culture that do resist will do so increasingly as "folklore," which no longer remains unpolluted, but is rather molded by the international market of images and symbols. To this must be added the fact that so-called formal instruction is considered a source of social prestige, so that to learn the language and the official knowledge transmitted in school increases the security of indigenous peoples and of peasants, expanding their marketability.[23]

However, the disenchantment which can be observed at present in Latin American culture should not be interpreted as an abandonment of political struggles in order to take on a nihilist lifestyle. Let us not forget that what has led to skepticism in Latin America is not weariness born of abundance or the dehumanization produced by scientific and technological development, but rather the failure of all the projects of social transformation associated with a "enlightened" worldview. It is therefore not a matter of an "ontological" disenchantment, but rather of a disillusionment with a certain understanding of politics and the exercise of power. This leads people to develop new ways of political participation in the public sphere.

Colombian sociologist Orlando Fals Borda is one of the Latin American thinkers who have best dealt with the topic of the New Social Movements.[24] These are grass-roots organizations looking for alternative ways to exercise political pressure, in order to decide for themselves how to live and work in accordance with their most personal needs. As Fals Borda points out, they distrust all institutions defined by eighteenth-century Enlightenment models: the nation-state, political parties, representative democracy, the virtues of the free market, the legality of public power, etc. They therefore attempt to build a public space in which they can try out self-administered economic models, new forms of federalism and direct democracy, the irruption of women into the public arena, elimination of the sexual division of labor and other alternatives for political participation. Their main objective is to substitute vertical relations of political power, which move hierarchically from top to bottom, with transversal networks, shaped by pluralist, multiclass values. In short, the New Social Movements represent a decentralization of political power, in the sense that solutions to concrete problems are not dictated by a "central" body, but rather are based on decisions made by small grass-roots citizen groups.

This dialogue with some of the most recent Latin American analyses allows us to come to at least two conclusions: in the first place, that postmodernity is a "state of the culture" with deep roots among us, even though its *causes are different* from those which produce the *same phenomenon* in the North-Atlantic countries. This should be enough to refute (at least in part) the simplistic opinion according to which postmodernity is an "ideology of late capitalism" adopted in Latin America by intellectuals alienated from their own cultural reality. Secondly, postmodernity is not necessarily allied with neoliberalism or with the unfolding of "instrumental reason," since it represents precisely an attitude of profound distrust in the face of technocratic and burocratic modernization projects pushed by political and financial elites in Latin America. As Martín Hopenhayn has shown so well, postmodern disenchantment is not the ideological correlative of a liberal transnational offensive (with the slogan of "anything goes"), but rather the expression of a cultural openness in which the social subjects constitute identities no longer determined by state hypertrophia and public sector giantism.[25]

3. LATIN AMERICA AND POSTMODERN CLICHÉS

Having established that the discussion on postmodernity in Latin America is more than an intellectual fad, but rather is based on a particular "state of the culture," I will now consider more deeply some of the criticisms described above (part 1), attempting to respond to them from a standpoint "within" the dialogue with postmodern proposals.

I say "within" because I am convinced that most of the criticisms of postmodernity are based on four or five clichés rather than on a rigorous consideration of what thinkers as varied as Vattimo, Lyotard, Derrida, Rorty, Foucault, Baudrillard, Welsch, Virilio, Deleuze, Bauman, or Guattari are trying to tell us. Unfortunately, in Latin America philosophical discussions often evoke a sense of personal loyalty or rejection rather than deep reflection. Because I am convinced of the superficiality of such statements, I will go over four of the most common truisms: (1) the "end of modernity," (2) the "end of history," (3) the "death of the subject," and (4) the "end of utopias."

1. Perhaps the most recurrent of the clichés consists in presenting postmodernity as the "end of modernity." Certainly, the prefix "post" suggests periodicity, and furthermore Vattimo's most well-known book is entitled precisely "the end of modernity." But nothing could be more inexact than understanding this "end" as the fulfillment of one era and the beginning of another. Postmodernity is not what comes after modernity but rather means becoming aware of the crisis which characterizes modernity. Arturo Roig sees this very clearly when he says that "postmodernity is the way in which modernity puts into practice something it always has exercised: self-criticism."[26] Leopoldo Zea aptly describes postmodernity as "modernity's modernism."[27] Postmodernity is, in other words, the reflective return of modernity to itself and not a transition to another era. It is therefore fallacious to suppose that in Latin America the project of modernity would first have to be "realized" as Habermas would put it in order for us then to be able to consider the meaning of postmodernity (P. Guadarrama).

Admittedly, it is true that modernity, as a specific historical age characterized by transformations and schisms, is in crisis. But the crisis pointed to by postmodern thought has a different, deeper dimension than the crises originated for example by Copernican astronomy, Bacon's *Novum Organum*, or Kant's criticism of metaphysics. The crisis to which I am referring is that of modernity's self-image as an enlightened conception supposing a kind of "preestablished harmony" between the scientific-technological, ethical-political, and esthetic-expressive development of society. This unitary understanding of progress constituted the ideological basis for modern consciousness from the seventeenth century up to our days. This was the ruling idea of the liberal bourgeoisie in Europe and Latin America during the nineteenth century: the ideal of a synthesis between the accumulation of capital, technological progress, and the ethical and artistic needs of culture. It was believed that behind all of these processes there existed a "rational order" able to guarantee the indissoluble unity between the true, the good, and the beautiful.[28] Already toward the end of the nineteenth century, a consciousness of the essentially antagonistic, fragmented character of modernity began to arise. Marx, Bergson, Dilthey, Husserl, Ortega y Gasset in Europe; Rodó, Martí, Vasconcelos, and Mariátegui in Latin America: all of them were aware of the crisis of modern culture, yet still very much attached to the political and esthetical ideals of the Enlightenment. They tried in various ways to recuperate the lost unity of society. It took the experience of the two World Wars and the resulting ideological conflict for people to realize that any attempt to "harmonize" the dynamics inherent to the different levels of society tends to result in military terror, the social discrimination of minorities, the destruction of nature and political intolerance.

Postmodern philosophers teach us that modernity's unitary ideal cannot continue to function as a "master narrative" which legitimatizes political praxis, and urges us to try out new ideological legitimations. It is, then, to the loss of credibility of this type of narrative that the expression "the end of modernity" refers, and not to the cancellation of modernity as a historical epoch. What is searched for is not to bid farewell to the project of modernity but to continue it on the base of *another type of narrative legitimation* that derives *also* from modernity. Postmodernity does not entail the abandonment of the emancipatory ideals of modernity, as Hinkelammert and Sánchez Vázquez affirm, but instead the rejection of the totalizing and essensialist language in which those ideals have been articulated. As Ernsto Laclau so well put it, what is questioned is not the validity of the emancipatory contents of modernity, but the *ontological status* of its discourses.[29] What it concerns, then, is of disabusing enlightened language of its fundamentalist glimmer, in order to relocate it in a discursive context.

2. When we use the expression "the end of history" a similar distinction to the one above becomes necessary, since it actually has little to do with postmodernity. The thesis about the "end of history" has two versions: One is the idea of "posthistory," developed in the 1950s by the German sociologist Arnold Gehlen as a critique of the inability to innovate shown by advanced industrial societies. According to Gehlen, these societies have reached such a sophisticated state of material reproduction, that the creation of new impulses and ideas is already totally exhausted. The only thing that advances is the technical-institutional machinery, which guarantees perpetual satisfaction to masses no longer able to think.[30]

The other version is that of the North American political scientist Francis Fukayama, who, basing himself on a Nietzschean interpretation of Hegel, asserts that the "end" of universal history is none other than liberal-capitalist democracy. In this case the word "end" is used both in the sense of "finality" (*telos, Zweck*) and in the sense of "termination" (*eschaton, Ende*). His thesis is therefore that human history necessarily leads to a universal culture of consumerism orchestrated by liberal democracy and the market economy. Fukayama leans on Hegel to state that the conflict between masters and slaves, that is to say, the irrational struggle of all against all to be recognized as superior to everyone else, constitutes history's meaning and motor. The desire to be recognized is also the psychological basis of two extremely powerful passions which for centuries have given impulse to fanaticism, war, and hate: nationalism and religion. But in the mid-seventeenth century in England, a conception of the state began to arise that established the superiority of reason's cold calculation to the irrational desire to be recognized by others. It is the liberal tradition of Hobbes and Locke, determined to instill in the population a series of rational habits, in order to ensure a peaceful, prosperous society. Fukayama tells us that towards the end of the twentieth century there seems to be a general consensus accepting the claims of liberal-capitalistic democracy as the most rational form of government. Monarchy, aristocracy, theocracy, fascism, communism—all these forms of government, which still emphasized the struggle to be recognized, have ceased to be the ideological rivals of liberal democracy.

The triumph of liberal democracy therefore means that the desire to be recognized has been rationalized and leads to the end of that which had been the force moving history. History has come to its end, for the desire to be recognized is satisfied through massive consumerism guaranteed by the market economy.[31]

As shall be seen in a moment, the thesis about the "end of history" in either of its versions is far from being the same as postmodern criticism, which tries to point out not the finalization of history as such, but rather the deep crisis of a specific understanding of history: i.e., a vision of history which uses identical criteria to measure the transformation and unfolding of all human societies. Let us take the case of Foucault, who, on the basis of the new developments in historical theory beginning in the 1950s, tells us that we should no longer think about history in terms of continuity and universality, but rather in terms of discontinuity and particularity. Documents as used by contemporary historians are no longer understood as signifieds but rather as signifiers, that is to say, as open always to new and different interpretations. This means that the events in the various planes of society no longer can be understood on the basis of a material or formal principle that gives them coherence and unity. For this reason it is now impossible to continue speaking of a logic inherent to history, as Fukayama does, or of a model of social development through which all the peoples of the earth must necessarily go. What remains is, according to Foucault, a multiplicity of "small histories" which coexist simultaneously, without the historian being able refer to a transcendental criterium which would permit him or her to put them in an given order of importance.[32]

Foucault's critique, which was also picked up by Vattimo, Lyotard and Derrida, allows us to see firstly, that human societies are not the result of a qualitatively ascending historical process which necessarily leads from the traditional to the modern, from myth to logos and from barbarity to civilization. Precisely this was what the liberal elites in Latin America in the nineteenth and twentieth centuries believed. They were convinced that "modernization" programs would be enough to leave behind all the irrationality inherent to the ethos of Hispanic colonial society. The "theory of dependence" reacted critically to this expectation, only to fall into an equally totalizing interpretation of history. The dialectics of development-under-development became the "inherent logic" that not only explained the riches and the poverty of the nations but also the meaning of all the artistic, philosophical and cultural expressions of a given society.

Secondly, postmodern criticism, in showing that different human societies do not function according to a sole underlying "logic" and thus cannot be thought of as participants of a single historical current, precludes any pretension of establishing a particular history, for example, European history as a paradigm for "universal history." This was what happened in the grand historical narratives of Hegel and Marx, who tried to explain human history as a whole, without realizing that what they considered "universal" was actually determined by particular historical circumstances. To be sure, twentieth-century Latin American philosophy, both the historical and the liberationist school, carried out a strong, appropriate criticism of Marx and Hegel's eurocentrism. And yet, blinded by a romantic "Third-Worldliness" which in those days was much the fashion they ended up by simply inverting the traditional roles: instead of looking at all of human endeavor from the point of view of the conquerors, they decided to look at everything from the perspective they called "the backside of history," i.e., from the point of view of those conquered and oppressed.

This shows that both the "theory of dependence" and the "philosophy of liberation" still remained trapped in the Enlightenment pathos of modernity which postmodernity tries to leave behind. The latter attempts to look at the past without trying to discover a fixed Archimedean point, thus avoiding the idealization of any given particularity. But wouldn't this mean denying all the historiographic work carried out by Latin American philosophy in the twentieth century, as held by Arturo Roig? By no means, for, as mentioned above, postmodernity does not imply the cancellation of the past but rather, quite on the contrary, leads to the renaissance of the "small histories." Precisely this constitutes the challenge to the new generations of Latin American philosophers who dedicate themselves to the task of interpreting our intellectual history: to look for and disinter those "small histories," yet without trying to integrate them in all-inclusive discourses. This means specifically to avoid subsuming them in abstract categories such as "people" (pueblo), "nation," "economic dependence," or interpreting them based on dualistic hermeneutical structures (oppressor/oppressed, center/periphery), since such categories cover up struggles that need to be understood in their particularity. It is time for us to realize that the Latin American societies are not a homogeneous fabric of events that can be observed from a single point of view, but rather a collage of multiple, irreducible histories that reflect each other.

3. Another one of the slogans applied to postmodernity is the "death of the subject," which would imply, according to some, the neutralization of any kind of critical thought opposed to the reigning "instrumental reason." This is why Habermas refers to the postmodernists as "the young conservatives," linking them to the political right.[33] But what does the "death of the subject" actually mean? Is it a logical consequence of the "death of God" proclaimed by Nietzsche as Hinkelammert supposes or is it a new ideological strategy used by the centers of power to "disarm consciences," as Arturo Roig suspects?

When Foucault states, for example, that the human being is a recent invention which is about to be erased "like a face drawn in sand at the edge of the sea," he is not referring to the subject as such but rather to the vision of the human being characteristic of the Enlightenment, as it has been expressed by the natural sciences and the humanities since the eighteenth century.[34] Foucault is speaking of the monological, omnipotent subject, able to decipher all the mysteries of the universe by means of reason. It is a Faustian subject conceived of as an "ego cogito" which places itself in the center of history and which can transform the world in accordance with its will. It is a patriarchal subject which empowers the conquest and domination of other peoples and cultures under the pretense of taking them the benefits of "civilization." And it is, ultimately, an authoritarian subject that is at the root of a disciplinarian society whose control model is, according to Foucault, Bentham's Panopticon.

But the new directions taken by the social sciences have been showing that this kind of subject is a giant with clay feet. Freud teaches that the thinking subject is not at the center of human activity, but rather that reason interacts with unconscious forces that determine our behavior to a great degree. Linguistics shows that the distinction between subject and object arises from the contingent combination of various language games. Foucault himself has shown that the relationship between power and truth is much more complex than had formerly been believed, for science itself is sustained by power relationships. Clinical medicine, psychiatry and pedagogy are disciplinary systems constituted by a field of knowledge, investigation techniques, and the gathering of data, on the basis of which the object's epistemological statute is "created." Not even the natural sciences work today on the assumption of truth as a mirror-image, but rather knowing that our theoretical edifices are subject to chance and causality.

Is this leading us to the anarchic irrationality so feared by certain Latin American intellectuals? I believe not, because postmodern criticism does not attempt to do away with the subject, but rather to decentralize it. While the subject of the Enlightenment be it the solipsistic subject of Descartes's cogito, the subject of classic German philosophy or the Marxist "collective subject" was once placed at the center of cognitive, political and moral power, it is now important to open the field to a plurality of subjects that do not demand centrality, but rather *participation* in the public life of the increasingly multipolar, interactive society which can be expected in the twentieth century. Neither the state, nor the church, the market, the political parties, the army, the intellectuals, the parliament, the workers and peasants nor any other particular group should continue to claim its right to centrality. Instead, power relations and participation in public life need to be extended to all sectors of society. In late modernity the subject does not disappear; quite on the contrary: it is multiplied. Neither does reason disappear: it opens up a space for the coexistence of different *types of rationality*. The decentralization of Enlightenment reason does not open up the gates to irrationality but rather favors a more ample vision with regard to sociocultural, politico-ideological and economic-productive heterogeneity, as well as a greater indulgence in the face of differences of all kinds.

It is important to recognize that Latin American philosophy, especially liberation philosophy, very opportunely initiated a critical distancing from the Enlightenment subject characteristic of the first phase of modernity. Before Foucault, Vattimo, and Derrida in Europe, Argentine philosopher Enrique Dussel had already recognized the consequences of Heidegger's criticism of Western metaphysics, pointing out the intrinsic relationship between modernity's Enlightenment subject and European colonialist power. Behind the Cartesian ego cogito, which inaugurates modernity, there hides a logocentrism through which the Enlightenment subject divinizes itself, becoming a kind of demiurge able to determine the world of objects. The modern ego cogito thus becomes will to power: "I think" is equivalent to "I conquer." This is the ideological base of European expansion in the world and is directly responsible for the misery suffered by millions of persons all over the planet. For this reason, Dussel tells us, it is necessary to advance toward the formation of a new kind of society which does not retrace the paths of modern subjectivity. It will therefore be a postmodern society which will have as its main characteristic what Emmanuel Levinas has called "the humanism of the Other." A society in which differences are no longer seen as part of a totality, but rather as valuable in themselves.[35]

Up to here, Dussel's critique anticipates almost at every point that of European and North American postmodern authors. It could be said that he reduces European modernity to its purely "instrumental" version, without recognizing in it the unfolding of other models of rationality and subjectivity. But the real problem starts when Dussel begins to deepen the Levinasian concept of "alterity" on the basis of the theory of dependence and of liberation theology. Totality's "other" is the poor, oppressed person who, because he or she is located "outside" of the system, becomes the only fountain of spiritual renewal. In the "periphery" of the oppressed people's ethos, very different values are experienced by those prevailing at the "center:" love, communion, solidarity, face-to-face relationships, a sense of social justice. This leads Dussel to a second reduction: that of identifying the world of the poor with "community ethics," without recognizing the presence there of other models of rationality, including strategical rationality. Here we find ourselves at the opposite pole from postmodernity, for what Dussel is attempting to do is not to decentralize the Enlightenment subject but rather to replace it with another absolute subject. According to him, society's moral reserves originate exclusively from poor, outcast sectors of society, and any other type of morality is an ideological justification of the existing order. The capitalist system with all its institutions is an "aberrant idol" that demands human victims in order to stay alive. For this reason it is only possible to "destroy" the "oppressive totality" from the perspective of these victims.

Although Dussel's claims in favor of the poor may sound justified, I submit that it is extremely problematic to speak of such a thing as a "good power" and a "bad power," the former originating "below," in the world of the poor, and the latter originating "above," in the selfish interests of capitalism. In the first place, power, as Foucault has shown, is not an attribute linked to the state, to an oppressive social class or to a given "mode of production," but rather a web which touches both the dominators and the dominated. Power relations do not depend on any given person's "bad faith," for these relations have always been indissolubly united to discourse and truth.[36] For this reason the different kinds of knowledge including practical-moral knowledge are not "external" in relation to the strategies of power. In the second place, in the planetary society in which we live, it is no longer possible to speak of cultural forms as if they were a "veil" that covers up the "true" function of economic relations. Images, representations and cultural symbols cannot be subsumed into a given "mode of productions," but rather have become autonomous signs that are not emanations from some "fundamental" sphere. That is to say that cultural signs, transnationalized by the mass media and by information systems, no longer cover up or pervert a supposed "basic reality" of which we should "become conscious," for money (capital) itself has become a sign and signs have become money.[37] This means that it is not possible to look back nostalgically upon a decapitalized culture (or "popular culture"), as Dussel wants, for identification with these signs is a desire internalized by all sectors of society, especially by the poorest.

We still need to resolve the question posed by Arturo Roig about whether the crisis of the Enlightenment subject leads to the neutralization of critical rationality. This can be answered simultaneously with "yes" and "no." Yes, if we understand "critical rationality" to mean the philosophical tradition of the *Ideologiekritik*, i.e., the idea of reason able to discover the ultimate causes and mechanisms of human "alienations." No, if we understand "critical rationality" as *resistance* in the face of all the forms of political, ideological, or social organization which impede human beings from being the subjects of their own lives. In the first case, the exercise of such a criticism presupposes the existence of a subject able to place itself "externally" with regard to all alienations. But as we have already seen, such a point of view is impossible to sustain because there is no form of knowledge able to divorce itself from the strategic relations of power which make up the social fabric. The consequences of such a position are familiar: to suppose the possibility of moral knowledge above good and evil means positing the need for an absolute subject (the Church, the State, the People, the Leader, the Oppressed, the Party, etc.), able to lay down the law unconditionally in all matters having to do with morality and social justice. The second position, on the other hand, leans on contingent subjects that struggle from different perspectives to remodel existing power structures, without claiming to possess cognitive, ethical or aesthetic absolutes. Criticism is therefore no longer realized starting from a unique, absolute transcendental reason, by whom the aspirations of all particular rationalities must be judged, but is rather oriented toward the possibility of communication between various forms of rationality. In this sense we can speak, with Wolfgang Welsch, of a *transversal reason* which does not part from unity but rather from plurality and multiperspectivism.[38] This criticism does not lead to resignation in the face of reality but rather teaches new ways of understanding and undertaking the struggle for an autonomous life.

4. Lastly, I would like to refer to one of the most popular accusations toward postmodernity: to have proclaimed the "end of all utopias." Here it would again be important to ask to which authors the critique refers and about what kind of utopia they are speaking. Let us examine the specific case of Lyotard, one of the most contro-

versial authors. Taking Wittgenstein's analyses as his starting point, Lyotard points out that all human language games are structured in such a way that it is impossible to use them to construct a human community devoid of injustice. Games such as "arguing," "describing," or "asking" are built on the foundation of extremely complex chains of statements, which can be interconnected in different ways. Since there is no linguistic metacriterium which allows us to know which connections we should carry out, the selection of one or several possibilities is always made to the detriment of others. The result is inevitable conflict between various types of discourses and discursive forms, or what amounts to the same thing, between different ways of life. Heterogeneity and the *différend* are, therefore, an essential part of human language and cannot be eliminated. According to Lyotard, any attempt to "reconcile" the differences that exist between language games and the various ways of life shaped by them necessarily ends in dictatorship and terror.[39]

Almost all the "future utopias" found at the threshold of modernity conceived of the ideal society as that in which unity would reign, in which there would no longer be any differences and in which communication between people would not be affected by power relations. Happiness in that future society would be experienced as the total *lack of diversity.* Harmony and homogeneity would characterize a community which no longer would have room for the presence of conflicting orientation values. But if heterogeneity and difference are innate to all social communication, as Lyotard has shown, then it is clear that this type of utopia had to degenerate into authoritarian models of social interaction, in which homogeneity and consensus could only be ensured by means of the despotic application of a religious, economic, political, or social overarching criterion.

What does the end of this kind of totalizing utopias mean for Latin American philosophy? Would it mean rejecting the "future-oriented discourse" as the essential narrative form on which the largest part of "our thought" is based, as Arturo Roig suggests? Probably so, if the "future-oriented discourse" is identified with the "New World utopia," the origin of which has been explained very well by Uruguayan essayist Fernando Ainsa.[40] Ainsa identifies four levels in the development of this narrative form: (1) the transposition to the New World of classical topics and myths such as the biblical Paradise, bucolic Arcadia, the Golden Age, the earliest Christian community in all of which human beings lived in absolute harmony with themselves and with nature; (2) the notion of alterity, in the sense that because it is completely different, the New World becomes the depositary of all the hopes of perfection which had not been realized in Europe; (3) the millenialist dreams of the religious orders who attempted to try out a theocratic model of society in the American continent; (4) the dream of bettering the individual and collective situation of the indigenous peoples by means of their conversion to Christianity, that is to say, by being assimilated to lifestyles dictated by a superior authority. Unfortunately, this discourse, which formed the foundation of the "New World utopia" and which was characterized by its totalizing claims, has been reproduced since then by a great number of Latin American intellectuals as the social utopia par excellence: Latin America understood as the "absolute other" of European rationality, as the continent of the great synthesis, as humanity's spiritual reserve, as the future of the Christian Church, as the land of mystery, magic and poetry. If Roig is referring to this "future-oriented discourse," then we welcome its disappearance, for it is a rhetoric that has served to legitimize authoritarian and populist regime of all stripes in Latin America.

Yet, in proclaiming the end of totalizing utopias, are we not undermining an essential concept in Latin America, namely "social justice"? Is this concept not based precisely on the idea of a society in which oppression and inequality will *no longer* exist? I think that this concept of justice as the "absence of all evil," is part of the legacy of the Judeo-Christian chiliastic eschatology that is necessary to abandon the belief in the coming of the millennium, in the reconciliation of humanity with nature, in the emergence of a redeemed 'man'.[41] I believe, with Lyotard, that any attempt of transposing this idea to social reality almost always degenerates into its opposite: some of the most authoritarian regimes known in the history of Latin America have been established in the name of "equality" and of "social justice." For this reason, what we need to do now is to recognize that we cannot go beyond ourselves (we are condemned to the

différend) and that "social justice" is only possible in a framework
made up of fallible political structures that allow dissent. Such structures are not legitimated by the utopia of "total emancipation" but
rather by new criteria for action which make clear that the struggle
against injustice always necessarily brings with it new injustices. The
question would therefore be: Which injustices are more or less tolerable for society as a whole? But that is a question which cannot be
decided a priori on the basis of universal criteria, but which has to be
submitted to consideration in a public debate, in which all conflicting
parties can legitimately represent their interests and in which dissent
can be regulated in a rational fashion.

Of course, to imagine such a society necessarily means proposing
a utopia. But fortunately, the utopian dimension is not only limited to
modernity's totalizing narratives. Other kinds of narrative forms also
exist, which even while they carry out a utopian function, do not
emphasize values such as consensus, harmony, homogeneity, the
absence of injustice, and reconciliation. It is the utopia of a necessarily conflict-ridden and peaceful coexistence between different
forms of knowledge and different moral criteria of action. It is the
utopia of a polycentric world (seen from an economic-political point of
view); and of a pluralist world (seen from a cultural perspective). It is
the utopia of a world in which different, alternative roads to modernity can run parallel to each other. It is the utopia of a society able to
modernize tradition without destroying it. It is the utopia of a religiosity lived intensely yet not desirous of re-enchanting the public
sphere. It is the utopia of a society, in which all people can have the
opportunity of making their voices heard and of struggling legitimately
to better their quality of life. It is the utopia of an economic development which does not result in the destruction of nature. Because they
are not linked to the heroical pretensions of the Enlightenment, these
utopian models could form the foundation for realistic, nontotali-
tarian policies. The "end of the utopias" announced by postmodernity, therefore, does not mean the absolute decease of the utopian
dimension, but rather, quite on the contrary, the rewriting and rein-
terpreting of old utopias according to the new needs of contemporary
Latin American society.[42] To dare to imagine the future in utopian

ways continues to be a source of change and of struggle for change. But after Auschwitz, Hiroshima, and Ayacucho,[43] we can only understand that change under the paradigm of heterogeneity and diversity, lest we repeat the temptation to transform reason into irrationality.

NOTES

1. As a matter of fact, the thesis of a "farewell to the theory of dependence" had already been presented in 1974 at the II Latin American Sociology Congress, cf. J. L. De Imáz, "¿Adiós a la teoría de la dependencia? Una perspectiva desde la Argentina," *Estudios Internacionales* 28 (1974): 49–75. Among the reasons advanced by José Luis De Imáz for announcing this farewell are (1) the theory of dependence's pretensions of offering a comprehensive explanation of a heterogenous phenomenon such as underdevelopment, thus surpassing any possibility of empirical verification, and (2) the tendency toward an "externalism" that prevents one from assuming a responsibility for the problems in our societies.

2. H. Cerutti Guldberg, "Posibilidades y límites de una filosofía latinoamericana después de la 'filosofía de la liberación', in *La filosofía en América. Trabajos presentados en el IX Congreso Interamericano de Filosofía*, vol. 1 (Caracas: Sociedad Venezolana de Filosofía, 1979), pp. 189–92.

3. G. Vargas Lozano, "Reflexiones críticas sobre modernidad y postmodernidad," in G. Vargas Lozano, ed., *¿Qué hacer con la filosofía en América Latina?* (México: UAM/UAT, 1991), pp. 73-83.

4. A. Sánchez Vázquez, "Posmodernidad, posmodernismo y socialismo," in *Casa de las Américas* 175 (Havanna 1989): 137–45.

5. F. Hinkelammert, "Frente a la cultura de la postmodernidad: proyecto político y utopía," in F. Hinkelammert, *El capitalismo al desnudo* (Bogotá: Editoral El Búho, 1991), pp. 135–37.

6. Ibid., pp. 130–35.

7. Pablo Guadarrama González, "La malograda modernidad latinoamericana," in P. Guadarrama González, *Postmodernismo y crisis del marxismo* (Mexico: UAEM, 1994), pp. 47- 54.

8. Ibid., p. 47.

9. Ibid., p. 52.

10. A. A. Roig, "¿Qué hacer con los relatos, la mañana, la sospecha y la historia? Respuestas a los postmodernos," in A. A. Roig, *Rostro y filosofía de América Latina* (Mendoza: EDIUNC, 1993), pp. 118–22.

11. Ibid., pp. 126–29.

12. Allow me to point out that I am not adhering to positions such as

that of José Joaquín Brunner, for whom Latin America sets the precedent for the "postmodern condition" long before it makes its entry onto the European and North American stage (cf. "Notas sobre la modernidad y lo postmoderno en la cultura latinoamericana," in *David y Goliath* 17 ([1987]). When I speak of postmodernity as the "state of the culture" I am referring, rather, to a nonenlightened form in which modernity has been experimented in Latin America during the last thirty years.

13. [This is a reference to Eduardo Galeano's book *Las venas abiertas de América Latina* (Montevideo: Universidad de la República, Departamento de Publicaciones, 1971). Trans.]

14. On this paradigm change in the Latin American social sciences see B. Scharlau, ed., *Lateinamerika denken. Kulturtheoretische Grenzgänge zwischen Moderne und Postmoderne* (Tübingen: Gunter Narr Verlag, 1994); G. Yúdice, J. Franco, and J. Flores, eds., *On edge. The crisis of contemporary Latin American culture* (Minneapolis: University of Minnesota Press, 1992); W. Rowe and V. Schelling, eds., *Memory and Modernity. Popular culture in Latin America* (London: Verso, 1991).

15. N. Richard, "Latinoamérica y la postmodernidad," in H. Herlinghaus and M. Walter, eds., *Postmodernidad en la periferia. Enfoques de la nueva teoría cultural* (Berlin: Langer Verlag, 1994), pp. 210–22.

16. Ibid., p. 212.

17. D. García Delgado, "Modernidad y posmodernidad en América Latina. Una perspectiva desde la ciencia política," in D. J. Michelini, J. San Martín and F. Lagrave, eds., *Modernidad y posmodernidad en América Latina* (Río Cuarto: ICALA, 1991), pp. 43–61.

18. R. Follari, *Modernidad y posmodernidad: una óptica desde América Latina* (Buenos Aires: Rei, 1991), p. 146.

19. Ibid., p. 145.

20. N. Lechner, "La democratización en el contexto de una cultura posmoderna," in N. Lecher, *Los patios interiores de la democracia* (Santiago: F.C.E., 1990), pp. 103–18.

21. B. Sarlo, "Basuras culturales, simulacros políticos," in *Posmodernidad en la periferia*, pp. 223–32.

22. J. J. Brunner, "Un espejo trizado," in *América Latina: cultura y modernidad* (Mexico: Editorial Grijalbo, 1992), pp. 15–72.

23. J. J. Brunner, "Cultura popular, industria cultural y modernidad," in *América Latina*, pp. 135–61.

24. O. Fals Borda, "El nuevo despertar de los Movimientos Sociales," in Id., *Ciencia propia y colonialismo intelectual. Los nuevos rumbos* (Bogotá: Carlos Valencia Editores, 1987), pp. 131–52. See also: M. D. París Pombo, *Crisis e identidades colectivas en América Latina* (Mexico: Plaza y Valdés S.A., 1992).

25. M. Hopenhayn, "Postmodernism and Neoliberalism in Latin

America," in J. Beverley, J. Oviedo, and M. Aronna, eds., *The Postmodernism Debate in Latin America* (Durham / London: Duke University Press, 1995), pp. 93 ff. See also: M. Hopenhayn, *Ni apocalípticos ni integrados. Aventuras de la modernidad en América Latina* (Santiago: F.C.E., 1994).

26. A. Roig, "Posiciones de un filosofar. Diálogo con Raúl Fornet-Betancourt," in *Rostro y filosofía de América Latina*, p. 212.

27. L. Zea, "Modernización y Estado en Latinoamérica," in *Modernidad y postmodernidad en América Latina*, pp. 63–72.

28. Cf. E. Subirats, "Transformaciones de la cultura moderna," in J. Tono Martínez, ed., *La polémica de la postmodernidad* (Madrid: Ediciones Libertarias, 1986), pp. 103–18.

29. E. Laclau, "Politics and the Limits of Modernity," in A. Ross, ed., *Universal Abandon? The Politics of Postmodernism* (Minneapolis: University of Minnesota Press, 1988), pp. 66–67. See also E. Laclau, and C. Mouffe, *Hegemony and Socialist Strategy: Towards Radical Democratic Politics* (London: Verso, 1985).

30. A. Gehlen, "Ende der Geschichte?" in Ch. Konrad and M. Kessel, eds., *Geschichte schreiben in der Postmoderne* (Stuttgart: Reclam, 1994), pp. 39–57.

31. F. Fukayama, "El fin de la historia. El más frío de todos los monstruos fríos" in *Revista Foro* 18 (1992): Santafé de Bogotá, pp. 5–19.

32. M. Foucault, *Archäologie des Wissens* (Frankfurt: Surkamp, 1973), pp. 9–30 (French original: *L'archéologie du savoir*, 1969).

33. Cf. J. Habermas, "Die Moderne: ein unvollendetes Projekt," in Id., *Philosophisch-politische Aufsätze 1977-1990* (Leipzig: Reclam, 1990), pp. 32–54.

34. M. Foucault, *Las palabras y las cosas. Una arqueología de las ciencias humanas* (Barcelona: Planeta-Agostini, 1985).

35. See E. Dussel's interesting study *Para una de-strucción de la historia de la ética* (Mendoza: Universidad Nacional de Cuyo, 1971), and also *Filosofía Etica Latinoamericana* (México: Edicol, 1977), vol. 1–3.

36. Cf. M. Foucault, *Die Ordnung des Diskurses* (Frankfurt: Fischer, 1991) (French original: *L'ordre du discours*, 1972).

37. Cf. J. Baudrillard, *Crítica de la Economía Política del Signo* (Madrid: Siglo XXI, 1972); F. Jameson, *Postmodernism or the cultural logic of Late Capitalism* (Durham: Duke University Press, 1991).

38. Cf. W. Welsch, *Unsere postmoderne Moderne* (Weinheim: VCH Acta humaniora, 1991), pp. 295–318. See also: W. Welsch, *Vernunft. Die Zeitgenösische Vernunftkritik und das Konzept der transversalen Vernunft* (Frankfurt: Suhrkamp, 1995).

39. J. F. Lyotard, *Der Widerstreit* (München: Wilhelm Fink Verlag, 1987) (French original: *Le Différend*, 1983).

40. F. Ainsa, *De la Edad de Oro al El Dorado. Génesis del discurso utópico Americano* (México: F.C.E., 1992), pp. 131ff.

41. On this see the reflections of Hugo Felipe Mansilla, "Las utopías sociales y sus consecuencias totalitarias," in H. F. Mansilla, *La cultura de autoritarismo ante los desafíos del presente. Ensayos sobre una teoríca critica de la modernización* (La Paz: CEBEM, 1991), pp. 59- 67.

42. As a matter of fact, postmodernism favors the revindication of the imaginary and poetic spheres in the face of what is empirically given. What is to be left behind is not, therefore, utopia, but rather the messianism of erudite vanguards with their pretensions of leading Latin America along the "true path of liberation." Cf. T. Escobar, "Postmodernismo/Precapitalismo," in *Casa de las Américas* 168 (1988): 16.

43. ["Ayacucho" is a Peruvian city whose name in the Quechua language means "cemetery, place for the dead." The Peruvian theologian Gustavo Gutiérrez uses the word as a symbol for the poverty in the "Third World" which kills millions of people each year. Cf. G. Minervini and K. Renna, eds., Dossier: Dire Dio dopo Auschwitz, durante Ayacucho. Dialogo tra Jürgen Moltmann e Gustavo Gutiérrez, in: *mosaico di pace* 4 (1993): 11–26, especially 23–24. Trans.]

Ofelia Schutte

LATIN AMERICA AND POSTMODERNITY
Ruptures and Continuities in the Concept of "Our America"

ostmodern thinking is generally thought to put on trial the stability and legitimacy of the philosophical and political categories of modernity, either by taking these categories as objects of analysis with a view to questioning their basic presuppositions, or by subjecting their meaning to irreverent critiques which reject the legitimacy of modernity's established order. To some theorists, the postmodern moment essentially symbolizes exuberant, creative festiveness, regardless of the cost to the subject. In this vein, metatheoretical claims have been offered involving the so-called death of the author (Foucault, Barthes) or the end of metanarratives on history and society (Lyotard). Others look upon the postmodern festiveness as an accelerated form of modernity's already inherent nihilism. One Latin American critic preoccupied with the theme of modernity and postmodernity characterizes the nihilism in the European version of the latter as a "fake skepticism" that "would attempt to liberate itself from the fetishes of the philosopher, the historian, the moralist, and the creative genius."[1] The effect of postmodern inquiry so far has been to question the most fundamental assumptions on which stable Western identities had been grounded—the subject, the self, the notion of "progress" (the metanarrative of emancipation), the autonomy of reason, and the objectivity of the sciences. If not catapulted altogether, at a minimum such foundational categories are replaced by others indicating their previously unsuspected fragility.

Among the salient topics of postmodernity one finds those of the fragmented and split subject, the end of the metanarratives of emancipation, the social construction of knowledge, and the engendering of
reason, to name only a few of the themes which have captivated the
attention of poststructuralist intellectuals and scholars.

Postmodern discourse attends to the ruptures, gaps, inconsisten-
cies, and displacements of meaning occuring in modern Western
thought as well as to the technological and material conditions
whereby the systematization, dissemination, reception, and utiliza-
tion of information is produced and distributed in global and local
networks. When these techniques of analysis and interpretation are
applied to ethical and sociopolitical issues, it is possible to draw different political positions from postmodern analysis. On one hand, the
analysis can favor a highly apathetic stance toward politics, given the
loss of belief in a metaphysics of the subject and in the foundational
metanarratives of human and political emancipation. On the other
and alternatively, the analysis can favor a deepened and radical questioning of Western modernity's concepts of subjectivity, politics, and
emancipation. If the latter option is taken, special attention can be
focused on issues concerning the displacement and exclusion of marginalized individuals and subaltern groups from society's representational structures and from its codes of power.[2]

Critics of postmodern thought have warned that the latter involve
reactionary political positions and that the cultural politics of its
"reception" in Latin America may indicate one more instance of the
"latest" ideas from Europe seeking hegemony in the Latin American
region. Our discussion, however, will not take it for granted either
that the Latin American postmodern, whatever this means, is necessarily a replica of the European postmodern, or that the European
postmodern is insufficiently differentiated internally so as to prevent
its association with politically progressive positions.[3]

To clarify the point regarding the differentiation of political positions in and toward the postmodern, this discussion of Latin American postmodern thought begins by distinguishing two modalities or
streams of philosophical concern in postmodern thought—the metaphysical and the political. In this view, depending on the way meta-

physical and political discussions are interwoven, different political orientations will be adopted and different political conclusions reached. For example, a postmodern text may argue that the concept of identity is a metaphysical fiction. But from this standpoint it does not follow necessarily that all claims to identity, including claims to personal and political identity, must be abandoned. For it is possible to hold that even if there is no such "thing" as identity in the traditional metaphysical sense, *identity constructs* are very important. They are ways of indicating senses of "self," values, habits, and preferences that individuals and groups use to distinguish where they stand in differentiation from others. In such a case, although one might no longer wish to invoke the category of identity in the foundational sense understood by the epistemic and/or metaphysical paradigms of modern philosophy, claims to identity in a qualified sense will continue to operate as philosophically relevant. What such claims lose in the epistemic shift from modernity to postmodernity is the legitimation associated with a (modern) foundationalist metaphysical system. From a postmodern standpoint, the intersection of a political interest in identity together with the rejection of a metaphysics of identity could mean and in fact has been taken to mean, however, that questions of national identity (for example) need to be rethought outside of a framework assuming essentialist preconceptions about a national character or patrimony. Postmodern critiques of foundationalism and essentialism have helped to spur on progressive political debates in transnational cultural theory by emphasizing the complexity of issues, categories, and themes such as marginality, gender, race, ethnicity, and popular culture. These new perspectives have systematically challenged the political and economic assumptions about a white, male propertied citizen-subject, derived from the European Enlightenment and typical of a modern Eurocentric philosophy and methodology.[4]

Thus, from the questioning of a metaphysical concept or category (is there such a thing as identity?), different political attitudes and conclusions may be drawn. One possibility is to decide against accepting the language of identity, since at best this term would point to an unreliable construct. This position can lead to such reactions as: what if colonized people lose their so-called (precolonized) identity? It does not matter. There is no such thing as identity and never was. No identity can be imposed by the conqueror, and no identity has been lost by the conquered, since identity as such is a metaphysical fiction. The political resonances of this approach are apathy and possibly aversion toward issues of oppression and cultural imperialism. In contrast, a very different reaction might be to question the legitimacy of the cultural order that claims hegemony in any political struggle. According to this approach, identities rising to dominance are always on trial and therefore always already subject to deconstructive criticism. The political effects of this reading of identity, rather than leading to apathy regarding conquest, can result in precisely the opposite endeavor: a continuing examination of the identities-on-trial, a thorough-going rethinking and critical examination of the material and political relations whereby some identities end up being superimposed over others, and an exposure of the complicity between systems of philosophical and juridical legitimation and class, racial, gender, ethnic, or other interests.

On the first reading of postmodernism, the postmodern turn in cultural and critical studies would be frivolously apolitical; it would not care to differentiate between tyranny and democracy, since it would have a relatively cynical attitude toward questions regarding the legitimation of power. On the second reading, the effect of postmodern thought would be to enhance and expand the modern concept of democracy, by arriving at an ultracritical attitude regarding the types of justifications of power accepted in modern politics. This means that a focus on issues and categories excluded by previous "identities" would be in order. This focus on the exclusions inherent in the determination of any "identity" in turn opens up a new discursive field for marginal and previously invisible or undetected actors in a political field. What modernity calls "underrepresented groups" (women, racial and ethnic minorities, those discriminated on account of sexual orientation, and so on), postmodern thought problematizes even further by questioning the politics of "representation," and therefore calling attention to the differences not only *among* but *within* such groups.[5] This line of thinking privileges the proliferation of meaning over the centralization (and the attempted totalization) of meaning, in part because it sustains the value of a democratic resistance to the totalization of meaning.[6] This line of thought interprets itself to be not liberal-democratic, but radical-democratic.[7]

If the postmodern turn in theoretical analysis admits of extensive political variation and differentiation, then considerable suspicion can be cast on arguments holding that all postmodern (or, for that matter, all modern) thought carries the same political agenda. True, various historical epochs display what Foucault calls the *historical a priori*, that is, the existence of a set of presuppositions which are taken for granted in the legitimation and negotiation of knowledge claims. But, within such broad paradigms as well as at the intersections of paradigms, particularly at points of historical and cultural intersection, differentiated and conflicting political effects can be generated. I have just shown how two very different political positions (one completely uncritical, another highly critical, of established politics in the West) can be generated out of the lack of belief in metaphysical identity. In the case of Latin American postmodern thought, what are some key elements that will allow us to distinguish these two streams of thought—the metaphysical and the political—from each other? At the intersection of the two general categories, "Latin America" and "postmodernity" where does one locate the trends in cultural politics?

GENEALOGY, RENOVATION, DECOLONIZATION

For postmodern thought the question of how to theorize decolonization is vital if an ideological movement different from the emancipatory paradigms of modernity is going to be articulated and sustained. Understanding decolonization, however, requires that a corresponding understanding of colonization take place. Indeed, we can ask, retrospectively, what did colonization mean to the Europeans who settled in America? In response to this question, one could represent the erection and establishment of a colonized space, for the colonizer, as a "new haven" for those dissatisfied Europeans who settled in America, seeking what they did not have or could not obtain

in Europe. In actuality, though, the cost of attaining such safe
haven—which never was as safe as the civil compacts adopted may
have declared it as being—was to achieve the success of the subject at
the expense of "the other," of what was other to the subject. America
represented a "New World" which, in the minds of Europeans, symbolized the renovation of their civilization via the extensive conquest
and colonization of other peoples and land.

The renovation that some nonWestern cultures have undertaken
by emphasizing spirituality and/or by appreciating the ever-renewing
cycles and seasons of nature was not a typical process for Europeans.
In the West, the renovation of the self has all-too-often been linked in
a practical way to the material exploitation of the non-self. The renovation and strengthening of Western culture, in a pattern still
detectable today, has all-too-often been accomplished by means of the
exportation of this culture and by its imposition on whatever appears
ready to accept (or unable to resist) its expansion. While there are,
and have been, counterhegemonic movements to this pattern of dominance within the West itself and while expansion through dominance
and conquest have also been traits of other civilizations in earlier as
well as recent periods of history, the problems generated by this
mechanism of the imposition of subject-over-other as experienced by
Latin Americans and Europeans is a culture-specific one. In other
words, it is the Europeans who conquered America and it is against a
Eurocentric, and later, Anglocentric, understanding of history that
the counterhegemonic movements in Latin America, by virtue of
these specific conditions, place themselves.

Ironically, though, the more radical counterhegemonic movements that disputed the political order of the colonizers, like their
hegemonic predecessors, had learned well the lesson of using the
power of subject-over-other. This is reflected in the style of Caliban,
a figure appropriated by many Latin American critics, who is remembered for stating: "[Master], you taught me your language, and now
I use it to curse you."[8] In this dialectical confrontation, colonization
and decolonization appear in the American historical scenario hand-
in-hand. The logic of one entails the counterlogic of the other. The
power of the colonizer is invoked in the curse uttered by the politi-

cally awakened colonized. Yet which is the greater curse, one might ask, the initial conquest or the necessity of invoking its memory even as one cries out in repudiation of it? Postmodern thought relieves the tension and impasse of this stance by proclaiming: there is no privileged origin, time is not linear, displacement and hybridity are as productive for the self as stability of lineage; the ultimate source of legitimacy, the name of the Father, is socially constructed; power is unstable and traverses all regions of historical and social space.

The postmodern "subject," born of the impasse arising from the exclusion of hybrid, nonnormative, and deviant subjectivities from the pure categories of "universal" thought, belongs to a different genealogical script than the one recounted by (traditional Western) history. Its recognition has become imminent due to the temporary and partial eclipse of the ostensibly dominant and all-too-visible subject of history, the subject of modernity.

WHY LATIN AMERICA?

Despite the changes a postmodern turn in thought brings to questions of the subject, identity, history, nationality, progress, emancipation, and so on, from a cultural standpoint the challenges raised by such thinking in specific texts do not seem to undermine very much the texts' general cultural positioning and identification. By this I mean that discussions of postmodernity, whether explicitly or implicitly, are still marked by their point of cultural origin—whether their cultural identification is strictly European, as in the texts of Jean Baudrillard, Michel Foucault, or Jean-François Lyotard, or whether it is fully or predominantly Latin American, as in the work of Nestor García Canclini or Nelly Richard. For García Canclini and Richard, this cultural "mark" is also (and perhaps inevitably) a political, or better yet, a politicized stance which, when explicitly confronted, will place in relief the specificity of Latin American vis-à-vis European or North American cultural production. In other words, the politization of Latin American perspectives is bound up with the question of *differences* characterizing modernity and postmodernity in Latin

America, both internally within the region and vis-à-vis the cultural, economic, and political trends found in the European continent.

Within Latin America, the postmodern turn represents a break with past institutional politics and its corresponding political ideals, principally the conservative and liberal views of national identity and its cultural patrimony.[9] A process of de-essentializing both national and regional (Latin American) "identity" is in order, allowing not only the examination of concrete differences in its modes of living and of production, but also the positive recognition of differences as part of the healthy cultural texture of these societies and their heterogenous and shifting components. García Canclini reminds us that the question of how a society comes to appropriate the meaning of its historical past for the sake of its present representation of itself is of primary importance. He charges that in the past, Latin American political theory regarding the nation has oscillated between "dogmatic fundamentalisms and abstract liberalisms."[10] The first congeal around the region's early Hispanic-American legacy, Catholicism, and social hierarchy, elements used to sabotage the concept of modern development, while the latter subordinate the diversity of Latin American cultural productions, including the history of indigenous production and the contribution of the native populations of the Americas, and of all marginal sectors of society, to the unifying discourse of modern science and of the modern nation-state.

In this newer political framework, differences are again hierarchized, only under the terms permissible to abstract liberal political categories. Of what use, says García Canclini, is the turn to a postmodern analysis at this juncture of understanding the national patrimony? He suggests, and rightly so, that the postmodern contribution "offers the occasion of rethinking the modern as a relative project, [a project that] can be doubted, that is not antagonistic to traditions nor destined to overcome them by any unverifiable evolutionary law. It is useful, in sum, to put us in charge at once of the impure itinerary of traditions and of the displaced [desencajado], heterodox realization of our modernity."[11] In other terms, postmodern theory is useful in allowing us to understand and take up a position of radical democracy devoid of political fundamentalisms and cultural essentialisms.

In this transformed understanding of Latin American culture resulting from the postmodern turn, the regulation and legitimation of identity is released from its former associations with hierarchized social order as with the liberal abstract concept of political power, to be reconceived and reconfigured in terms of "hybrid," multifaceted, heterogeneous, and shifting appearances. The recognition of the variability of processes of identity formation and change becomes prominent. This recognition opens up the range of political and cultural positions that may be assumed legitimately by Latin Americans of all social sectors, just as it alters the meaning of the "authentic" used by modern thinkers. For example, in *Profile of Man and Culture in Mexico*, Samuel Ramos argues that one of the traits of a culture's authenticity is its ability to retain central values that outlast the test of time.[12] Today's postmodern cultural production, however, is not tied down by such criteria of authenticity. Indeed, the issue of what is authentic is undergoing questioning, with terms such as "original" and "authentic" losing the privileged, hierarchized aspects of their meanings. Today the dichotomy between "original" and "copy" is rejected by some critics, such as Nelly Richard, because for so long these categories and terms have been associated with a foundational hierarchy in which the center-defined cultural product is always seen as original vis-à-vis the copies, the products of the periphery.[13] The center maintains the illusion that it is the seat of universal science or value, while the cultural products pushed to the periphery are represented as inessential to the system of universal truths promoted by the center.

Richard recognizes that theoretical categories of postmodern thought (as of previous Western thought) have been launched out of Europe and, as such, at least in their European version, have not emerged directly out of the so-called peripheries of Latin America. She asks, "How are we to make use of international theoretical conceptualizations—knowing that they form part of the systematic normative standards of the center—but without, for all that, yielding to its grammar of authority?"[14] She argues that by appropriating the language of postmodernism and by claiming the space reserved for resignifying "local and self-directed operations," the periphery can use postmodernism to its advantage through the discursive strategy of "countermimesis."[15] For example, the periphery can use the post-modern language of the figure of the Other to speak about itself. In so doing, it can change the character of otherness, pointing to its internal differences, that is, not resting on yet one more essentialized version of the other of the Western self. For Richard, Latin American postmodernism is insistently and radically democratic, intent on breaking up the discursive credibility of semantic totalities all across the political spectrum.[16] Through avant-garde poetry, irreverent art, and transgressive discourse, postmodern cultural production constantly decenters and deconstructs authoritative totalities. What is left is, again, a hybrid way of creating and resisting hegemonic European trends, but one which is also inventive, transgressive, and defiant. The center's normativity is not countered by a peripheric normativity, but rather by diverting the hegemonic readings from the center toward resignifications beyond its control.[17] In this way, the Latin American postmodern cultural product maintains its relations to the "origin" in the form of a question and a puzzle: not claiming to represent the universality or originality of the center, or the site where these can be rediscovered in some distant periphery, but performing the mascarade of the original and thereby continually subverting its signs and symbols of power.

RUPTURES AND CONTINUITIES IN THE SYMBOLIC REPRESENTATION OF "OUR AMERICA"

Granting that the notion of cultural authenticity has been problematized—and, in some cases, entirely laid to rest—along with some of the other legitimating constructs of modern thought, need we raise the question of why many Latin Americans still want to name our region of the geographical and cultural world *nuestra América* (our America) and to protect its admittedly fragile identity from conceptual disintegration? Is this an inconsistency on the part of a Latin American postmodern approach, given the well-known tenet of the end of the metanarratives of emancipation and the critique of the politization over what is considered authentic? In answer to this question, the themes of decolonization, hybridity, and the pursuit of radical democracy in Latin America seem to converge in the deciphering of one problem: should a Latin American postmodern critical practice limit itself to acts of countermimesis and to deconstruction of the center's discourse, or is there still a place for a kind of "standpoint" position whose aim is to identify and negotiate our specific differences (as we perceive them) from the prevailing NordoEurocentric "universal" order of culture? For example, does the notion of *nuestra América*, as used by José Martí at the end of the nineteenth century to refer to a decolonized Latin American continent, people, and culture, continue to have a meaning for us as we look to the twenty-first century? What form or forms of appropriation by Latin Americans of our social reality is possible or desirable, given a context in which a global capitalist economic system and its associated political and cultural values are ever more increasingly penetrating into the most remote regions of the continent?

Indeed, it is in a context such as this one that Luis Britto-García proposes, in a distinction that prioritizes the political over the metaphysical aspects of postmodernism, that the "true" meaning of postmodernism lies only in the creation of alternative geographical, political, and cultural spaces to modernity—not in the metaphysical debates regarding the end of the subject and of history. "The loudly proclaimed [metaphysical] End of History is the beginning of histories in the plural: not the forced paralysis of the future of the world in accordance with the interests of a hegemonic power, but the right to alternatives."[18] Britto-García argues that in struggles to assert their own character and identity in contradistinction to the Europeans, the nations of the periphery have been engaging in a "postmodern" practice all along, long before the concept of the postmodern evolved in the second half of the twentieth century in Europe. The true critique of a European conception of history and of its narrative of progress, he states, has been carried out by people and nations of the periphery which have struggled, among other things, to "conserve their signs," to assert their own goals and values in terms of their local traditions and needs without mixing them indis-

criminately with the demands of a global market economy.[19] Britto-
García therefore distinguishes between mainstream European postmodernism, which he characterizes as "nihilistic," a mere extension
of the colonizing European legacy of modernity, and Latin American
cultural politics and popular movements of resistance, which he characterizes as engaging in the "true critique of modernity" by carrying
out "a struggle over the constitution of free spaces for creation."[20]

Britto-García does well to remind the Eurocentric reader that
modern history is not merely a unilinear narrative moving from West
to East and from North to South, as modern thought represented it.
He claims the topic of the "end of history," as it arises in the postmodern discourse of the West, is not a negation of this narrative but
parallels the modern view which placed the European subject as civ-
ilizer and protagonist of history. Implicit in Britto-García's position
is that history cannot end, precisely because mankind is still engaged
in the task of overturning the effects of modernity's colonization. In
Britto-García's view, it is crucial to emphasize that the West's narrative of world history has been resisted both in the center and in the
periphery.[21] This resistance alone, he argues, merits attention as an
instance of the "postmodern," now understood in its essential
meaning as the creation of alternative spaces to modernity.[22]

Britto-García's redefinition of the meaning of the postmodern is
not without problems. For instance, although he discards modernity's teleology of history as oriented toward "progress," on his view
history continues to be subject to a teleological political narrative
wherein the good or "authentic" side rightfully struggles against the
nihilistic other. This time, however, the movement is the reverse of
the Eurocentric account of progress. This time the point of origin is
the struggle of the peripheries against modernity and specifically
against its expansion via the capitalist international exchange
market. Rejecting the notion of the end of history (a metaphysical
premise), Britto-García's account favors a political historical objective, namely, the disappearance of the market and of "mercantile reasoning."[23] This aim would be accomplished by movements of political
resistance (including theoretical critiques of modernity and the work
of aesthetic vanguards) against global capitalism both in the

periphery and in the West itself. Assuming that there are other names by which one can designate the process Britto-García is referring to—names such as "socialist criticism," "indigenous uprisings," or "revolution"—why, one will ask, refer to such processes as signifying the "true postmodernity"?[24] Isn't this a somewhat misleading use of the term "postmodern"? It seems that if modernity deployed a linear concept of history with certain protagonists in place (West over non-West), to change the protagonists while retaining a progressive sense of history (creative humanism versus Eurocentric market rationality) is not to depart too far from the paradigm of modernity. The concept of history that is assumed in such a discussion is still a modern civilizing one, especially if "truth" is said to be on the side of those struggling against Western dominance, while "nihilism" is said to characterize the civilization of the dominant.

TIME, NARRATIVE, AND IDENTITY

Nevertheless, Britto-García has identified an important problem that needs to be addressed in a discussion of Latin American postmodernity. The problem is: how should indigenous, grass-roots, non-Eurocentric political projects be classified by postmodern thought if, by intent, such projects are or have been decolonizing projects, yet their official historical location has been the modern age? In examining this problem, I believe the analytical concept of "multitemporal heterogeneity" offered by García Canclini can be of some assistance.[25] Basically, García Canclini argues that due to economic dependence and resistance to complete assimilation to modern European cultural expectations, modernization in Latin America has retained the characteristic of incompleteness. Modernization has not been able to reach a completely hegemonous control over an entire continent. The result is the coexistence of modern and premodern art work, cultural values, and forms of life. Today, elements of the global (transnational, postmodern), the national (modern), the colonial (early modern), and the pre-Columbian may coexist so as to create, for those who experience their proximate presence, a *hybrid* reality or identity. At a time when there is a transnationalization of the economy and of culture, he states, "to limit our options to dependence on nationalism, modernization or local traditionality, is to simplify the actual dilemmas of our history."[26]

This hybrid notion of identity breaks down the concept of the linearity of Western history. The breakdown is made possible by the awareness that the same moment in time may be traversed by multiply-situated cultural interpretations of the events taking place at that moment. In our ordinary lives in the West, if there are two narratives of the same event, it is usually the case that both narratives belong to the same framework of temporal reference. For example, if two persons are having a conversation, they will generally use temporal terms such as "now" and "later" in approximately the same sense. Even if one were to describe an oppositional political practice, such as attending a political demonstration, the policy being protested and the act of protesting it would be understood in the same narrative time frame. This time frame is usually conceived in linear time, by reference to the month, day, and year. Suppose, however, that I had a friend from a different culture who marked the differences between one day and another by reference not to linear time but to various feasts or holidays named after a variety of mythical figures. If my friend also lived in the modern world, she would be able to handle two narrative time-frames the same way some people are able to speak two languages. She could date the same event by the modern calendar and by the feastday-based calendar. An epistemic rupture would indicate the shifts between the narratives which use one or another way of marking time and relations in time and space.

Hybridity involves being able to handle and to shift back and forth between and among two or more sets of narrative-identity frameworks, e.g., an indigenous one and a modern one. At the least, it involves appreciating the possibilities of doing so. Postmodern hybridity, in particular, involves noticing and handling the epistemic ruptures and shifts between modernity and postmodernity. Perhaps, as García Canclini suggests,[27] modernity's very incompleteness in the appropriation of all ancient culture makes room for the postmodern hybrid condition to assert itself. Postmodern hybridity is not simply the ability a modern liberal education would give one to appreciate the value of different cultural and artistic products from a broad-minded perspective. Postmodern hybridity involves the ability to shift in and out of differently constituted narrative discourses and practices, whether the motive for doing this is out of a sheer need to survive in a highly complex postmodern world or as an informed option based on a choice between a modern and a postmodern approach to one's thinking and living.

In this spirit of acknowledging the cultural sensibilities of a postmodern hybrid self, how would we classify the position of Latin Americans who, prior to postmodernity, attained certain positions which bear a certain family resemblance to some of the phenomena associated with cultural hybridity? What shall we call a nineteenth-century Latin American writer who is a radical democrat (that is, neither merely liberal or conservative, as in García Canclini's model), who rejects colonialism and proposes an alternative vision of Latin American cultural identity? What relationship would the product of such a person's work bear on our understanding of the connections or lack of connections between modernity and postmodernity? The temptation to want to call certain past movements or figures with whom one has certain political affinities "postmodern," as Britto-García tends to do, should be approached with caution. In the remaining discussion, I suggest a more appropriate conceptualization of the relation between such a figure—for whose prototype I will use the thoughts of José Martí as represented in his essay, *Nuestra América*—and our present postmodern concerns with identity, both political and cultural. I argue that between ourselves and Martí a dual movement of proximity and distance can be conceptualized: on the one hand, there is a political continuity based on certain practices of radical democracy and conceptualizations of hybridity; on the other hand, there is a noticeable epistemic rupture with regard to conceptual schemes distinguishing modernity from postmodernity. Both the continuities and the ruptures are important to remember, lest one is led to dismiss the nature of the political continuities due to the epistemic rupture or to dismiss the nature of the epistemic rupture due to an emphasis on political continuity. Perhaps a brief analysis of Martí's celebrated essay will yield some clues and insights into this paradoxical problem.

In "Nuestra América" (1891), Martí argues, in terms that antedate the postmodern critiques of Eurocentrism, that the study of Latin America's own history and culture as well as of the social reality of each individual country are major prerequisites for those interested in the governance of their country.[28] He observes that the local mayor who believes that as long as he runs things in his village, the universal order of government is a good one, ought to beware of political giants who at any moment may intervene to get what they want out of his little village. He asks Latin Americans to put their divisions aside and unite, to value their culture and particularly the study of the indigenous roots of their culture above the origins of Western culture in ancient Greece, and to use their knowledge to create a government that will work to preserve these values rather than try to import from Europe the criteria on how to govern. Martí supports the diversity of different traditions and peoples, but warns that when things get out of balance in the weaker countries, they will be in danger, because already those who govern the stronger countries are predisposed to think the weaker ones are inferior and not likely to last as long as they. In tactful terms Martí describes the conditions that allow for cultural imperialism to penetrate into Latin America, at the same time that he encourages Latin Americans to resist it by becoming more aware of their strengths and by communicating these to North Americans who "do not speak our language . . . and who are dissimilar to us in their political faults, which are different from ours."[29] Martí's essay, though appealing to the categories of moral judgment and political opinion prevalent in his time (modernity)—such as universal respect for humans of all races, government by and for the people, attaining cultural strength through education, and so on—inserts into these categories a standpoint of radical critique of Eurocentrism and of the naïve acceptance that the so-called universal order of government is a benign one. I would suggest that in Martí's perspective we can find a *political continuity* between Latin American postmodern thought critical of Euro- and Nordocentrism and those Latin American emancipators, who, like Martí, saw themselves as writing and acting from a modern standpoint. At the same time, we can also find an *epistemic rupture* distinguishing the writings of a nineteenth-century liberator like Martí from today's postmodern writings, even if both share a kindred perspectival awareness of Latin America's marginality and the need to sustain and strengthen its fragile yet nonetheless "indigenous" cultural profile.

Martí was aware that if our knowledge—that is, the knowledge derived from our specific cultural differences—does not count, we do not count in the West's paradigm of universal knowledge. And, if our knowledge does not count, then we are ripe for the imposition of someone else's laws, someone else's knowledge, even someone else's religion. Perhaps this is why Martí stressed the concept of "el hombre natural" (the natural man) and of the harmony and correspondence between a new Latin America that would be the product of the quest for freedom and the natural environment of the continent.[30] For Martí, culture and nature were to work toward common aims, not against each other—that is, culture would not justify the exploitation of nature as is typical of the culture/nature dichotomy of modern thought. Moreover, Martí referred to the continent that nourished the projects of emancipation of its people as *madre América* (mother America), using the figure of a mother as a unifying symbol of "our America" to represent independence from the Eurocentric colonizer.[31] Despite many of the conventional ways in which Martí used the figures of woman and mother in his writings, I think the fact that he used the feminine figure, *madre América*, as a symbol of powerful inspiration for a decolonized America is sufficiently indicative to show the radical overtones of his earth-bound, grass-roots concept of identity and democracy. His alignment is with the nonprivileged *pobres de la tierra* (the poor of the earth), for whom he would reserve a dignified place in the newly constructed social order.[32]

Three characteristics of Martí's cultural-political position in "Nuestra América" may be helpful in situating his view at the somewhat contradictory site marking both the epistemic rupture and the political continuity between Latin American modern and postmodern thinking. Martí's essay shows (1) the promotion of intracultural solidarity, (2) the affirmation of specific cultural differences and the cor-

responding appreciation of the situation of oppression experienced
by ethnic and racial minorities, and (3) the use of a racially decentered concept of the human species, insofar as he ultimately appeals,
beyond all racial differences, to a "universal identity" of the human
being.[33] While Martí appeals to unity among Latin Americans as a
way of strengthening their vulnerable cultural and political situation,
he insists this unity must be built on the positive acknowledgment and
inclusion of indigenous and black cultural production to their respective societies. He uses the expression *desestancar al indio* (to free up
the Indian's economic and social stagnation), just as he argues for the
incorporation of blacks into the free life of the society.[34] He observes
that "neither the European nor the Yankee book can offer the key to
the Hispanic American enigma."[35] In decentering the importance of
Europe and the United States for Latin Americans, and in raising the
importance of the indigenous and black populations of the region,
Martí tries to balance the specific differences of the margins of
Western culture against the powerful influences of the center. He is
aware that to some extent the popular culture will act as a buffer
between the decolonizing self-determination of *nuestra Americanistas*
and the "exotic creole" who will want to import Latin America's
models from abroad.[36] His work shows a constant involvement—to
the point of giving up his life for Cuba's independence—with the issue
of how and why to preserve that image and reality of America, toward
which, as Latinos, in our deepest decolonialized spirit, he sensed we
felt a maternal bond.

CONCLUSION

The question of the relation between postmodern issues of identity
and culture, and Latin American critiques of Euro- and Nordocentric
modernity and postmodernity cannot be easily resolved. Still, certain
approaches to this question can be tentatively ruled out by our
analysis. I would like to reemphasize that not much is gained either
by the move to judge the political status of postmodern thought as a
whole or by dividing postmodern thought into authentic and nihilistic

oppositional sides so as to pass moral judgment on both aspects. It is important to note that there are political differences (just as there surely are differences in moral perspective) among postmodern authors; this is not unusual. There is no reason to reject all or part of postmodern thought on account of the political ambiguities of postmodernism. Rather, the point of criticism can be to reach, via postmodern thought and analysis, a better understanding of Latin American and global cultural, economic, and political realities.

On the positive side, as has been shown, there are political continuities between modern and postmodern authors in Europe, Latin America, and North America, all of whom favor differing expressions of radical democratic politics without ignoring the geographical/cultural locations from which they write. Among the continuities in political discussion there is the question of cultural identity. The concept of Latin American identity has been around much longer than postmodernism and is not reducible to postmodern treatments on the subject; nevertheless, today's postmodern debates on identity are of considerable importance and often occupy the forefront of discussion in the fields of critical and cultural studies. Without the use of contemporary research on postmodern cultural theory, debates on Latin American identity and the so-called relation between center and periphery would become dated, either confined to past conceptual frameworks or to ahistorical generalizations.

Modernity lay the roots for the theorizing of the concept of *nuestra América*; postmodernity has relativized the terms of the debate and has brought forth such concepts as hybridity, countermimesis, and multitemporal heterogeneity to describe the new ways Latin American identity constructs continue to be negotiated in the unavoidable interaction between center and periphery and in the light of the complex relationships among North American, Latin American, African American, European, and indigenous cultural production. The metaphysical tenets of the end of history and of the subject should not be used as pretexts for shunning contemporary postmodern theory. These tenets do not ring true even for much of the postmodern thinking produced in the West—much less for studies on Latin America where, as long as the economic-political projects of modernity remain unfinished, it makes no sense to bring concepts of subjectivity and history to self-cancellation or closure. For this reason I believe that the process of appropriation of cultural identity should also not be brought to a closure and that, in fact, the rethinking of a figure like Martí is a relevant exercise in the pursuit of our claims to hybridity. If this hybridity includes some elements— as it must—of the modern, why not let there be an affirmation of our cultural roots in a style that takes into account the better insights of Martí's concept of *nuestra América*, particularly if we adopt such a style of thinking as a conscious appropriation of our signs of difference?[37] Why not assert and confront the terms of our displacement from the mass media messages imparted by the global producers of identity, as we study and articulate the terms and values of our appropriated differences?

Martí's concept of *nuestra América* can help ground (when grounding is necessary) those hybrid identities displaced from an original or permanent home and yet not altogether homeless. There are changing, shifting ways of abiding as we make note of our multi-temporal perceptual experiences. The main epistemic rupture between the modern emancipators and ourselves, I think, has been the rupture with the belief that one universal state of freedom would be reached, past which only minor adjustments and modifications would be needed to create and maintain a just and democratic political and social system. Postmodernity has taught us that the expectation of such a universal had many flaws—both in its conceptual articulation and its practical implementation. Postmodern existence has shown that, for the most part, local struggles have much more of a presence in people's lives than grand struggles. The reality of what is contingent and changeable, and the inquiry into the identities constructed and lost in response to these types of demand, has become, in postmodern times, perhaps our most pressing issue.

NOTES

1. Luis Britto-García, "Critiques of Modernity: Avant-Garde, Counterculture, Revolution," *The South Atlantic Quarterly* 92 (1993): 522.

2. Gayatri Spivak, "Can the Subaltern Speak?" in *Marxism and the Interpretation of Culture*, ed. C. Nelson and L. Grossberg (Urbana: University of Illinois Press, 1988), pp. 271–313; Judith Butler, *Bodies that Matter: On the Discursive Limits of "Sex"* (New York: Routledge, 1993).

3. See, for example, the debate on feminism and postmodernism in Linda Nicholson, ed., *Feminism/Postmodernism* (New York: Routledge, 1990).

4. See, for example, Inderpal Grewal and Caren Kaplan, eds., *Scattered Hegemonies: Postmodernity and Transnational Feminist Practices* (Minneapolis: University of Minnesota Press, 1994).

5. The problematization of essentialist constraints on categories and widely used terms such as *woman/women, the Indian, the Latin American*, and so on, is an important benefit provided by postmodern research strategies.

6. Nelly Richard, "¿Tiene sexo la escritura?" *Debate feminista* [Mexico City] 9 (1994): 134–35.

7. "Se trata de averiguar . . . cómo ser radical sin ser fundamentalista" ("It is an attempt to inquire . . . how to be radical without being fundamentalist"), Nestor García Canclini, *Culturas híbridas: Estrategias para entrar y salir de la modernidad* (Mexico City: Grijalbo, 1989), p. 348. With these words which speak to the purpose of his study, García Canclini concludes his book.

8. See, for example, Roberto Fernández Retamar, *Caliban and Other Essays*, trans. E. Baker (Minneapolis: University of Minnesota Press, 1989). The short quote above, though popularly used, is not an exact quote from Shakespeare's *The Tempest* (1.2.362–64). Retamar (pp. 5–6) cites the actual quote: "You taught me your language, and my profit on't/ Is, I know how to curse. The red plague rid you/ For learning me your language!" See also O. Schutte, *Cultural Identity and Social Liberation in Latin American Thought* (Albany: SUNY Press, 1993), pp. 128–29.

9. García Canclini, *Culturas híbridas*, pp. 188–90.

10. Ibid., p. 189.

11. Ibid., p. 190.

12. Samuel Ramos, *Profile of Man and Culture in Mexico*, trans. P. G. Earle (Austin: University of Texas Press, 1973), pp. 10–14.

13. Nelly Richard, "The Latin American Problematic of Theoretical-Cultural Transference: Postmodern Appropriations and Counterappropriations," *The South Atlantic Quarterly* 92 (1993):455.

14. Ibid., p. 454.

15. Ibid., p. 457.

16. Ibid., pp. 456–57.

17. Ibid., pp. 458–59.

18. Britto-García, "Critiques of Modernity," p. 526.

19. Ibid.

20. Ibid., p. 527.

21. Ibid., p. 516.

22. Ibid., p. 527.

23. Ibid., p. 527.

24. Ibid., p. 516.

25. García Canclini, *Culturas híbridas*, pp. 71–73. Cf. García Canclini, "Memory and Innovation in the Theory of Art," *The South Atlantic Quarterly* 92 (1993): 428–31.

26. García Canclini, "Memory and Innovation," 431.

27. García Canclini, *Culturas híbridas*, p. 71.

28. José Martí, "Nuestra América," in *Política de Nuestra América*, Preface by Roberto Fernández Retamar (Mexico City: Siglo XXI, 1979), pp. 35–44. Translations are my own.

29. Ibid., p. 44.

30. Ibid., pp. 39, 41. Martí expresses the view that to be a tyrant is to act against the natural intelligence and goodness of humanity.

31. José Martí, "Madre América," in *Política de Nuestra América*, 44–52.

32. José Martí, "Versos Sencillos," in *Poesía Completa: Edición Crítica*, vol. 1 (2 vols.; Havana: Centro de Estudios Martianos y Editorial Letras Cubanas, 1993), p. 238.

33. Specifically, Martí states: "The soul emanates, equal and eternal, from bodies diverse in form and color. Whoever encourages and propagates the opposition and hatred among the races sins against humanity" ("Nuestra América," pp. 43–44). Martí, however, uses the notion of racial difference to specify the oppression of races and to argue for their emancipation. When he mentions there are no races on this same paragraph, what he means is there is no natural reason on which to base racial hatred. In nature there is only "the universal identity of man" (p. 43). Although Martí's metaphysics of nature would of course not be shared by postmodernists, interestingly, his position allows him to agree with the thesis of the social construction of "race."

34. Ibid., pp. 41–42.

35. Ibid., p. 42.

36. "El mestizo autóctono ha vencido al criollo exótico" (The autochthonous mestizo has conquered the exotic creole), "Nuestra América," p. 39.

37. The appropriation mentioned would nevertheless acknowledge the existing ruptures between a modern and a postmodern epistemic framework in the treatment of such concepts as identity, authenticity, and nature.

Walter Mignolo

LOCAL HISTORIES/GLOBAL DESIGNS
Geohistorical Spaces and Epistemological Locations

The following quotation from Darcy Ribeiro describes the problem I explore in this article:

> In the same way that Europe carried a variety of techniques and inventions to the people included in its network of domination . . . it also introduced to them its equipment of concepts, pre-concepts and idiosyncrasy which referred at the same time to Europe itself and to the colonial people.
>
> The colonial people, deprived of their riches and of the fruit of their labor under colonial regimes they suffered, furthermore, the degradation of assuming as their proper image the image that was no more than the reflexion of the European vision of the world, which considered colonial people racially inferior because they were Black, (Amer)Indians or "mestizos." . . .
>
> Even the brighter social strata of non-European people got used to seeing themselves and their communities as an *infrahumanity whose destiny was to occupy a subaltern position* because of the sheer fact that theirs was inferior to the European population. (Ribeiro 1968: 63)

Although the notion of "subalternity" was introduced by Gramsci to account for class relations, it is no less obvious that before the consolidation of the structure of labor under capitalism, ethnicity played a major role in the configuration and consolidation of the modern world. Not only at its inception do we find the retrenchment of the

Amerindian population and the African- slave trade to supply labor, but also the expulsion of the Moors and the Jews from the Iberian Peninsula. Before the consolidation of the modern nation-state, with liberalism as its ideological form and the consolidation of class relations based on exploitation of labor in a capitalistic economy, subalternity was mainly localized at the ethnic level, be it in the context of the Religion of the Book (Christians, Islamic Moores, and Jews), be it at the level of African slaves or Amerindian indigenous populations. The crisis of the liberal/socialist ideology of the state after 1989 (interpreted by some as the final triumph of liberal democracy), together with an exacerbation of technology which makes possible for some to talk about a postwork society (López 1994) and for others about immaterial labor (Lazzarato 1996), have brought ethnicity to the fore again and theorized as "The Clash of Civilizations" (Huntington 1996). Colonial legacies are still alive and well as central strategies of subalternization. Subalternity, based on ethnicity as Ribeiro's paragraph makes clear, was not only economic but intellectual as well, as far as a concept of humanity linked to intelligence first and the concept of reason later were attributed to certain groups of people and denied to others. In a parallel form, certain languages were considered appropriate to express certain levels of intelligence or reason, and other languages were considered inferior, as the people who spoke them. Cultures of scholarship were the privileged or certain languages and not of others; and even among those languages with long histories to qualify as languages of scholarship, hierarchies were established. For instance, Latin in the sixteenth century established itself and set the stage for the emergence of modern/colonial languages as vehicles of new forms of scholarship.

All of these are alive and well today and moving toward the future. Ethnicity and cultures of scholarship have been linked, by colonialism, under the correlation of "purity of blood" and the "unity of language." Still today, in the United States as well as in Spain, France, or England, it is of the utmost importance to celebrate and defend the unity of the language, more so now when all kinds of migrations are constantly putting the language in danger; not to mention the purity of blood, now reformulated in geocultural (and not only sexual) and medical categories by the emergence of AIDS. Medical discourse was always entrenched with ethnicity, although it became predominant at the end of the nineteenth century with the consolidation of the nation-states, national languages and national literatures/cultures. Thus, if "territorial gnosis" is the tendency that characterizes the formation and transformation of modernity and its justification of colonialism, "borderland gnosis" is what we need to elaborate toward a future free from the prejudice of purity, unity, and authenticity. If knowledge is power, it is so for different reasons. The equation power/knowledge that is crucial in this article is manifested in geohistorical categories and their complicity with languages and cultures of scholarship. To undo the "natural" link between them is, at the same time, to undo networks of power that create new spaces of interventions by those who have been left out in a world constructed by geohistorical colonial categories and colonial geopolitic of knowledge. In this article, I explore "borderland gnosis" (border gnosis for short), as a new platform for thinking beyond the control of modern/colonial categories of thought.

Border gnosis, then, is used in dialogue with the debate on the universals/particulars on the one hand, and with Michael Foucault's notion of "insurrection of subjugated knowledges" on the other. Furthermore, border gnosis could serve as a mediator between the two problematics: universal/particular and the "insurrection of the subjugated knowledges."

My intention in this article is to move subjugated knowledge to a different space, the space of colonialism and colonial legacies, where the question is no longer of subjugated but of subaltern knowledges. That is, the question is how knowledge equivalent to European disciplinary knowledges (e.g., what Luis Vives conceived as "the disciplines" in the sixteenth century, or the rearticulation of the social sciences and the humanities in the nineteenth century), not only subjugated but placed them in a subaltern position and justified the colonial effort to "discipline" (e.g., Christianize, civilize) non-European communities. My reflections here start from where a previous study left off, and where I elaborated on the subalternization of knowledge in language, space, and memory (Mignolo 1995). Although my focus was the Spanish Empire in the Americas and chronologically the second half of the sixteenth and the first half of the seventeenth centuries, similar strategies were at work in English and French colonizations of India and Africa (Suleri 1992a; Mudimbe 1988; Mudimbe et. al. Africa and the disciplines) and, of course, in the past fifty years with the Three World Division and the corresponding distribution of scientific labor (Pletsch 1981; Mignolo 1992c, 1996), and the creation of area studies in the United States (Lambert 1990). In a sense, this article is also the continuation of the project started by Darcy Ribeiro (1968) before Foucault's notion of "subjugated knowledges" and of Edward Said's productive displacement of Foucault's archeology of knowledge to reveal the epistemological production of "Orientalism."

Culture and Imperialism (1993), "Intellectuals in the Post-Colonial World" (1986) are, without Said knowing it, basically about Ribeiro's "subaltern knowledge." And the fact that Said in *Orientalism* did not engage Ribeiro's reflections on colonialism and subaltern knowledge, and that in *Culture and Imperialism* (1993) Said introduces the notion of "contrapuntual analysis" without engaging Fernando Ortíz's "contrapunteo" (Coronil 1994), is a clear example of colonialism and unintentional subalternization of knowledge. Subalternization of knowledge in this context means simply that the practitioner of a given discipline (let's say, history, anthropology, comparative literature) in the "First World" (that is, working mainly within the languages of modern colonialism, English, French, and German) does not have to know what is produced in other languages and in other parts of the world (thus, the question of geocultural spaces and epistemological locations), although a practitioner of a given discipline, say in India or Brazil, has of necessity to know the canon of the disciplines, or the literary canon. What Darcy Ribeiro perceived as "subaltern knowledges" at the end of the sixties, and why he called himself "anthropologian" instead of "anthropologist" to mark the difference between an anthropologist who studies the Third World and an anthropologian who is, lives and works in the Third World, was more recently rearticulated by Dipesh Chakrabarty from his own experience as a historian of India, in India:

In the academic discourse of history—that is, "history" as a discourse produced at the institutional site of the university—"Europe" remains the sovereign, theoretical subject of all histories, including the ones we call "Indian," "Chinese," "Kenyan," etc. There is a peculiar way in which all these other histories tend to become variations on a master narrative that could be called "the history of Europe." In this sense, "Indian" history itself is in a position of subalternity; one can only articulate subaltern subject-positions in the name of history. (Chakrabarty 1992: 337)

I am trying to think, and get out of, subaltern knowledges through border gnosis. Subaltern knowledges as articulated by Ribeiro and Chakrabarty are precisely at the crossroad of local histories and global designs, or geohistorical spaces and epistemological locations. The border, conceived both as a space of physical and epistemological violence, is not the frontier. The difference between a "frontier" and a "border" epistemology is that the first is "territorial" and located on one side of the frontier, the hegemonic side, the side that advances civilization. "Border" epistemology is transient, moving and acting on both sides of the border, situated at the threshold, in the liminal space of the border, constantly revealing the relation of power while constantly undoing the epistemology of the frontier as an epistemology grounding the advance of civilization, modernization and development.

Thus, the basic difference between subjugated and subaltern knowledge that I would like to stress is the following: the configuration of the humanities in the European Renaissance and of the human sciences after the European Enlightenment in complicity with colonial and imperial expansion made possible the subalternization of "similar" kinds of knowledge in different geohistorical locations, and that subalternization continues today and is visible in the conflict between disciplinary practices and colonial legacies articulated by Ribeiro and Chakrabarty. This is what I call subaltern knowledges, which I analyzed in detail, for the sixteenth and seventeenth centuries in the domain of language (grammars and politics of language), space (mappings) and history (memories). "Subjugated knowledge" in Foucault's sense, is the operation presupposed and needed in the very constitution of the humanities and its transformation into the human sciences.

And this naturally brings me to the question of border gnosis in dialogue with the question of "universal/particular." Global or universal history needs an observer who is not attached to any particular history but who can transcend them all. That was precisely the program of G. W. F. Hegel in his *The Philosophy of History* (1822).

Let's bring Frantz Fanon into the picture. When in *The Wretched of the Earth* (1961: 205–207) he talks about the revolt of imperialist forms of knowledge, which will transform the passive spectators subdued with inessentiality into privileged actors, he is at the same time locating his own contribution to the liberation of both subjugated knowledge (à la Foucault) and subaltern knowledge (à la Ribeiro and Chakrabarty). Indeed, Fanon (1961) contributes to the sense of Ribeiro's (1968) and Chakrabarty's (1992) claim for a de-subalternization of disciplinary knowledge. Fanon's emphasis on the "particularity of the colonial experience" is a constant guard against the violence of universalizing knowledge, the universal/colonial knowledge that for five centuries "narrated" the culture, people, and knowledge that needed to be placed in a subaltern position in relation to the knowledge possessed, practiced, and imparted in the very process of colonial expansion.

The dialectic between universal and particular is complex, and it also has a long history that I cannot summarize here. A quotation from Ernesto Laclau will take us through a shortcut to the point I am trying to make. Laclau devised three alternatives connecting knowledge and politics, linking philosophical discussion with a future society that needs to rearticulate the universal/particular, for in order to be democratic has to deal with the current problem of multiculturalism. So, says Laclau:

> Differences and particularisms are the necessary starting point, but out of it, it is possible to open the way to a relative universalization of values which can be the basis for a popular hegemony. This universalization and its open character certainly condemns all identity to an unavoidable hybridization, but hybridization does not necessarily mean decline through the loss of identity: it can also mean empowering existing identities through the opening of new possibilities. Only a conservative identity, closed on itself, could experience hybridization as a loss. But this democratic-hegemonic possibility

has to recognize the constitutive contextualized/decontextualized terrain of its constitution and take full advantage of the political possibility that this undecidability opens. All this finally amounts to saying is that the particular can only fully realize itself if it constantly keeps open, and constantly redefines, its relation to the universal. (Laclau 1996: 65)

If we accept to the last consequence that the universal, as defined by Laclau, is an empty space ("the place of power is empty and we can conceive the democratic process as a particular articulation of the empty universality of the community and the particularism of the transient political forces incarnating in it"; 1996: 64–65), then we can understand Fanon's relentless call for the "particularity of the colonial experience" not as a divisive statement as a strong claim to the universal, his claim to "unleashing the human being." In order to do so, knowledge has to be unleashed, subaltern knowledge de-subalternized. The particularity of the colonial experience has then two sides that have to be rearticulated: the particularity of the colonial experience in the colonies, where knowledge and people have been subalternized and reduced to the local; the particularity of the colonial experience in the metropolis, where the subalternization of knowledge was practiced and a claim to universality was constantly made without recognizing its own particularity. In this second case, the locus of enunciation was emptied of is historicity in order to fill the space of the universal, at the same time that the locus of enunciation of the colonies was filled with particularities in order to underlie its localism and to prevent its entry to the universal. Border gnosis could help us in thinking the universal/particular otherwise, and Fanon's work is indeed a pioneering effort in this direction.

In this precise sense, my own notion of border gnosis is inscribed in Enrique Dussel's "transmodern project" in which a decentering and subsumption of modernity is articulated. The "transmodern project—states Dussel—really subsumes modernity's rational emancipative character and it negates alterity even as it rejects modernity's mythic character and its irrational exculpation of self and inculpation of its victims" (Dussel 1996: 138). If, on the one hand, the larger frame of border gnosis is at the intersection of local histories and global designs, where places are articulated and space conceived, the more specific historical one is the transmodern modern in which the liberatory legacy of modernity encounters its limits as it is taken over by and in local histories imbedded in colonial legacies. In this sense, border gnosis and transmodernity do not think in terms of negation, as Dussel makes clear, but in terms of multiple subsumptions in which the liberatory legacies of modernity are being swallowed and remapped by the particularity of local histories embedded in colonial legacies all over the planet. While a negative dialectics is indeed a necessary critical (Adorno 1966) reflection on the classical legacies of European modernity, subsumption and border gnosis is the necessary critical perspective "from" modernity embedded in colonial legacies. Nevertheless, if negative dialectics could be historicized, and instead of focusing on the "subject" and "object," so crucial for Hegel's conceptualization of the master/slave relation, the accent is placed on the denial of coevalness (Fabian 1982) as a crucial strategy of colonial discourse, the transmodern project could be complementary to negative dialectics. In other words, transmodernity and border gnosis are proposing to think in terms of "the denial of the denial of coevalness." To negate the negation of coevalness does not imply either a positive thinking or a happy synthesis. Subsumption and border gnosis are not another name for hybridity but, rather, the restitution of what has been negated by the denial of coevalness and the rearticulation of the legacy of modernity from the perspective of what is being restituted. In Dussel's words:

> I propose two contradictory paradigms: mere Eurocentric modernity and modernity subsumed in a world horizon. While the first paradigm functions ambiguously as emancipative and mythically violent (e.g., Dussel's "genocidal reason"), the second, transmodern paradigm embraces both modernity and its alterity. (Dussel 1996: 139)

"Alterity," it should be stressed, is not just the opposite of the "same": it is both the incorporation of the "same" into the fashioning of the "other." That tense subsumption in which alterity is, at the same time and in creative tension, the "other that incorporates the same" from the perspective of the subaltern is what I understand by border gnosis; the analectic moment in Dussel's philosophy of liberation.

The title of this article maps a geohistorical space crossed and cruised by the colonial situations and legacies, from the memories that are and can be retrieved to present-day thinking, feeling, and action. It also maps a curve between René Descartes's linking languages and geometry, disembodying thoughts from material locations, and doing so in Amsterdam at the moment that Dutch colonialism began to displace Spanish and Portuguese ones. The other end of the curve is the delinking of language and geometry, returning language to the body and doing so at the moment in which global capitalism is detaching economy from territory. The guiding metaphor is the "borderland" in the sense introduced and explored by Chicano/as writers, artists, theoreticians, and activists. The particular colonial legacies are the Spanish and the United States and in between them, the period of nation-building. Borderland gnosis, border gnosis in short, is the expression under which I indicate the complex relations implied in the title. The main concern is the relationship between geohistorical location and the production of knowledge, colonialism/imperialism/globalization as the expressions under which the geopolitics of knowledge I am exploring can be understood.

Border gnosis is a commodity, a space for critical reflection from the perspective of the transient (immigrants, exiles, and refugees), as well as the sedentary ones, those who do not move but for whom movement comes to them (e.g., the "frontier" between Mexico and the United States); and finally, border gnosis is a keyword in Raymond Williams's sense. It is a commodity because at the end of the twentieth century we find ourselves in a global marketplace to which intellectual and scholarly production cannot escape. It would be too romantic to criticize capitalism and consumerism, assuming an intellectual location that is itself outside of the market and consumerism. Thus, border gnosis as a commodity has to compete in the market, while being a constant reminder of the supreme alienation of a social and cultural organization whose main goal is to accumulate money-wealth (those managing financial capital and means of production) and object-wealth (those needing financial capital to consume the objects they produce). Border gnosis as a commodity also has to compete with other intellectual commodities while offering a space for a transformative position of dissent. Border gnosis as a critical form of reflection from the perspective of the itinerant, immigrants, exiles, refugees, and sedentary communities experiencing globalization (like Amerindians in the sixteenth century or Aymara communities in Bolivia in the twentieth century [Rivera Cusicanqui 1990] is both a reflection on structures of domination and relations of subalternity. Or, if you prefer, border gnosis is thinking from the borders between imperial and subaltern reasons; and it is the grounding for intellectual and political projects to dismantle and replace the principles upon which imperial reason produced subalternity: a longing toward subaltern reasons. Border gnosis as subaltern reason is the reason that thinks from both sides of the border, which knows both the locus of the empire and the locus of the subalterns. Imperial reason knows only one side, the side that in its building suppresses the other. Finally, keywords in Williams's view are not concepts, in the sense that philosophy of science or philosophical reasoning are (e.g., the Kantian supreme and regulative principle of pure reason), but tools for thinking through.

What called for thinking from the borders was the situation I found myself in when I came to the United States and realized that I was a Latin American and a Latinamericanist. In Argentina I did not have this problem, perhaps because I was a graduate student but mostly because my mentors, even when their concern was Argentina or Latin American cultural history, did not considered themselves Latinamericanists. To feel Latin American, on the other hand, comes second to being associated with one specific country, whether that feeling is passive or conflictive. Being in the United States since the late seventies, early eighties makes me feel Hispanic or Latin American. Once during a graduate seminar at Duke, a student questioned the identity label "latinoamerican" because, she said, one does not know what a "latinamerican" is. I agreed with her in that I did not know what a "latinamerican" is either, but I was pretty darn sure that I felt "latinamerican." In any event, what was important was the double side of a geocultural identity when one is, among other features, a subject identified as "latinamerican," the object of an area studies configuration called "Latin America," and at the same time a member of a disciplinary community that has Latin America as an object of study. It was a conflictive awareness that through the years led me to the notion of border gnosis. In this context, border gnosis means, for instance, to deal constantly with the tension between intellectuals, scholars, writers, social scientists, social movements, etc., working *in* Latin America and scholars, intellectuals, officers of government, etc., in this country working *about* or *on* Latin America. This scenario was particularly uneasy before the end of the Cold War, the configuration of area studies and the overarching and related world order, organized in First, Second, and Third. In the case of Latin America and Latin American Studies, it so happened that Latin America was located in the Third World, an area, and Latin American Studies in the First World.

The situation is changing now. The Cold War is over, at least in terms of how it was structured until 1989. Area Studies is also being disarticulated, even by research institutions supporting problem-oriented rather than area-oriented research. Thus, new ways of thinking are needed. Two interrelated aspects come forth. One is the suspicions of the distinction between subject and object, so prevalent in modern epistemology and so pervasively questioned in postmodern thinking. The other is the transnationalization of the economy that prompted a radical criticism of, again, the assumed one-to-one relationship between national (or regional, continental, or subcontinental) cultures and territories. Kuan-Hsing Chen (1992), facing a similar problem in Taiwan after he returned from pursuing graduate studies in London, conceptualized in terms of "international localism," which I will translate into "transnational localism." International maintains the distinctiveness of the nation-state, while transnational (which I correlate in this book with the use of transdisciplinary) presupposes the undoing of nationally based presuppositions. "Localism" has the double advantage of being part of the articulation global/local and the politics of location, which underlines the locus of enunciation and interaction. Thus, "transnational localism" has the advantage of breaking up the complicity between a seemingly universal epistemology that is articulated in the subject/object distinction and a geopolitical configuration of knowledge according to which the subject is located in the First and the object in the Third World. My first formulation of this idea was stated in the context of colonial and postcolonial studies:

> My concern is to underscore the point that "colonial and postcolonial discourse" is not just a new field of study or a gold mine for extracting new riches but the condition of possibility for constructing new loci of enunciations as well as for reflection that academic "knowledge and understanding" should be complemented with "learning from" those who are living in and thinking from colonial and post(neo)-colonial legacies. . . . Otherwise, we run the risk of promoting mimicry, exportation/importation of theories, and internal (cultural) colonialism rather than promoting new forms of cultural critique and intellectual and political emancipations—of making colonial and postcolonial studies a field of study instead of a liminal and critical locus of enunciation. In the apportionment of scientific labor since World War II, which has been described well by Carl Pletsch [1982], the Third World produces not only "cultures" to be studied by anthropologists and ethnohistorians but also intellectuals who generate theories and reflect on their own culture and history. (Mignolo 1992c: 131)

In research-granting institution lingo, what I called here "thinking from" has been rendered in terms of "area-based knowledge." The question now is not just to change the name as a sign of recognition that knowledge is not only produced in the former First World, as the last version of an extended modernity (from the early modern period to postmodernism, in Fredric Jameson's sense), but to make local knowledge sustainable and to accept the complementarity of local and global knowledges. Border gnosis is necessary and a necessary tool to think at the intersection of the local and the global, of areas as object and area studies as a disciplinary configuration of knowing subjects. Border gnosis is also a useful way of establishing a dialogue between those who, like Kuan-Hsing Chen, studied in the former First World and returned to the former Third World, and those like myself, who studied and remained in the former First World and made colonial/imperial legacies not an object of study but a space of critical reflection. Border gnosis is post-subaltern thinking.

I will locate border gnosis in three specific examples and expand on them: Gloria Anzaldúa's articulation of *borderlands*; Stuart Hall's (1991a and 1991b) inscription of a critical postcolonial/imperial reason in the "original" frame of globalization (which I will refer to as "Hall's turn"); and, finally, Fernando Ortíz's notion of "transculturation."

First, then, Gloria Anzaldúa and a disclaimer. Border gnosis should not be conceived in terms of a master or universal concept that absorbs all kinds of situations in which forms of knowledge from both sides of the frontier could be generated and expanded. Such a conception would replicate and maintain a modern, monotopic kind of epistemology from which all known cases of border gnosis attempt to escape. Instead, border gnosis shall be conceived as an empty category allowing for a transnational and international grounding of communication and alliances; the empty space in which not only different forms of local critical knowledge can be connected, but also the empty space that allows for inscribing new geopolitics of knowledge that are an extended meditation to escape all forms of authoritarianism being the secular and modern concept of reason, as well as all forms of fundamentalism based on the authority of the Sacred Book; to forms of nationalism grounded on the defense of the authenticity of national glories and traditions. Thus, instead of defining border gnosis in abstract terms, I will ground it locally, in local histories and memories linked to particular colonial legacies.

I need to take a detour here before coming back to Anzaldúa. When Spain took over the Christian mission at the end of the fifteenth century, the border of humanity began to be traced in terms of a concept that embodied (almost literary) race and religion: "purity of blood" became a signpost to distinguish Christians from Moors and Jews both in terms of religion and race. The "unity of language" that accompanied the "purity of blood" was grounded in the first grammar of a vernacular, modern language written by Antonio de Nebrija in 1492, and by the first history of Castilian language written by Jose de Aldrete in 1606. Now, while the purity of blood and the

unity of language were a serious concern in Spain, their exportation
toward the New World had a different configuration. In Spain the two
principles (purity of blood, unity of language) justify the expulsion of
the Moors and the Jews. In the New World, the two principles justified the colonization of Amerindian languages and the enactment of a
legal and religious system for controlling the population. "Mestizaje,"
however, was unavoidable and certainly more controllable than
"mestizaje" between Christian Castilians and Moors or Jews. Thus,
at the end of the sixteenth century we find in the New World a significant group of Amerindian and Mestizo intellectuals dealing with the
conflictive situation of rearticulating the memories of their communities not only with the memories imposed upon them by missionaries
and men of letters, but also with the fact that men of letters, missionaries, and soldiers took the liberty to write Amerindian memories.

Purity of blood and the unity of language were two fundamental
principles to frame, both in Spain and in its colonies, a world in
which the exterior could be controlled and tamed by the interior. To
establish a kind of expanding frontier, governable communities were
kept in its interior and the ungovernable was relegated to the exterior. *Frontier* enacted the violence that *border gnosis* tried to overcome. This scenario also set the stage for a future melodrama: the
specific terms in which nineteenth-century nationalism conceived the
nation not only as surrounded and enclosed by geographical frontiers, but also the complicity with an encapsulated space as well. At
this point, the leading metaphor no longer came from Spain but from
England, Germany, and France. The complicity between the image of
the nation and epistemology impinged on the cultures of scholarship,
which also contributed to tracing the frontiers of the nation. Greg
Calhoun offers a useful description of this complicity:

> Under the influence of nationalist ideas, they developed notions of
> societies as singular, bounded, and internally integrated, and as
> realms in which people were more or less the same. On this basis, a
> great deal of modern social theory came to incorporate perfectly the
> notion that human beings naturally inhabit only a single social
> world or culture at a time. People on borders, children of mixed
> marriages, those rising through social mobility, and those migrating
> from one society to another were all constituted for social theory as

people with problems by contrast to the presumed ideal of people who inhabited a single social world and could therefore unambiguously place themselves in their social environments. The implicit phenomenological presumption was that human life would be easier if individuals did not have to manage a heterogeneity of social worlds or modes of cultural understanding. An ideal of clarity and consistency prevailed. (Calhoun 1994: 44–45)

Calhoun makes this observation to trace the path of social theory and critical thinking. It is precisely at the intersection of colonial legacies, nation-building and knowledge production that border gnosis becomes an important keyword: if national ideology was constructed, in part, on the foundation of the unity of national languages and cultures of scholarship and the modern worlds, which were manufactured on both national and imperial languages, then modern epistemology is implicitly monotopic and enclosed within the frontier of the nation. The current crisis of national principles, including the questioning of national languages, naturally leads to a new foundation of knowledge and understanding housed across borders, in the impurity of blood and in fractured languages, like Anzaldúa's varieties of English, mixed with Spanish and Nahuatl, or Khatibi's "double pensée," grounded on the historical crossing between Arabic and French, between the Sacred Book and the Secular text. This new foundation of knowledge is what calls for border thinking, for border gnosis.

I am now in a position to return to Anzaldúa's first question by introducing another, longer one:

The U.S.-Mexican border *es una herida abierta* where the Third World grates against the first and bleeds. And before a scab forms it hemorrhages again, the lifeblood of two worlds merging to form a *third country—a border culture* (italics mine). Borders are set up to define the places that are safe and unsafe, to distinguish *us* and *them*. A border is a dividing line, a narrow strip along a steep edge. A borderland is a vague and undetermined place created by the emotional residue of an unnatural boundary. *It is a constant state of transition. The prohibited and forbidden are its inhabitants* (italics mine). *Los atravesados* live here: the squint-eyed, the perverse, the queer, the troublesome, the mongrel, the mulatto, the half-breed, the half dead; in short, those who cross over, pass over,

or go through the confines of the normal. Gringos in the U.S. Southwest consider the inhabitants of the borderlands transgressors,
aliens—whether they possess documents or not, whether they're
Chicanos, Indians, or Blacks. Do not enter, trespasser will be
raped, maimed, strangled, gassed, shot. The only "legitimate"
inhabitants are those in power, the whites and those who align themselves with whites. *Tension grips the inhabitants of the borderlands
like a virus* (italics mine). Ambivalence and unrest reside there and
death is no stranger. (Anzaldúa 1987: 3–4)

In this paragraph Anzaldúa describes a scenario similar to the
one described by Calhoun: in both cases the interior and the exterior
of the nation, as the official discourse of the state and the object of
the social sciences, is underlined. In Calhoun's description of the two
sides of the border, he remains within a monotopic epistemology,
monotopic because even when the two sides of the frontier are perceived and described, Calhoun maintains the purity and consistency
of the disciplinary locus of enunciation. Anzaldúa, however, takes us
to another realm: there is no longer a division between the object of
study and the disciplinary subject of understanding. The object of
study, so to speak, emerges in the very construction of the speaking
subject; the imaginary construction is no longer detached from the
locus of enunciation. Calhoun maintains a disembodied and monotopic gnosis; Anzaldúa announces and enacts a pluritopic and
embodied one. But, the reader may note, Calhoun is a well-known
sociologist, while Anzaldúa is a well-known Chicana writer with no
particular disciplinary affiliation (e.g., social sciences or humanities)
with academic institutions. Such observations, if they arise, will be
based on a problematic distinction between academic/disciplinary
forms of knowledge and those forms of knowledge beyond the border
of academia. Border gnosis may help us in thinking this dilemma otherwise: the implicitly transdisciplinary (and I use here "trans-" as in
trans-vesti) dimension in Anzaldúa's quotation, the possibility of
thinking beyond the complicities between imperial and national languages, beyond disciplinary norms and institutional foundations
ingrained in economic modes of production and state policy. But,
even if such thinking is possible, it could be argued that it will always
be absorbed by the authoritarian system of a global economy without

nation-state grounding. Such a thinking will play into the hands of a wild economic system for which there are no national limits for consumerism, where the differences are—at their turn—commodified. But if this is the case, then border gnosis should not be conceived as a point of arrival but as an extended meditation to overcome subalternity and fundamentalism, as a relentless thinking toward a post-subaltern world.

Let's explore this issue further by looking at the links between border gnosis and postoccidental/colonial/imperial reason in Anzaldúa's case. Postoccidentalism, in its extended form (postimperialism, postcolonialism), is a particular kind of border gnosis: a geocultural border gnosis, where geocultural stands for a crossing of space-time configuration saturated with particular geographical and historical memories, the colonial memories. The geocultural border articulated by Anzaldúa is clearly inscribed in a double colonial history that produces both the borderland and the *new mestiza*, as a reinscription of old memories of mestizaje in the early colonial period and in the nineteenth century.

The *new mestiza* is a singular articulation of border gnosis that consists of claiming an identity without being claimed by it. The first colonial history is the history of Spanish colonization of Mexico. The second is the U.S. recolonization of the Spanish colonization of Mexico. In this complexity of colonial legacies there coexists the imperial conflicts managing native imperial populations as well as producing new communities occupying the space in between former colonizer-colonized configurations. This story is told by Anzaldúa around two dates: 1521 and 1846.

> (a) 1521: At the beginning of the 16th century, the Spaniards and Hernán Cortés invaded Mexico and, with the help of tribes that the Aztecs had subjugated, conquered it. Before the conquest, there were twenty-five million Indian people in Mexico and Yucatan. Immediately after the Conquest, the Indian population had been reduced to under seven million. By 1650, only one-and-a-half-million pure-blooded Indians remained. The *mestizos* who were genetically equipped to survive small pox, measles, and typhus (Old World diseases to which the natives had no immunity), founded a new hybrid race and inherited Central and South America. *En 1521 nacio una*

nueva raza, el mestizo, el mexicano (people of mixed Indian and Spanish blood), a race that had never existed before. Chicanos, Mexican-Americans, are the offspring of those first matings.

Our Spanish, Indian, and *mestizo* ancestors explored and settled parts of the U.S. Southwest as early as the sixteenth century. For every gold-hungry *conquistado* and soul-hungry missionary who came north from Mexico, ten to twenty Indians and *mestizos* went along as porters or in other capacities. For the Indians, this constituted a return to the place of origin, Aztlan, thus making Chicanos originally and secondarily indigenous to the Southwest. Indians and *mestizos* from central Mexico intermarried with North American Indians. The continual intermarriage between Mexico and American Indians an Spaniards formed an even greater *mestizaje*.

(b) 1846: In 1846, the U.S. incited Mexico to war. U.S. troops invaded and occupied Mexico, forcing her to give up almost half of her nation, what is now Texas, New Mexico, Arizona, Colorado and California.

With the victory of the U.S. forces over the Mexicans in the U.S.-Mexican War, *los norteamericanos* pushed the Texas border down 100 miles, from *el rio Nueces* to *el rio Grande*. Separated from Mexico, the Native Mexican-Texan no longer looked toward Mexico as home; the Southwest became our homeland once more. The border fence that divides the Mexican people was born on February 2, 1848, with the signing of the Treaty of Guadalupe-Hidalgo. It left 100,000 Mexican citizens on this side, annexed by conquest along with the land. The land established by the treaty as belonging to Mexicans was soon swindled away from its owners. The treaty was never honored and restitution, to this day, has never been made. (Anzaldúa 1987: 5–6)

I am not offering this long quotation simply for historical information. The events are narrated in more detail in any historical account of U.S.-Mexican relations. My point could be better phrased by asking: *how do you think from the wounds of colonial legacies?* Which would be equivalent to asking, in a different colonial legacy, how do you *think in* Jewish as J. Boyarin does? In the same vain, one can ask, *how do you think from the celebration of classical legacies?* Or, to use a comparative example, what and how do you think from two historical rapes (1521, 1846), or from a pair of shoes painted by Van Gogh and the Hotel Buenaventura, as magisterially as Fred

Jameson does in his introduction to *Postmodernism or the logic of late capitalism* (1990)? The answer is simple: the paradigmatic examples of your thinking not only offer the location of itself but also offer its political grounding as well. Finally, I make this comparison not to oppose one to another but on the contrary, to indicate the force in the coexistence of thinking from the borders and thinking from within the limits of the system you are criticizing. Both examples have, for me, the same provocative effect and ground-breaking power. Both lunge toward post-subaltern thinking.

Neither case, Anzaldúa's nor Jameson's, are implicated in "thinking from the celebration of classical legacies," the foundation and the location of cultures of scholarship in the early modern/early colonial and modern/colonial periods. In these periods, from the humanistic *trivium* (in the early modern/early colonial periods) to the postenlightenment emergence of the social sciences and rearticulation of the humanities (Foucault 1966), cultures of scholarship went hand in hand with colonial expansion. As such, they were from the very beginning an exportable merchandise. From 1500 until after World War II, cultures of scholarship worked in a modern world-system like the railroad system in Argentina. When the rail system was established, it connected Buenos Aires with several terminal points in the interior of Argentina, although none of the points was connected to the other points within the country. Buenos Aires was directly connected with London by an ocean liner that crossed from the South to the North Atlantic. Much like an inverted image of Argentina's railroad system in Buenos Aires, cultures of scholarship emanated from the center of Europe and stretched outward (connecting Spain, Portugal, Italy, and the exportation of the *trivium* first; England, France, and Germany later; and the exportation of literature and the disavowal of poetry [in the *trivium*] and Christianity [Viswanathan 1989]) to all points in the system, but none of the terminal points was connected to the other points. Thus, social sciences and the rearticulation of the humanities in Europe would not be exported until after the end of World War II.

Border gnosis, the common and simultaneous thread connecting colonial histories among themselves and negating the negation to which they have been submitted, is enacting a rearticulation of cultures of scholarhip and their classical/imperial legacies. The classical tradition in Europe has been constructed as a straight and ascending line from ancient Greece to the French Revolution and it was exported to different parts of the world. Local histories began to emerge (in Mexico, Peru, India, Algeria, etc.) from the tensions between the European effort to export the classical tradition to America or Asia. Thus, thinking *from* what is today called the Americas and, more specifically, from the border between Northern Latin America and Southern United States, neither implies nor naturally presupposes that the point of departure of American memories should also begin in Greece instead of in Mexico-Tenochtitlán, in 1521, when the Aztec men of wisdom encountered themselves in the mirror of another cosmology, Greek/ Christian (which means, Greek translated into Christian); or in 1846, when nation builders in Mexico had to face an emerging nation-state and take possession of territories that belonged to the Spanish crown. Anzaldúa's text is a foundational one for thinking from the border, geo-cultural as well as sexual. I will, however, pass over sexual border gnosis for the time being but come back to it after describing Hall's and Khatibi's contribution to border gnosis.

At first glance, it is not clear which way Stuart Hall's thoughts could be cast in terms of border gnosis, since there is no clear-cut case of borders or frontiers like Anzaldúa's. The frontier in Hall's case is the Atlantic, the black Atlantic of Paul Gilroy (1993) a border-water rather than a border-land. In all evidence, it is a space between Jamaica (and the English Caribbean) and England, which becomes clear as a space in between when Hall compares England with Jamaica, Jamaica with England, bringing to the foreground the entire colonial history and experience. Border gnosis begins to emerge as soon as the colonial experience is invoked by someone from the colony who moves to the metropolis. It is no longer a colonial history narrated from a disciplinary perspective, but a critical reflection on it from the perspective of those who have experienced subalternity and elected to speak from that experience. Hall (Jamaica), George Lamming (Barbados) and Jean Rhys (Dominica), Aimé Césaire, Frantz Fanon, and Edouard Glissant (Martinique) have, one way or another, theorized (although in narrative forms like Rhys's and several of Lamming's novels), colonialism and took it as the foundation of postcolonial theorizing, as French Enlightenment philosophers took Greek thought as their foundation. Border gnosis is at the core of their thoughts articulated in essays, poetry, or narratives. It cannot be otherwise, since border gnosis not only emerges from but it is the most effective way to deal culturally with colonial experiences from the perspective of those who received and endured colonialism.

Hall's articulation of border gnosis is apparent in his way of thinking about the emergence of new forms of identity and identification in the last thirty or so years, when the growing power of transnational corporation provided a new twist to the increasing process of planetary interconnections we refer to as globalization (1991a; 1991b). For Hall, the historical references are not, of course, the Spanish and U.S. successive colonization of Mexico, but the rise and fall of the British Empire and the consequences for some particular areas of "The Commonwealth." England is a postcolonial country, too, like all the countries that were under its domain until the middle of the twentieth century. But when the British Empire fell, the United States rose to a new role of global prominence. In this change of hands there was also a significant change in the global articulation of the world order:

> As an entity and national culture, the United Kingdom rose with, and is declining with, one of the eras or epochs, of globalization: that era when the formation of the world market was dominated by the economies and cultures of powerful nation states. It is that relationship between the formation and transformation of the world market and its domination by the economies of powerful nation-states which constituted the era within which the formation of English culture took its existing shape. (Hall 1991a: 20)

The declining power of England went together with decolonization, and decolonization in some ways was, from the British perspective, to "get rid of them." Paradoxically, when decolonization began to take place, massive migrations moved toward London, most remarkably migrations from those countries that (contrary to Australia or New Zealand) make the difference felt at the very moment of

arrival. For Hall, this is a very important time to understand globalization in the constant interaction between global designs and local
histories, and the constant double-side of nation and empire in the
metropolis, and nation and imperialism in the colonies or ex-colonies:
the history of Jamaica cannot be detached from England, just as the
history of England cannot ignore its debt to Jamaica. But the double
history of England, as a colonial power and the dominant one until
1950, roughly corresponds to a stage of globalization, in Hall's view,
which is significantly different from the new stage lead by the United
States, where mass culture (instead of importation of raw material
from the colonies) is one of the dominant forms of global intercon-
nection. Hall underscores two features of this new form of globalization. First, global mass culture remains centered in the West (technology, concentration of capital, concentration of advanced labor,
and the stories and the imagery of Western societies) and in that sense
"it always speaks English" (1991a: 28), although not the "Queen's
English" anymore but a broken, fissured English—an English that is
no longer the mother tongue and an emblem of national identity for
all those who speak it:

> It is a new form of international language, not quite the same old
> class-stratified, class-dominated, canonically-secured form of stan-
> dard or traditional highbrow English. That is what I mean by "cen-
> tered in the West." It is centered in the languages of the West but it
> is not centered in the same way. (Hall 1991a: 28)

The second feature of global mass culture is, for Hall, its form of
homogenization. And by that he means its form of operation, or organizing and policing the system while absorbing local capitals and
working through them rather than eliminating them. There is more to
say about Hall's view of the new face of globalization, but the main
point here is: what are the consequences of his interests in globalization for our purpose and in relation to border gnosis? In this new
stage of globalization, multinational and decentered, we are moving
not toward "the unity of the singular corporate enterprise that tries
to encapsulate the entire world within its confines, but much more
decentralized and decentered forms of social and economic organiza-

tion" (Hall 1991a: 30). And it is precisely at this junction, of a decentered and decentralized form of capitalism, that local histories began to emerge. With local histories comes the need of new forms of thinking capable of articulating, on one hand, people's experiences across languages and cultures and, on the other, the emergence of those who have been suppressed by old forms of globalization and who are faced with the problems of articulating local with global knowledge, local histories with global designs. In that junction, border gnosis is a necessary epistemology in order to avoid reproducing the colonization of knowledge imposed by modern epistemology, or to resist it by restitution of local knowledge untouched by colonization, global expansion, and global designs.

Let me push this argument a little bit further. Hall insists on the distinction between two forms of globalization still struggling with one another:

> An older, corporate, enclosed, increasingly defensive one which has to go back to nationalism and national cultural identity in a highly defensive way, and to try to build barriers around it before it is eroded. And then this other form of the global post-modern which is trying to live with, and at the same moment, overcome, sublate, get hold of, and incorporate difference. (Hall 1991a: 33)

Border gnosis emerges as a need to understand the second form of globalization, to resist its drive toward homogenization, to find new avenues for social transformation, which shakes the increasing forms of control imposed by the new form of global economy in the second format, while keeping in the horizon the utopian bent toward superseding it. On the other hand, border gnosis offers new ways of thinking and resisting the principles enacted by the celebration of national cultural identity and the fundamentalist defense of national values. Hall's own formulation of this comes about when he thinks of local histories and the rearticulation of old/new identities and old/new ethnicities. This is a phenomenon not just strictly related but a consequence of the transition between an old form of globalization (old identities and ethnicities) and the new form of globalization (new identities and ethnicities). I quote Hall at length:

For it would be an extremely odd and peculiar history of this part of the twentieth century if we were not to say that the most profound cultural revolution has come about as a consequence of the margins coming into representation—in art, in painting, in film, in music, in literature, in the modern arts everywhere, in politics, and in social life generally. Our lives have been transformed by the struggle of the margins to come into representation. . . .

Paradoxically in our world, marginality has become a powerful space. It is a space of weak power but it is a space of power, nonetheless. . . .

The emergence of new subjects, new genders, new ethnicities, new regions, new communities, unable to locate themselves except as decentered or subaltern, have acquired through struggle, sometimes in very marginalized ways, *the means to speak for themselves* (and I would say that Hall himself is an example of what he is talking about, WM) for the first time. . . .

Face to face with a culture, an economy and a set of histories which seem to be written or inscribed elsewhere, and which are so immense, transmitted from one continent to another with such extraordinary speed, the subjects of the local, of the margin, can only come into representation by, as it were, recovering their own hidden histories. They have to try to retell the story from the bottom up, instead of from the top down. And this moment has been of such profound significance in the post-war world that you could not describe the post-war world without it. You could not describe the movements of colonial nationalism without that moment when the unspoken discovered that they had a history which they could speak; they had languages other than the languages of the master, of the tribe. (Hall 1991a: 34–35)

It is not necessarily the first time that marginal subjects are able to locate themselves or to speak for themselves, as we will soon see in colonial Latin America. It is the first time, however, that the marginal voices get to circulate on their own, escaping the colonial control, cutting off the possibility for the subaltern to speak. It is also the time in which the emergence of new identities go together with a move to end subalternity. The affirmation of ethnic identities is, at the same time, the negation of all forms of subalternity. Now, when people in and from the margin began to speak (as Hall himself), the stories and histories they recover are also the construction of new places for thinking, they are places that call for new forms of thinking. When people in the margins reconstruct those forgotten and suppressed stories, thoughts, and cultural practices, they are in a privileged location for thinking: they know both, the stories of the master and their own, and they know from that double experience how to subvert the single, monotopic experience of modern epistemology engrained in the colonial/imperial reason. And this is what constitutes border gnosis and what explains the very logic of Hall's argument that I have been trying to reconstruct—not to show border gnosis thematically, when Hall thinks from some place in the Atlantic, in between Jamaica and England but, better yet, in the logic of his own argument. This aspect perhaps came into full force when Hall brought his notion of new ethnicities to the foreground. The shorter statement is: "Ethnicity is the necessary place or space from which people speak" (Hall 1991a: 36), and what he means by this is the self-discovery, after releasing the closure of the imperial reason in its old as well as new forms (e.g., "blacks" in the sense Hall describes it in London after colonization; "Hispanics" in the United States after 1970), or histories that had been negated by imperial histories. The negation of the negation (e.g., the denial of the denial of coevalness, Mignolo 1995: 6) of imperial histories, come with people who began to realize the value of the grounding that Hall calls "ethnicity." In his own words, "Ethnicity is the necessary place or space from which people speak. It is a very important moment in the birth and development of all the local and marginal movements of rediscovery of their own ethnicities" (1991a: 36). Hall is certainly aware that celebration of ethnicity can have the same dangerous effect as celebration of national values. Nevertheless, as Hall himself notes, it is not the only way that ethnicity has to go. And certainly, I cannot stress enough what ethnicity, in the sense and history described by Hall, has brought to dismantling the underlying natural belief in the power of modern reason. And that is the moment when Hall links ethnicity with enunciation: "Modern theories of enunciation always oblige us to recognize the enunciation comes from somewhere. It can be unplaced, it cannot be unpositioned, it is always positioned in a discourse. It is (unpositioned only) when a discourse forgets that it is placed, that it tries to speak for everybody else. It is exactly when Englishness is the world identity, to which everything else is only a small ethnicity. . . . So, the moment of the rediscovery of a place, a past, of one's roots, of one's context, seems to me a necessary moment of enunciation. I do not think the margins could speak up without first grounding themselves somewhere" (Hall 1991a: 36). That grounding is in Hall's grounding, which I submit is the geocultural of border gnosis, thinking from ethnicity in the frontiers of European Christian modernity, when in the sixteenth century Christianity separated itself from Islam (e.g., expulsion of the Moors from Spain), and set the stage for the three subsequent and logically related genocides: the Amerindians, the African slaves and the European Holocaust, exploding five centuries after the expulsion of the Jews from Spain, at the same time the Moors were expelled, Amerindians decimated and African people uprooted and transported to the New World. This is the deep sense of the groundings Hall calls "ethnicity" and is also the grounding of geocultural border gnosis. I specify geocultural, because border gnosis is not limited to geocultural dimension, as we will see later on, although geocultural border gnosis is the main concern of this article.

Finally, it is important to stress that the discovery of ethnicity as grounding is not a longing for authenticity or nostalgia in the recovering of a past destroyed by colonialism. On the contrary, it is this grounding that allows us to transgress national, regional, and imperial geohistorical categories: to be Jamaican, Caribbean, and English. But also, and mainly, to reveal the subaltern status of ethnicity and denounce colonial legacies and subalternity. In other words, it is precisely the force of creolization of the world that can be better theorized from the double experience, and the double grounding in the new discovery of ethnicity. "The primitive has somehow escaped from control" observes Hall (1991a: 39), and that primitive, the barbarian theorizing, is the moment in which the local interrupts in the global, that global designs could be interfered by local critical stories. That is why globalization is not a violent process, and although the new discovery of ethnicity grounding border gnosis is not necessarily promising a paradise in the near future without subalternity and without violence, it is at least a place of resistance, a place for resistance, a place for creativity, a place of hope, a place of extended critical reflection and action to transform nostalgia into celebration.

"Transculturation" is the concept coined by Cuban anthropologist Fernando Ortíz in the early 1940s to deal with economic structures and cultural interactions engendered by colonialism. As an anthropologist, Ortiz did not engage himself in the type of philosophical explorations that we have seen in Khatibi, the free-floating linguistic and discursive undertaking of Gloria Anzaldúa, or the critical inquiries carried on by Stuart Hall and Paul Gilroy. However, as a Cuban anthropologist reflecting on Cuban cultural and economic history, Ortíz does not have the epistemological problems of "writing cultures." He is not writing about some remote cultural community, which he visited and then wrote about in London, Paris, or Los Angeles. He did not write about the other; he wrote about themselves, the Cubans, Ortíz's thoughts *in* Cuban. He did not write in terms of national foundations, that is, on the unity, purity, and coherence of Cuban culture. The concept of transculturation is precisely the negation of any claim to purity and unity. But was it, for Ortíz, transculturation?

Ortíz first defines transculturation and then uses it in constructing the narrative of tobacco from a natural-growing plant to ritual, colonialism, and, finally, to a commodity. In the first case, "transculturation" is offered as a corrective to the by then (1940) current concept of "acculturation" in anthropology, introduced by influential anthropologist Branslaw Malinowski (Polish by origin, British by professional residence). "Acculturation," says Ortíz, "is used to describe the process of transition from one culture to another, and its manifold social repercussions" ([1940], 1995: 98). Ortíz doesn't say it, but it is implied in the concept, that transition means from traditional to modern societies made possible by the spread of—at that point in time—capitalism and civilization. "Transculturation" is more fitting, he says, to "express the highly varied phenomena that have come about in Cuba as a result of the extremely complex transmutations of culture that have taken place here, and without a knowledge of which it is impossible to understand the evolution of Cuban folk, either in the economic or in the institutional, legal, ethical, religious, artistic, linguistic, psychological, sexual, or other aspects" (1995: 98). He then extends this consideration to the rest of Latin America. Knowing the history of Latin America and reading the extended attention that Ortíz pays to colonialism, it is not difficult to conclude that: (a) transculturation points toward the mixing of cultures brought about by colonialism and the construction of the modern world, and (b) transculturation conceives transitions not as a unidirectional process, but as a complex interaction where everybody loses some and wins some. Thus, transculturation is indeed a double process of "deculturation," where people and communities in mutual contact lose some of their way of being before entering in contact; and also a process of "neoculturation" where new cultural forms emerge from the creation that follows processes of "deculturation." "Neoculturation" is not, of course, a happy mestizo or hybrid new state of affairs. Since people and communities in contact because of colonial and imperial processes never met on equal terms, transculturation is always performed in power structure, in the tension between hegemony and subalternity. The universal history Ortíz traces of tobacco and sugar is centered around the history of Cuba, which since 1500 has been a history of changing imperialisms.

Once defined in terms of different people mixing with each other through history, Ortíz locates transculturation in the history of tobacco. How should we understand transculturation in this context?

> Tobacco, which aside from its physicochemical properties and its individual physiological effects, formed part of a social structure of a predominantly religious character among the American Indians, took on among the European Americans and later among other peoples a structure that was principally economic by reason or a very curious, swift and complete phenomenon of transculturation (pp. 192);
>
> The transculturation of tobacco from the society of the Indians to that of the Africa Negroes was much easier than between Indians and whites. (pp. 192, 195)

The most telling observation in connection with the argument I am developing here is Ortíz's analysis, several pages long, of the moment in which four alkaloids (tobacco and chocolate from the Americas; coffee from Abysinia and Arabia; tea from the Far East), interact in the construction of Europe. At this point, Ortíz observes:

The coincidental appearance of these four exotic products in the Old World, all of them stimulants of the senses as well as of the spirit, is not without interest. It is as though they had been sent to Europe from the four corners of the earth by the devil to revive Europe when "the time came," when that continent was ready to save the spirituality of reason from burning itself out and give the sense their due once more. Europe was no longer able to satisfy its senses with spices or sugar, which aside from being rare and, because of their costliness, the privilege of the few, excited without inspiring, strengthened without lifting the spirits. Nor were wines and liquors sufficient either, for although they nourished daring and dreams, they were often the cause of degradation and derangement and never of thoughtfulness or good judgement. Other spices and nectars were needed that should act as spurs of the senses and the mind. And the devil provided them, sending in for *the mental jousts that initiated the modern age in Europe* the tobacco of the Antilles, the chocolate of Mexico, the coffee of Africa and the tea of China. Nicotine, theobromine, caffeine, and theine—*these four alkaloids were put at the services of humanity to make reason more alert.* (p. 207)

Modernity suddenly appears not as a European phenomenon, but as a *process of transculturation*, upon which the very reason that the four alkaloids from the non-Christian world may have helped to nourish constructed itself as, Dussel (1992) would say, a genocidal reason. A monotopic and genocidal reason that survived building frontiers to oversee and patrol the safety of the interior. A paradoxical example of, on the one hand, transculturation and the social life of things and, on the other, transculturation and the articulation of modernity and colonialism in the early modern period. Thus, transculturation reintroduces a pluritopic perspective in our understanding of modernity/coloniality and contributes to the planetary border thinking, border gnosis.

A final note on border gnosis, cultural studies, and the human sciences (e.g., social sciences and the humanities). Border gnosis, as an attempt to think from subaltern positions or perspectives (following Gilroy's terminology), offers a space of contestation, of a constant and renewed counterhegemonic position. Thinking from a subaltern perspective does not mean to "represent the subaltern," thus maintaining a problematic distinction between intellectuals, on one hand, and subaltern workers on the other. I talk of subalternity as a structure of power relations rather than as an identifiable social class. Certainly, workers and peasants are in relation of subalternity, but so are women or blacks or Hispanics even when they are not working in the assembly line or in the cotton fields. Intellectuals and scholars could also be in subaltern positions, even when they talk or analyze economically subaltern communities. If we do not break the correlation between subalterns as an object and subaltern studies as an (inter)disciplinary locus of study, we remain within the subject/object modern epistemological correlation and its geocultural version of cultural area/area studies. One of the three antinomies under which social sciences functioned for almost two centuries was the antinomy between civilized and barbaric worlds (the other two being the antinomy between past and present and ideographic and nomothetic disciplines, Wallerstein et al. 1996: 95), which is the antecedent of First/Third World antinomy. In other words, academic and scholarly knowledge production is not outside the object, the area or the subaltern. Thus, border gnosis is one way to think otherwise and to link knowledge production with political intervention and social transformations.

Thus, the links between border gnosis and cultural studies and, by extension, with the social sciences and the humanities. Cultural studies as a challenge to the configuration of the social sciences and imperial global designs has been pointed out recently by the report from the Gulbenkian Foundation (Wallerstein et al. 1996), a report indirectly implicated with the organization of area studies. Accepting the mapping the relationship between cultural studies and social sciences (Wallerstein et al. 1996: 65), I would like to underline that: (a) cultural studies, in my view, is not a discipline or quasi-discipline but an institutional locus allowing for thinking across disciplines. In that sense, border gnosis could be linked to the space in between disciplinary organization (in the social sciences and humanities) and transdisciplinary thinking; (b) as an institutional locus for thinking across disciplines, and justifying a different kind of knowledge, or producing and transforming it, cultural studies should not be thought of in terms of disciplinary control in "ought to be" terms, but rather as an institutional justification for what really counts at the level of intellectuals and scholars: the formation and framing of new questions and new problems that cannot be policed by disciplinary norms. Therefore, border gnosis is the space of negotiation between the rigor we expect in any investigation and the personal involvements that have been controlled by disciplinary claims to objectivity and detached observation. Border gnosis, in consequence, will allow us to think from the double consciousness of the subaltern vis-à-vis hegemonic thinking in the domain of the social, and to think from the demands of social problems (and our personal involvement in them), bypassing the empty demands of disciplinary control without relinquishing the intellectual rigor that we all learned from disciplinary training.

BIBLIOGRAPHY

Adorno, Theodor W. *Negative Dialectics*. New York: Continuum, 1983 [1966].

Anzaldúa, Gloria. *Borderlands/La frontera: The New Mestiza*. San Francisco: Spinsters/Aunt Lute, 1987.

Calhoun, Craig. *Critical Social Theory*. New York: Blackwell, 1995a.

———. *Critical Social Theory: Culture, History, and the Challenge of Difference*. Oxford, 1995b.

Chakabarty, Dipesh. "Provincializing Europe: Postcoloniality and the Critique of History." *Cultural Studies* 6, no. 3 (1992): 337–57.

Chen, Kuan-Hsing, "Voices from the outside: towards a new internationalist localism." *Cultural Studies* 6, no. 3 (1992): 476–84.

Coronil, Fernando. "Transculturation and the Politics of Theory: Countering the Center, Cuban Counterpoint." Introduction to Fernando Ortíz's *Cuban Counterpoint*. Durham: Duke University Press, 1995, pp. ix–ivi.

Dussel, Enrique. "Eurocentrism and Modernity." *Boundary 2*, 20, no. 3: *The Postmodernism Debate in Latin America*. Edited by J. Beverley and J. Oviedo (1992): 65–76.

———. "World System, Politics, and the Economic of Liberation Philosophy." In *The Underside of Modernity: Apel, Rorty, Taylor, and the Philosophy of Liberation*. Translated and edited by Eduardo Mendieta. Amherst, N.Y.: Humanity Books, 1996, pp. 213–39.

Fanon, Frantz. *The Wretched of the Earth*. 1961. Reprint, New York: Grove Weidenfeld, 1991.

Foucault, Michel. *Les mots et les choses: Une archeologie des sciences humaines*. Paris: Gallimard, 1966.

———. *Power/Knowledge: Selected Interviews and Other Writings, 1972–1977*. Edited by C. Gordon. Brighton, Sussex: Havester Press, 1980.

Gilroy, Paul. *Black Atlantic: Modernity and Double Consciousness*. Cambridge: Harvard University Press, 1993.

Hall, Stuart. "The Local and the Global: Globalization and Ethnicity." In *Culture, Globalization, and the World-System*. Edited by A. D. King. Binghamton: Art and Art History, 1991, pp. 19–39.

———. "Old and New Identities, Old and New Ethnicities." In *Culture, Globalization, and the World-System*. Edited by A. D. King, pp. 40–68.

Huntington, Samuel P. "The Clash of Civilizations." *Foreign Affairs* (1993): 22–43.

Jameson, Fredric. *Postmodernism: Or the Logic of Late Capitalism*. Durham: Duke University Press, 1991.

✓ Kaplan, Caren. *Questions of Travel: Postmodern Discourses of Displacements*. Durham: Duke University Press, 1996.

Khatibi, Abdelkebir. *Maghreb pluriel*. Paris: Denoel, 1983.

Laclau, Ernesto. *Emancipation(s)*. London: Verso, 1996.

Lambert, Richard D. "Blurring the Disciplinary Boundaries: Area Studies in United States." *American Behavioral Scientist* 33, no. 6 (1990): 712–32.

Lazzarato, Maurizio. "Immaterial Labor." In *Radical Thoughts in Italy: A Potential Politics*. Edited by P. Virno and M. Hard. Minneapolis: The University of Minnesota Press, 1996, pp. 132–46.

Lopez, Milagros. "Post-Work Society." *Social Text* 34 (1994): 23–35.

Mignolo, Walter. "Colonial and Postcolonial Discourse: Cultural Critique on Academic Colonialism?" *LARR* 28, no. 3 (1992c): 120–34.

———. "Colonial Legacies and Postcolonial Theories." In B. Gonzalez (Com.), *Cultura y Tercer Mundo*, vol. 1 (1996): 99–136.

———. "Espacios geográficas y localizaciones epistemológicas o la ratio entre la localización geográfica y la subalternizacion de conocimientos." *Disenso*, 1997.

———. "Semiosis Colonial: La dialéctica entre representaciones fracturades y hermenéuticas pluritópicas." B. Gonzalez, et. al. (Coord.) 1992d, 29–47.

———. *The Darker Side of the Renaissance: Literacy, Territoriality and Colonization*. Ann Arbor: University of Michigan Press, 1995a.

Mudimbe, V. Y. *The Invention of Africa Gnosis, Philosophy and the Order of Knowledge*. Bloomington: Indiana University Press, 1988.

Ortíz, Fernando. *Cuban Counterpoint: Tobacco and Sugar.* 1940. Reprint, Durham: Duke University Press, 1995.

Pletsch, Carl E. "The Three Worlds, or the Division of Social Scientific Labor, circa 1950–1975." *Comparative Studies in Society and History* 23, no. 4 (1981): 565–90.

Ribeiro, Darcy. *Las America y la civilizacion. Proceso de formacion y causas del desarrollo desigual de los pueblos americanos.* Caracas, 1992, p. 57.

Rivera Cusicanqui, Silvia. "Liberal Democracy and *Ayllu* Democracy in Bolivia: The Case of Northern Potosi." *The Journal of Development Studies* (1990): 97–121.

Said, Edward. *Culture and Imperialism.* New York: Knopf, 1993.

———. "Intellectuals in the Post-Colonial World." *Salmagundi* 70–71 (1986): 43–64.

Suleri, Sara. *The Rhetoric of English India.* Chicago: Chicago University Press, 1992a.

Viswanathan, Gauri. *Masks of Conquest.* New York: Columbia University Press, 1989.

Wallerstein, Immanuel, et al. *Open the Social Sciences, Report of the Gulbenkian Commission on the Restructuring of the Social Sciences.* Palo Alto: Stanford University Press, 1996.

Young, Robert J. C. *Colonial Desire: Hibridity in Theory, Cultures and Race.* New York: Routledge, 1995, pp. 29–54.

PART 3

The "Postmodern" Apertures in Latin American Alterity

Politics, Spirituality, the Politics of Literature, and Identity Politics

Iris M. Zavala

TIRESIAS'S PARADOX
IN THE THIRD MILLENNIUM

Saying it all is literally impossible: words fail. Yet it's through this very impossibility that the truth holds onto the Real.

Lacan

In Greek mythology, Tiresias is the Theban who was transformed for nine years into a woman for killing the female of a pair of snakes. Having had this unusual experience, Zeus and Hera referred to him the pressing question of whether man or woman derives more pleasure from love, and when Tiresias supported Zeus's opinion—that it was woman—Hera struck him with blindness, but Zeus gave him long life and the gift of prophesy. He appears in texts by Sophocles and Euripides, and is also the subject of a dramatic monologue by Tennyson in which the poet recounts the story of his blinding by Athene, for excess in seeing. He is also reaccented by T. S. Eliot in *The Waste Land* as an androgyne: "throbbing between two lives,/Old man with wrinkled female breasts." But Tiresias became a sage man after Hera's condemnation, and understood that he should have returned the question, and not answered in terms of quantitative proportions; he should have maintained the question open.

My point is that what the Olympian gods were really discussing is

Lecture presented at the *Hispanics Cultural Locations* Conference, San Francisco, Calif., 10–12 October 1997.

the unthinkable irrepresentability of the Other's jouissance, the
enigma and impenetrability of the Other's desire.

Taking seriously Lacan's aphorism that desire is desire of the
Other, the enigma of the Other remains indeterminate, since we have
no image of the Other's desire. The Other has diverse shapes, but suffice it to say that it is the Other of language, as well as it can be the
Other of the symbolic order. But, by definition it is that which guarantees our consistency, and is nonetheless incomplete, and lacks universality. Our Tiresias, then, exemplifies the overlapping of the two
lacks Lacan discusses in *The Four Fundamental Concepts of Psychoanalysis* (1981)—that which the subject covers over by its identity
and that of the Other's incompleteness, both (following Laclau 1994,
1995) are the conditions of a radical democratic action in our contemporary world.

Tiresias paradox, in my reading, is the enigma of the Other's
jouissance, that which is "more than ourselves," that defines us, but
is simultaneously undefinable. In other words, the well-known
Lacanian formula of the "not-all" or excess of the feminine enjoyment; the logic of inconsistency, the unforeseen, since woman is not
fully submitted to the causal link, nor the symbolic order. The argument is that woman addresses an ambiguous question to the Other,
which articulates the perplexity of the subject itself confronted with
an impenetrable Other who wants something (see Copjec 1995: 227).
Woman as *enigma* is expressed in the perplexed *Che vuoi?—What do
you want from me?* Tiresias "not-all" and "something more" is analogous to this refusal to surrender. This "not-all" will help clarify the
paradoxes of the Universal grounded in an Exception, and the logic
of the universal and the particular. With this paradox we will explore
the fundamental impossibility which preventes social reality from
being fully symbolized, and approach the fantasy structure of
national identifications.

It is against the Tiresian paradox of jouissance that we shall consider problems of identity, nation, and gender for the millennium. All
three concepts present privileged domains of explosions of jouissance
in the social field, the way subjects of given ethnic communities organize their enjoyment through national myths, and sexuality, a

pressing subjective and, thereby, political problem of our time. We can go so far as to say that these notions, as part of our political imaginary, are desintegrating. Identity as a concept has suffered major transformations before our eyes, and it entails questions on particularism and universalism (Laclau 1994, 1995), whether they are seen as complementary, mutually exclusive or as creating tensions. In the United Sates arena multiculturalism has questioned all values of modernity, and as a result there is an assault of obsolete notions of holistic totalizations, through powerful argumentative strategies and paradoxical combinations. The problem can be formulated in terms of pure difference, or pure particularism doing away entirely with universal principles. Against this conception of difference, my proposal is a difference that is worked out through a relation to others, and which emerges once our appeals to the Other (the symbolic, the law) have been abandoned. The implications of accepting that "there is no Other of the Other," that nothing guarantees the Other's certainty, consistence, and completeness, that the Other possesses nothing to validate our existence, has fundamental implications for our contemporary democracies, specially for ethnic communities of different languages and cultures within large democratic states.

I evoked the twofold myth to retell the story of the postcolonial breakup of identities, and the paradoxical groups that manifest in the Real a nonbelonging. In doing so, we shall touch on questions of language, borders, and subjectivization; if the human subject is a product of discourse, and literature is an entrance to language—what Lacan calls the "treasure of signifiers," and Barthes "the galaxy of signifiers"—the networks have a plurality of entrances. Or to quote Lacan: "the things of the human world are things in a universe structured by words, that language, symbolic processes, dominate and govern all" (1992: 45). The double sexual identity of Tiresias exemplifies to me the bidirectional responsiveness of postcolonial subjectivization, in a sense, a schizophrenic world. If we consider the affinities between schizophrenia and language as division, everything I have just discussed seems to me to lead in the direction of the postcolonial subject, that we are to read retroactively. The continuous rewriting of its own past, including past signifying traces in new contexts which retroactively change their meaning, together with the priority of syn-chrony over diachrony, will help us understand that what was mean-ingless, retroactively acquires meaningful impact. We are addressing the signifier's synchrony as opposed to simple temporal simultaneity; synchrony designates such a paradoxical coincidence of present and past—a temporal loop where, by progressing forward, we return to where we always already were (Žižek 1994: 32). The Lacanian motif of temporal logic in the ambiguous French imperfect tense, the future anterieur of symbolization—the "will have been"—illustrates this deferred action or retroaction: subjects are forever suspended in a future anterior, which entails adopting or occupying a certain posi-tion. From this angle, texts become readable retroactively, from the future they prefigure. My point is to read backwards this developed identification of Hispanic communities at the end of the millenium, to be confronted with the fact that it entailed from the very beginning in the seventeenth century a fully articulated "not-all" as a radical eth-ical duty to protect the agalma, the ineffable secret of being.

Now, if a subject is that which is produced as a singularity, on the basis of imaginary identifications involving the body and assuming the laws of a culture, a given symbolic order, then the process of sub-jectivization can be described as the historical constitution of bodies into subjects, and the subject can be defined as the power of a singu-larity and as a contingent and recusable event. What follows is that this history is inseparable from a history of discursive forms and a history of forms of power. The situation of postcolonial subjects is altered—the double-tongued, split and transcultured Tiresias in the core of subjectivization resists the universalizing to celebrate partic-ularity and singularity.

IDENTIFICATION

At this point we must move to this register, and approach questions that affect the subject (as lack) and identity (objectivity), as a process mediated through identification (see Laclau 1994: 31 from another perspective). Identification (subject of an unpublished 1961 Seminar

X) is in Lacan linked to the image of the Other, while in Freud it denotes a process whereby one subject adopts attributes of another subject. He later developed the idea that the ego and the superego are constructed on the basis of identification, to the extent that it eventually came to denote "the operation itself whereby the human subject is constituted" (Laplanche and Pontalis 1967: 206). Lacan places special emphasis on the role of the image of the other, to recognize oneself in the image, and to appropriate the image as oneself. He also distinguishes between imaginary and symbolic identification; the first being linked to the mirror stage, involves aggressivity and alienation, fundamental human rivalry. While symbolic identification becomes in his 1961 seminar an identification with the signifier as the instance of the symbolic pact, he stresses that it is based in difference. Finally, Lacan also conceives the end of analysis as the destitution of the subject, a moment when the subject's identifications can no longer be maintained in the same way as before; he argues that it means identification with the symptom.

Through continuining elaborations of mathematical theory—the topology of the Borromean knot—and the intricate writing of James Joyce, in his 1975–76 seminar he states the "the symptom can only be defined as the way in which each subject enjoys the unconscious, in so far as the unconscious determines him" (18 November 1975, in Aubert 1987). The symptom is to be understood then as the trace of the particular modality of the subject's jouissance: a center of enjoyment immune to the efficacy of the symbolic. The sinthome is what allows one to live by providing a unique organization of jouissance. Joyce provides the example of an extended ainthome; art as a supplement. By refusing any imaginary solution, Joyce was able to invent a new way of using language to organize enjoyment. Jouissance in turn, and after continuous reaccentuation, expresses the paradoxical satisfaction that the subject derives from his or her symptom. Further aspects and changes need mention. The subject's entry into the symbolic is conditional upon a certain renunciation of jouissance through castration, or symbolic renunciation, a core of resistance that any ethics must take into account. By 1973 (Encore) Lacan asserts that there is a specifically feminine jouissance, supplementary, and beyond the symbolic, a jouissance of the Other. Such experience is ineffable, for women experience it but know nothing of it. This is the excess I have been tracing. With this scenario of excitement which stimulates and focuses the libido, Tiresias jouissance, which I am translating to suggest an homology with the postcolonial forms of jouissance, is supplementary, and beyond the symbolic order. I shall now proceed tentatively, and draw some conclusions from the previous developments. If the end of analysis means the destitution of the subject, a moment when the subject's identifications can no longer be maintained in the same way as before, and it means identification with the symptom—the particular modality of the subject's jouissance, an enjoyment immune to the symbolic, a provider of a unique organization of jouissance—it follows that the subject of the lack cannot fully achieve any identity. We are of course referring to the object a, what is the excess in the subject, which not only causes the subject to be eccentric, but other than itself.

Now what I have called this Tiresian feminine surplus, this excess and eccentricity or *jouissance* packed in the signifier, the Other as language, has been the symptom of nodal Hispanic texts, and helps understand that excess of enjoyment, and the discontent against the interdiction of pleasure, which is for society, the intolerable Other. Within colonial communities, this *jouissance* becomes a negative phobic projection, giving way to forms of despotism in the past, or to contemporary totalitarian modern forms of power. My point, however, is the individual colonial subject and the surplus of meaning that historically hybrid, *mestizo, transcultured* texts have produced in the struggle over the definition of the subject in order to reconstruct their own history, and to figure their own futures. To understand this position, let us return to the implications of transculturation—a notion coined by Cuban Fernando Ortíz—best understood as a dilemma, a point in which different paths converge. It could be defined as a Borromean knot, where the three Lacanian orders of the Imaginary, the Symbolic, and the Real converge, but it is also an *enigma*. In the symbolic order-law, language—it can be equated to the signifying chain; in the imaginary or specular image it corresponds to the universe of identifications of the heteroclitic ego; in the

Real or object of anxiety, to the traumatic and irrepresentable dimension which societies try to incorporate to the symbolic, through naming. Thus translated, every nation is equivalent to a fantasy or a fantasm, in the precise sense in which it is understood in psychoanalysis: forms of organizing *jouissance*. Therefore, national identifications are elements which can never be fully symbolized. It is the object of desire, that internal element which is in "us more than ourselves," the object which renders possible desire as the transferential structuring of the relation between subjects. What is crucial here, and I draw from Renata Salecl (1994) is that national identification is linked to the Real, to that which is always absent in the signifying chain. My final point is that transculturation is, thus, ambivalent and contingent, and does not determine a totality, and it responds to incorporations into the symbolic order which always exceed the symbolic dimension from where they originated.

The general conclusion to be drawn is that such hybridity and excess are the marks of a compulsion to reenact the traces of historical traumas. Lacan defines drive as the compulsion to encircle again and again the site of the lost Thing, to mark it in its very impossibility (Žižek 1996: 272). The best illustration of this can be found in some nodal texts which have challenged colonialism historically. Our focus in revising them will be the inherent political dimension of their forms of *jouissance*, or the way this core of enjoyment functions has functioned as a political factor to encircle over and over again the lost object. Now, at the verge of a new millennium, going through these ideological fantasies of liberation and new figures of democracy, we are forced to look from a certain distance at the paths that have guaranteed the very consistency of our symbolic universe, and question the logic of excess that still defines the parameters within which the colonial and postcolonial subject have rejected total assimilation. Language has been a twofold instrument of symbolic appropriation: on the one hand Spanish (since I center on Hispanic cultures) identifies the majority language shared by many postcolonial nations and communities; it has become the *object petit a*, the "more than ourselves" of Hispanics in the United States. Tiresias's postcolonial *plus de jouir* is double-tongued, and as a figure, Tiresias is composed of the mixtures and hybridities which only arise through *mestizaje*. Our contemporary Tiresias has taken the semblance of contemporary Hispanics.

The Greek myth will also help us explore the question of ideological identification; the aim is to point out that behind every ideology lies a nucleus of enjoyment that resists being integrated into the ideological universe. Fantasy, as Renata Salecl (1994) suggests, stages a scenario; when we identify with a certain political discourse we relate precisely to this fantasy structure hidden behind its ideological meaning. My thesis is to read the history of this center of enjoyment which has sustained our ideological fantasies retroactively, to grasp the libidinal economy of that "something more," that *plus de jouir*, which designates the symbolic community of any culture. The collective fantasies we have been elaborating are part of an ideology of cultural threat, constructed through what Lacan called in his early seminar on psychoses (1981) the "founding word," what we may also call the performative dimension of speech (Salecl 1994: 30). Such speech act, through its very enunciation, establishes a new intersubjective network that redefines the places of both speakers—what Bakhtin calls dialogical communication, or responsiveness, the creative structuring role of speech. What we are saying is that this fantasy read retroactively is "polyphonic," and deeply ironic: specially if we consider that feature of the difference Bakhtin (and later Oswald Ducrot 1984) established between speaker and enunciator.

Lacan's demarcative nuance between *the subject of the enunciation and the subject of the utterance*, which corresponds to Ducrot's distinction between speaker and enunciator (as Salecl 1994: 31 lucidly suggests), is essential to us here, in that it points to the decentered subject, to the division that separates the enunciation and the enunciator, as the central point of perspective of an utterance. The crucial notion is that not only is the subject of enunciation split—it is a vanishing point without any positive identity, therefore it can assume a series of positions—but, the addressee is strictly determined and defined. It is a discursive position constructed by the illocutionary act so that the empirical person will recognize itself as such, and thus obey or disobey the obligation implied. Such obligation only exists in the discursive universe, and concerns the addressee, the figure created by the discourse itself. This version of the polyphonic illocutionary act implies a split or divided subject, an "empty point striving to achieve positive identity by identifying itself with different enunciatior figures" (Salecl 32). Such a divided subject is relevant to our point, since it helps us approach the pressing question of how subjects recognize themselves as the addressees of cultural-political discourses, and thus identify with specific positions. Two further notions which Ducrot elaborates are also pertinent: the 'later discourse' which constructs the place of the subject's identification, and the 'surmise' of the illocutionary act which functions as a place for fantasy.

'Later discourse' delineates in advance the ideal, fictional place of the response to come; it works as a symbolic fiction, a network by means of which a certain discursive relationship is established, as new symbolic reality and new intersubjective network. Precisely this 'later discourse' designates the place of identification: the fact that we recognize ourselves as its addressee. What is essential is the distinction between present and later discourse, and from our perspective, how this discourse constructs a symbolic space, a point of view to be filled out by images of our ideal ego. Such a responsive discourse is well exemplified in the nodal points which symbolically reinterpret our social reality. We are of course dealing with ideal identifications, supported by the fantasy frame of symbolic, intersubjective relations and our place within them. The next salient feature is the place of the inscription of the addressee, since she/he assumes responsibility for the surmise, which emerges as an answer to the now famous question *Che vuoi?* Just one more thing, responsive discourse necessarily touches upon fantasy; retroactively, these identificatory cultural discourses have as a hidden surmise or presupposition an organized form of community enjoyment, a form that aims at the liberatory forces against the Other as *das Ding*. It has taken many forms historically, and after the nineteenth century it becomes the ideal of democratic politics. Always as a contested field. I do not think this is simple, there is an implied "You" in discourse, and the moment when it is spoken—as Lacan reminds us in his seminar on ethics (1992)—the Real that 'always returns to its place', the traumatic Otherness, the hard kernel which resists symbolization, is bound to appear.

NATIONAL IDENTITIES AND
HISPANIC NODAL TEXTS

I must now stress a point which will be my leit motif: since democracy
deals with national linguistic identities and values it is purely relational, and at its very core is the definition of the subject as free.
Changes in the last decades, together with the transformation in contemporary thought, have altered the classical notion of *democracy* as
formulated by the Greeks—"rule of the people," a government where
the people share in directing the activities of the state. The notion was
dormant for centuries; during the Enlightenment it was enriched by
new concepts: representation, doctrines of natural rights, and social
contract. The constructs of Locke, Hume, and Rousseau made democracy more tangible. During the nineteenth century the term consoli-
dated what is known as bourgeois-liberal democracy, characterized by
universal suffrage, political liberties, the rule of law and political competition. From the nineteenth century kind and gentle brand of
democracy advocated by Tocqueville, we know now that democracy is
neither a utopia nor a harmonious state, but an unavoidable conflictual space. For a century this ideal of a free subject, which privileges the individual, and ruled by a provident power, has left us with
a haunting question: "democracy"—yes—but, "for what class and
ethnicity?" (in Chantal Mouffe's 1993 pertinent question).

I have argued that the inheritance of such expectations of emancipation have been deeply affected by changes in history, and in contemporary thought the problem is how can the growth of popular
forces within bourgeois democracies, through political mobilization
and organization, might develop a counterhegemonic culture, and
encourage the expansion of whatever possibilities for socialist transformation the notions of representation and power may contain. Such
a view begins to come to grips with the problem of democratic consent
and how to win it for socialism, as Chantal Mouffe has recently
stressed (1993). The question of cultural identity among Hispanics
within the United Sates and elsewhere lies at the heart of such projects; at issue is whether those identities of gender, sexuality, ethnicity, race, class, and nationality are in decline, giving rise to new

forms of identification, as well as to new forms of democracy. What seems to be clear is that conflict preserves democracy, through the dissatisfaction and struggle over the definition of the subject; precisely this struggle prevents us from surrendering the definition of the subject and its relation to other subjects to the Other. The attempt is to reintroduce some notion of community and resist the mortal consequences of the fetishization of private *jouissance*.

I will now try to open some significant questions interrogating the links between democracy, social identity, and cultural texts throughout the last three hundred years within Hispanic communities. The crucial moments of the emergence of this question which addresses critically the notion of an integral, originary and unified identity can be found during the baroque, during the Wars of Independence, what is known as *Modernismo* or turn-of-the-century literature, and in the literary expressions of what is broadly named avant-garde (which would include in my conceptualization, the neobaroque and "magical realism"). What we are to follow are forms of struggle over the definition of the subject and of its relations to other subjects away from tutellary powers. The *baroque* will help us enact the relationship between values, poetics, and history, quite specifically in the Caribbean cultures, where the baroque and neobaroque have been more prominent. Nueva Espana—Mexico—appears as the modern horizon where the shift became more symptomatic: if we conceive the nation as what "always returns," as the traumatic element around which fantasies weave, Sor Juana's texts indeed stand as a struggle for a new rhetoric of self. It is almost superfluous to point out the scandalous character of this colonial mestizo baroque as a kind of ethical action: it works as a strategic marker to undermine the foundations of power, its authority, at the very moment when it gives the impression of supporting them. By relying heavily on metaphor—conceits, concepts, hyperbole, rich colorful images, mythological allusions, Latinistic vocabulary and syntax, even forms of grotesque pedantry—it makes mimetic narration an impossibility. Therefore, "representation"—a key concept of modern democracies—is made ambivalent and ambiguous, thus disrupting the idea of an organic, homogenous colonized identity. Reinforced by heteroglossia in colonial America the baroque involves the subject's radical splitting (Zavala 1997).

The exploration of this tension during the first stage of modernity in the seventeenth century leads to the very center of the problematic of the subject: the question was posed in terms of creativity. By relying on metaphor, speaking with the voice of another, multiplying voices, what is called baroque, illuminates interrelations, and helps understand the past as preparation for the present, at the same time that it makes evident the struggle for "symbolic capital." It can thus be interpreted as a value conflict, a distinctively modern problem, since contemporary societies accord great importance to values, and these, in turn cannot be separated from those signifiers associated with power. In Foucauldian terms, validity and values are always relative to a specific regime of truth, connected to power, in this very specific case, obliging the reader to ask questions in new ways; it serves as an 'ethical knowledge', dependent on the cultural and historical conditions current in the community.

The heterogeneous use of baroque strategies during the seventeenth century helps reformulate central problems on the inscription of ideology, the ideological orientation of communication, language usage, dialogical processes and the value of heteroglossia. In my reading the term *baroque* is equivalent to a bricolage of plurality of voices, dialog of difference as difference, irreducible to the concepts of identity and representation. It is difficult to imagine a 'representation' better suited to capture the paradoxes of seventeenth century colonial life than Sor Juana's individual use of the baroque, since she stands for the "not-all" within a politics of monarchical authority. In this juncture her strategies constitute something like a surplus of signifier, a space of exegetical excess, which through interpretive multiplicity enables to formalize the ideological dilemma of writing national identities through a polyphonous structure of language, where several voices are implied in one melodic line. Its effect hinges on the condensation (metaphor) of the multitude of voices in one line. We are referring to the "polyphonous structure of speech" (Ducrot 1984): any enunciation always contains a multiplicity of voices which relate to each other in the mode of questioning, ironic overtones, assent. It is evident that everything in our preceding analyses conspires to propose that the excess of this baroque fugue underscores the articulation of a subject, whose voice condenses an articulated bricolage. No reader of Hispanic texts can ignore or disregard this surplus of signifiers, essential to such heteroglossic polyhedral structure.

The most elementary understanding of ideological identification—mestizo, mulato, Chicano, niuyorican, Hispanic, Latin American—rests in the whole series of articulated but provisional combinational possibilities of identifying with a virtual place in discourse. Going back to history, Garcilaso el Inca and Mexican Sor Juana speak—like us—another tongue. Their discursive practices (and I must stress that el Inca coined *mestizo* as a positive form of identification) rework language to fashion the authority of the colonized over the colonizer other. They specifically lay bare the process of subject formation within the context of a gross imbalance of power. Their oblique rhetoric, the heteroglossia of resistance, their schizophrenic dialogism, are active displacements of power which bring to ruin colonial representations. Sor Juana's texts, exemplary of a canonical Caribbean baroque, figure explicitly modern texts: the strategy (similar to that of the modernists in turn-of-the-century literature) is to subvert the totality contradicting the official truth. The elementary axiom (paraphrasing Žižek 1994a: 121) is that *details* always contain some surplus which undermines the universal frame of the official truth. In Bakhtinian terms baroque texts can be read as exemplary cases of excess or surplus of vision (on the one hand), and outsidedness or exotopy and double-voicedness, on the other. The heteroglossia inherent to plural societies was being united by the very circulation of texts, addressed to the future.

Within this excess—of vision, of signifiers, of signs—in its new form, communities found a sense of self-identity which the emotional-evaluative forms of colonial discourse were articulating for the future. Its first arborescence in Nueva España made the "big Other" visible (that is, the symbolic order of colonialism). The most evident contradictory extremes can be found in Sor Juana's texts—spoken in a forked tongue—constituting a female subject in the context of Counterreformation Hispanic discourse, asserting at the same time her identity as a Mexican. Our Tenth Muse values difference, asserting, simultaneously, a Mexican language and inflection.

Sor Juana's forked tongue and schizophrenia can he overheard in the contemporary neobaroque, which can be identified with a new aesthetic sensibility based on ludic games, transgressive language, but also with the "ideological myth" (employing Žižek's term 1996: 211) produced by the baroque retroactively to explain its own genesis. What we encounter in the term neobaroque is a form of retroactive causality, a symbolic rewriting of the past, a space for reordering the past; in short, figuring a time when language games and a forked tongue defined a subjectivization.

A second stage of this fugue or "polyphonous structure of speech" which contains a multiplicity of voices relating to each other in the mode of questioning, ironic overtones, assent, reveal a further step in the articulation of a subject around 1809: this time, a chorus of voices from Mexico to Venezuela, Argentina, and all of Central America and South America, in that first phase of postcolonial discourse now directly addressed to a liberal form of democracy. If the baroque was pure ambivalence, for the nineteenth century liberals and romantics the point of fugue was to reconstruct new nations and forms of democracy. Feelings and tears seem to project the problematics of the pain that inheres in the very essence of our dwelling in language: the traumatic cut or 'castration', which marks our entry into a new language. The ethical stance here was to assume fully the impossible task of symbolizing the Real, inclusive of its necessary failure (I draw from Žižek 1994b: 200 in another direction). It is precisely in this field that we should situate Schelling's notion of "access to the Absolute" (as developed by Žižek), or the desintegration of one's horizon of meaning. Such experience allows us to realize the greatness of the Independence heroes, even of isolated warriors like Geronimo. In persuing a lost cause of the battle against whites until 1886 when the United States annexed Texas and California, he clearly experienced the limitation of the Native American horizon. Not withstanding his awareness of the fragility of this universe, he persisted—did not give up on his desire—displaying a true ethical attitude. Examples abound. What this Wars of Independence against Spanish rule made clear are the paradoxes upon which modern democracies are constructed—liberty and equality, which modernity placed on the horizon of legitimacy. On the level of ideological meaning, the different *caudillos* succeeded in uniting in the same discourse elements which were hitherto regarded as incompatible. What these discourses presuppose is a *bricolage* of heterogenous elements: the whole domain of fantasies on which racist enjoyment feeds. The paradox is that the racism inherent to liberal democracy has produced in most Latin American nations what can be called "totemic societies," ruled by tutellary powers (on totemism see Copjec 1995: 156–57), where justice was to be distributed, with the desire to dispense "charity and humanity" to carry modernity for-ward. The logic of paradox allows us to understand the contradictory positions of the *caudillos*, and of the societies founded on a nonrecog-nition of their own contradictions. The major cultural texts resorted to tears and whispers, while poetry became an enthymemic-dialogical discourse with a paradoxical effect; I am evoking Andres Bello's *Alocución a la poesía* (1823), an invocation to the muses to abandon a decadent Europe to try the wonders of a 'virginal' unspoiled nature. Once the Wars of Independence were over, anxiety increased with the emergence of another kernel of power. By mid century, the Anglo-Saxon model imposed by the United States became the *das Ding*—that extrawordly force, the realm that threatened the world. These attacks on utilitarianism found support in Baudelaire, who by 1862 had iden-tified in *Fusées* this triumphant modernity as he denounced what Rodó later called *nordamanía* in 1900, making it synonymous to util-itarianism, materialism, empiricism, plutocracy, and imperialism. A new America is produced through Romantic fantasies of national states, which by 1850 were clearly pro-Spanish, against the anxiety provoked by the "manifest destiny" of the Other. The point is that what appears as the hindrance to society's full identity is the "big Other," as manifested in discourse.

A third stance comes around 1898: with the modernists—from Mexico, to Central America to the Antilles. Modernism, in Latin America, acquires a two-fold lateral meaning as it is addressed to the "big Other," which had bifurcated from European colonization, to the form of the obscene *Das Ding*, or "radical evil" of U.S. neocolonialisms. This third stage which also deploys poetry as its major genre of discourse, includes Martí and Darío, among the best known. Poetic discourse was a choice of democratic identity, wherein modernization was understood as a form of subjectivity where the "big Other"— European or U.S.—would actually cease to exert hegemony (see Zavala 1992). Through their poetics, both lyrical and narrative genres, we are now able to delineate the inherent limitation of the liberal political ethics and its paradoxes: while attacking the unbearable of the Real of a new form of colonialism, liberal ethics disguised conflicts with the myth of humanity as a consistent moral unit across time and space, and accorded much weight to a homogeneous language. With the North American *Das Ding* functionalism became the historical partner of neocolonialism's "civilizing mission."

Cuban Jose Martí's essays around and about America—Our America—have been pivotal in sustaining fictions and narratives which participate in the constitution of the self. From different subject positions and evaluative points of view, modernists produced in the organic crisis of 1898 a *mise an scène* and an imaginary cognitive projection of their concrete social existence within the collective and its historical context. By a process of identification and its opposite of estrangement in the dialogical social imaginary, the reader identified with a *symbolic victory*. A recognition of Martí and Darío's politics of meaning and discursive practices are an exemplary illustration of modernism's anticolonial narrative (a social project which still remains collectively powerful). Martí believes that the object of literature is to make reality transparent: "The word is not to hide truth but to say it," he writes in 1875, firmly believing with the Romantics that rhetoric is profoundly ethical. Darío's swan poems in *Songs of Life and Hope* (1905) begin with a prologue which reads: "If there is politics in these songs, it is because it is universal. . . . Tomorrow we may be yanquis (and it is most probable); in any case, my protest remains written on the wings of the immaculate swans, as illustrious as Jupiter."

What both the seventeenth century and modernist postcolonials are exhibiting is the fantasy-space within which a community organizes its culture. Once again, we must consider the role played by antagonism in the activity of defining identity. In contrast to a universe of pure positivism and instrumentalization, modernists seem to hope to organize their way of life in the self-sufficient forms of ethnic communities, even when they caricature and parody old forms of identification. Within this new present juncture, metaphor best comprises notions such as respect and dignity. We must be particularly attentive to the background of inherent *racism* which structured the social space as the inclusive antagonism between "us" and "them." The dialogics we are pursuing is specifically this antagonism, always reenacted and rewritten, thus providing new and newer answers. To make my point more evident, I will quote Ramón Emeterio Betances, a Puertorican man of letters and politician, who wrote in 1892: "forgetting future generations and not thinking beyond anything, they dream that the apple tree would give tasty fruit in Havana and the palm juicy coconuts in Washington, as if under mortal climates both trees were not condemned to die" (1892). By 1898 Argentinean-French Paul Groussac wrote: "A democratic yanquism, atheist of all idea . . . invades the world." José Vasconcelos spelled it clearly in our twentieth century: "Hagamos que nuestra América sea hispánica, que sea ibérica, que sea India, que sea universal" (in Fell 1986: 121). The union of these countries, quoting positivist Vasconcelos again "must exclude the United States" (112). In his words: "Queremos la unión de los pueblos ibéricos sin excluir a España y comprendiendo expresamente al Brasil, y tenemos que excluir a los Estados Unidos, no por odio, sino porque ellos representan otra expresion de la historia humana" (112).

The fantasy-space we have been persuing is present in the wave of this postcolonial writers from turn-of-the-century novels, to the 1920s and 1930s, epochs of dilemmatic bourgeois democracy and capitalism. Elzbieta Slodowska (1997) has intelligently delineated the great modernizing leap some of our "traditional" novels propose, and the dreams of nationalism, a desperate search for new roots in an organic community, with all its paradoxes. It is also the time of the avant-garde, with César Vallejo and Pablo Neruda, as well as Nicolas Guillén and Julia de Burgos and Luis Palés Matos in the Antilles delineating a radical democracy from the scraps of the bourgeois liberal projects. Neruda's and Vallejo's voice are engaged with the con-

stitutive role of antagonism in social life, and the deficient understanding of the sources of political identity outside the narrowly
defined of politics itself. In Vallejo's *Trilce* and Neruda's *Residencia
en la tierra*, the private is the space of death, of futility, and redemp-
tion is only achieved through a new configuration of the social (see
Yúdice ed. 1992). Both are concerned with democracy—radical
democracy—and although there is a crises of these discourses, since
there is no point in rewriting the old polarities after the rise of the
debt crisis, the collapse of the welfare state, and the struggle for redemocratization, both poets have helped discern the cultural spaces.

José María Arguedas passionate *El zorro de arriba y el zorro de
abajo* (posthumous 1971), in Peru, significantly deals with the motive
of the dying community in a hybrid writing which combines autobi-
ography and fiction. After this uneven text, it is impossible to expect
that in the Andinization of modernity there is anything like emancipation (in Moreiras 1997), which both projects of Neruda and Vallejo
supported.

A more recent stance in this perspective is to be found in what we
know as neobaroque literatures after the 1970s. What this latest
impulse of postcolonial neobaroque suggest to me is a defense of
enjoyment, through the celebratory heterology of popular music. A
whole set of alternative histories is interwoven in Sarduy's (and
Guillermo Cabrera Infante, and Miguel Barnet, among others) texts
through *cha cha cha's*, boleros, *sones*. Rhythms help sustain the
scopic drive, and the symbolic dimension of Cubanism is parodized.
I could venture further to say that music is presented as the conventional stereotype in its relation to Antillean identity.

The Caribbean neobaroque of García Márquez posits yet other
challanges. *One Hundred Years of Solitude* makes the reader oscillate
between two extremes: on the one hand the question of the presence
of speech as truth in Melquiades, and the empirical historical certainty that capitalism is an obscure and somber story of violent
expropriation and plunder, of merchant adventurers; a story we do
not have to be acquainted with in order to grasp in its synchronic
function. As a voyage into the past, the subject fills out the "missing
link" of its genesis by enabling us to jump into the past and appear as

its own cause. García Márquez's neobaroque goes through the fantasy which keeps the character of the vicious circle unconcealed.

Those are the paradoxes about our social life the nodal texts we have reread have figured for the future. What we have been following is the sustained attempt among paradigmatic Latin American writers to place the project of a radical and plural democracy on more adequate foundations, while keeping the question of identity and emancipation open. Strategies from el Inca to Sor Juana have attempted to create specific forms of unity within the heterogeneity of different interests by relating them to a common project and by establishing a frontier to define the forces to be opposed, the 'enemy'. If ever since Independence the postcolonial constituted a basic motif of organicist ideology—an autochthonous culture and a common and shared language—the idea of identity and self-representation was part of the process of a democratic nation building. However, what has been made clear after the Cold War is the weak state of civil societies, and the disaggregating tendencies of the vast-mestizo, mulato and indigenous classes. The paradoxes and conflicts of the Wars of Independence, and modernists and avant-gardes have erupted; we are left with conflicts on the social, "totemic societies" and tutellary powers, which we must question.

Within Latin America, debates on the meanings and possibilities of implementing democracy—as George Yúdice (1992) has lucidly stated—are linked to the historical vicissitudes of modernization. The question now is not only to understand the limitations of past ideologies, but also to discern the cultural spaces within this new situation in which the oppositional practices we have followed are no longer well defined. The current integration of Latin American economies into the 'new world order', specially the death of traditional cultural forms, as we now know that tradition is in transition, and new intellectual and aesthetic practices demand political struggles on the social and a cultural politics attentive to the dispersed practices unleashed by economic reconversion. What Chantal Mouffe (1993) calls 'the return of the political' should and must be situated within a critique of the universalism, utilitarianism and individualism of liberal theory, as well as within the constitutive role of social antagonism and economic power in social life.

The task of rereading and writing then is to explore the redefinitions our cultural imaginaries have undergone after long periods of populism and nationalism since the nineteenth century. If the signifier always receives its signification retroactively, what was done can always be undone the past can have no permanent existence, as Lacan reminds us. Our challenge then is to place hopes on emergent social actors—never before considered—and in redemocratization processes themselves, with the awareness that democracy is not a utopia, and that it will never be harmonious, and that only by dissatisfaction over the definition of the subject, can one prevent surrendering definitions to the Other. Our task may be to construct a radical democracy within the reigning forms of transnational capitalism, and the pluralism and fetishization of *Jouissance* that haunts us, and to work for a new thinking of borders, a new experience of the home, the economy and enjoyment, unavoidably conflictual spaces. Tiresias's question marks the deadlock, the antinomy, the impasse of the Real as the traumatic antagonism our nodal texts have been encircling since the dawn of modernity in the seventeenth century, and which returns as the same, and throws us out of joint. His question is how to deal with the antagonism, the constitutive splitting of the political; quoting chicana Erlinda Gonzalez, who retroactively gives weight to the past: Chicanos, she says, have the right to "preserve our tongue and our culture, that is to say, our *latinidad.*" In other words, that which is "more than ourselves" that defines us, but is simultaneously undefinable; the "treasure," *agalma,* in us. She wrote "latinidad," emphasizing the particular tenacity of the subject's resistance; logically and structurally translated "Latin American," a definition which includes Central and South America, Brazil, the Antilles—many of them still colonies—and Hispanics within the United States. All with forked tongues: be it Spanish, Brazilian, English, Dutch, Papiamento, Creole, Spanglish. We all speak forked tongues and many clearly persist in the defiant "not-all." And, in connecting with shame, and ethical imperative, we all know since the nineteenth century that English has not been the language of poetry or of peace, but mainly multinational capitalism's tongue. "Tongue and culture" refer to particulars, not universals; in fact, in the contemporary world what we have is a new relationship between universality and particularism, grounded in the notion of rights. Clearly, a project worth fighting for.

CONCLUDING REMARKS

I started with a myth as a key to the Lacanian logic of the "not-all" of *jouissance*, with the awareness that a "myth gives epic form to that which works from structure" (Lacan 1990: 34). We moved to theoretical problems around the "not-all" and the "Other" to rethink notions of universality, then to the logic of speech, and finally brought those abstract considerations to specific nodal texts attempting a retroactive reading of their cultural-symbolic construction. I left aside the kernel of *jouissance* of popular music, as part of this construction. Tiresias, the "not-all" and "something more," who maintains the question open, has rendered visible the retroactive reading of our nodal texts, with their traumatic paradoxes, and their defiant *Che vuoi?* to the Other. How, then, do we progress from here to a "not-all" that enables us to dismantle universals, and to a performative dimension of speech in order to establish new intersubjective networks, and reintroduce some notion of community to resist the mortal consequences of the fetishization of private *jouissance*? This is the time to recall the dramatic and somber Martinian words: "because I live inside the monster, I know its entrails"; read retroactively they impose a conflictive and conflictual task to assert our "not-all" against all tutellary forms of interpellation in our *mestizo* polyphonous in harmony against the borders which asphixiate our conflictual space to preserve democracy. Perhaps the strongest political claim for the Lacanian analysis we have made through the Tiresian paradoxes is that the emptiness of the universal makes true democracies possible. Our history of "not-alls" provides the most vigorous means of discovering the effective relations of the subject, culture and the Real, thereby making it possible to develop new forms of *jouissance* and desire. The conflictual task is ours.

REFERENCES

Aubert, Jacques, D. *Rhetoric & Culture in Lacan.* Cambridge: Cambridge University Press, 1996.

Copjec, Joan. *Read My Desire. Lacan against the Historicists.* Cambridge/London: MIT Press, 1995.

Ducrot, Oswald. *Le dire et le dit.* Paris: Minuit, 1984.

Fell, Claude. "Panamericanismo a iberoamericanismo: el debate entre los intelectuales latinoamericanos." *Mexico.* Universidad Autónoma de México (1986): 112, 125.

González, Erlinda. "La deslatinización del pueblo neomexicano." In *La latinidad y su sentido en América Latina.* México, 1986.

Lacan, Jacques. *The Four Fundamental Concepts of Psychoanalysis.* New York: Norton, 1981.

―――. *Television/A Challenge to the Psychoanalytic Establishement.* Edited by Joan Copjec, translated Denis Hollier, Rosalind Krauss, and Annette Michelson. New York: Norton, 1990.

―――. *The Psychoses.* London:Routledge, 1993.

―――. *La identificación. Seminario X.* Unpublished seminar.

―――. *The Ethics of Psychoanalysis.* London:Routledge, 1992.

Laclau, Ernesto, ed. *Making of Political Identities.* London: Verso, 1994.

―――. "Universalism, Particularism, and the Question of Identity." In *The Identity Question.* Edited by John Rajchman. New York/London: Routledge, 1995, pp. 93–108.

Moreiras, Alberto. "The End of Magical Realism: Arguedas's Passionate Signifier." Lecture Canada 1997.

Mouffe, Chantal. *The Return of the Political.* London:Verson, 1993.

Salecl, Renata. *The Spoils of Freedom.* London: Verso, 1994.

Yúdice, George. "Postmodernity and Transnational Capitalism in Latin America." In *On Edge: The Crisis of Contemporary Lain American Culture.* Edited by G. Yudice, Jean Franco, and Juan Flores. University of Minnesota Press, 1992.

Zavala, Iris M. *Colonialism and Culture: Hispanic Modernisms and the Social Imaginary.* Indiana University Press, 1992.

―――. "The Baroque as Point the Capiton." Lecture Canada 1997.

Žižek, Slavoj. *Everything You Always Wanted to Know About Lacan (But Were Afraid to Ask Hitchcock).* London:Verso, 1994a.

―――. *The Metastases of Enjoyment.* London:Verso, 1994b.

―――. *For Them Know Not What They Do.* London:Verso, 1996.

Marcelo Paz

THE POSSIBILITY OF THE POSTMODERN IN THE ARGENTINIAN NARRATIVE OF THE LAST MILITARY DICTATORSHIP

Latin American postmodernity demands that attention be given to the heterogeneity that exists among the various artifacts produced under a variety of local social conditions and aesthetic traditions. But second, Latin American postmodernity demands that the "original," "native," or "unique" elements identified in those artifacts not be interpreted only in light of those local phenomena. They must simultaneously be interpreted in light of differentiating global, economic, and cultural processes.

Colás

It's not a matter of merely expressing how bad the postmodern is but rather to acknowledge that these are the times we are living and the times in which we have to work, and these are the new problems we have to face and not those glorious issues that moderns had to deal with.

Fredric Jameson[1]

My intervention in the inexhaustible debate about postmodernity will develop in the space made possible by Jameson's epigraph. The inclusion of his words is justified by two compelling arguments which will underpin most of what follows: first, postmodernism should be considered from a desacralizing point of view. Thus, I will be critical of the celebratory aura that characterizes much of the postmodern debate. Second, the postmodern reality, because it is problematic, must be thought of in provisional terms. I will thus try to protect myself from two reductive responses: one, in which my arguments would be seen as merely an imported gesture; and another in which I would be cast as an unequivocal advocate of the post-modern celebration. These two reductions represent both poles of the current debate: at one extreme, are those who reject postmodernity and at the other, those who celebrate the postmodern incursion.

Some readers, by habit, mistaking me for an obedient consumer, will wearily listen to the celebratory rolling of the postmodern drum. Their supposition is the consequence of a space that I have provided here for the "entrance" of the postmodern, but I do so, under an additional precaution suggested by Nelly Richard. I aspire to delin-eate a "differential entry" (characterized in her words as "transfor-mative and questioning").[2] I am thus not claiming a totalizing char-acterization of contemporary Argentinean narrative as postmodern. The provisional sense of the term, an important component of this reading, tends to save it from such all-inclusive assumptions. It also repudiates static classifications and remains on the fluid side of a potential reading.

My allusion to the postmodern is appropriate as long as some of its contents help to articulate certain paradigms. In some cases, I believe those paradigms are at work in the novels of the post-Boom; in others they must be brought to the surface of literary expression. Such is precisely the purpose of my quest. It would be misleading, however, to read my previous qualifications as an irrefutable denun-ciation of the category of a postmodern literature. The potential of my appropriation of the postmodern as a workable category is exem-plified in Santiago Colás's work, alluded to in the opening citation. Colás's understanding avoids the weakness of studies which under-stand postmodern literature only within the limitations established by postmodern thought. In much of the postmodern debate, the overuse of this word has increasingly eroded its semantic stability. As Umberto Eco remarks: "Unfortunately 'postmodern' is a term that can be used for anything." However, we should not react to this semantic overuse by dogmatically rejecting the term. Such rejection, far from repressing the postmodern, would conversely have the effect of sacralization. As I have said, I have no totalizing purpose in alluding to the postmodern in reference to certain Latin American authors; yet, I would be contributing to the taboo against the postmodern if I should refuse to admit that, in a certain provisional way, I am talking about a postmodern literature. By saying this, I hope to avoid falling into Urandibia's uneasy contradiction, blatantly expressed in his essay "Lo narrativo en la postmodernidad," wherein he warns:

> Que nadie espere que de lo dicho vaya a caer en el cretinismo de hacer un catálogo o un equipo de escritores posmodernos . . . me parece una verdadera payasada hablar, como lo hacen algunos, de literatura posmoderna.[3]

I do not think that the proposition of a postmodern literature is either cretinous or clownish; more importantly, Urandibia, in rejecting the proposition of postmodern literature, does nothing but theorize about postmodern literature. By referring to postmodern literature as disturbing (he calls it *desasosegada*) Urandibia uselessly pretends to avoid allusion to the postmodern. But by doing so, he actually addresses the postmodern by omission. It seems that if we are going to engage in the debate, we must use the term, although not uncritically. And I do want to engage in this debate. The impulse behind my desire is none other than the compelling need to point out a possibility: of using the term to defeat the solemnity hidden in any reference to the postmodern (the solemn representing the opposite pole of the empty imprint of the postmodern). Part of the problem lies in the difficulties of arriving at a comprehensive definition of the postmodern, in part because this arrival will result in a paradoxical "master narrative," a narrative saturated with an all-inclusive rationality. In Jameson's view, such a narrative would constitute a "nonpostmodern" theory of the postmodern, insofar as the postmodern implies a healthy resistance to the possibility of "pure" theorization.

From the perspective of Latin America, the postmodern can potentially inscribe its discourse in a reality that moves between a so-called premodernity and, better yet, a distorted modernity. This aspect of the debate is evidently pertinent to Latin America, a location that has been ceaselessly deprived of a place in history by the metropolis. The possibility of this postmodern inscription is outlined in the decentralizing work written years ago by Angel Rama. I believe that the Uruguayan critic would not have any problems accepting postmodernity as one more instance of Latin America's transculturizing genius, the capacity of the continent to appropriate and transform cultural imports.[4]

It seems to me of paramount importance to emphasize here that the characterization of the social process in Latin America as premodern or as a distorted modernity, as a way of restraining the viability of what is known as the postmodern, emerges directly from totalizing metropolitan discourses. The exclusionary notions of modernity espoused by the metropolis attempt to explain the tardiness of modernization in Latin America. These exclusionary notions foreground the following contradiction when postmodernity is inscribed in the periphery: if modernity has not yet arrived in Latin America, if Latin America has not yet entered modernity, how could we apply to it a logic that assumes the "total" realization of its antecedent? This reasoning articulates a view that is inclined to understand the periphery's cultural terms through the monological linearity of the West. If we agree that the postcolonial Latin American space is nonmodern, the agreement is a result of a mimetic identification of the centralizing and excluding discourse of modernity. Critics who believe in the tardiness of Latin America's modernity and at the same time who reject postmodernity as "foreign," fall into a contradiction: they cannot help but sustain their opinions upon an identity that is borrowed, precisely, from the foreign discourse that they censor when it comes to postmodernism. Among the views held by these critics, this is the logic that prevails: the Latin American subject is premodern, pseudomodern, it does not fit the norm designed by European *man* as the universal prototype in *his* dismissive construction of modernity. The subordination promotes the inapplicability of postmodernity's discourses to Latin America. According to Western thought, the Latin American subject remains behind in the process of emancipation. But in fact, this status results from a paralyzed project, a project drawn solely from the experience and welfare of the European man and the subjects of his north-Atlantic extension. I would like to point out not only the flagrant contradiction of such a rationale but also its somber consequence. The process of cultural recontextualization that has been taking place in our continent since its constitution, is—now, in postmodern times—as legitimate and material as it was during the conformation of modernity. Moreover it helps identify the mechanisms that have persisted in silencing otherness and by doing so encourages emancipatory trends.

Although much of this discussion is articulated in relation to literature, it is important to know that the postmodern discussion is not exclusively aesthetic but also political. In the light of the emancipatory impetus promoted by postmodernity and the politics of difference, what argument could those who promote silence and isolation have against postmodernity? Furthermore, if we keep in mind that social interdependence and globalization are prominent consequences of postmodernity, critics must reckon with it as an inevitable layer of Latin American reality.

FACING POSTMODERNITY: LATIN AMERICAN LEFT AND RIGHT

Those who denounce the postmodern as a mere proimperialistic and demobilizing infatuation align themselves mostly with the left. Such radical denunciation expresses a contradictory relation with the commitment to cultural independence and political liberation postulated by the left. The inconsistency occurs in that, among the different understandings raised by the postmodern, we may also find positions furthering the imperative articulation and "completion" of Latin American emancipatory projects. By embracing mechanisms that prompt a resurgence of a new kind of activism and include discourses that vindicate difference and the local, the postmodern expands the substantial realization of this emancipatory project by enlarging its constituency in a broad, inclusive, and less dogmatic emancipation. What is remarkable in the left's repudiation of the postmodern is its allusion to a Marxism that is "naturally" Latin American. It is not my intention here to counterattack the reference to a Marxism that is inherently Latin American. Contrary to the left's visceral rejection of postmodernism, they regard Marxism—also born in the metropolis—as a viable ideology for Latin America. Indeed, how not to think of Mariategui's and Vallejo's experiences as important examples of this viability? In practicing a now autochthonous Marxism devoid of any "foreign" residue, the left justifies its antagonism towards post-modernity. Among other things this antagonism views the postmodern as the result of realities far removed from what Latin Americans must face in their daily lives. The exclusion of this specific "other" (in a reflex of critical protectionism) does not strive for a contextualized reading and revision of the postmodern phenomenon.

An alternative to the left's dogmatic rejection of postmodernity would then attempt to go beyond this indiscriminate rejection, and consider the signs of postmodernity in order to interpret them, taking into account our specific needs. To enter the discourse around the post-modern does not imply an uncritical adherence to a neoimperialist global project (the so-called International New Order). This task involves reconsidering the mobilizing energies of a logic that includes, among other insights, "the immorality of speaking on behalf of the other" (a prevalent gesture in the metropolitan discourse that sees Latin America as a frozen example of the center's crisis). However, the postmodern logic also manifests a genuine concern to articulate the other and its site of enunciation. Postmodernity aims at taking a stand for the victim's perspective, as Marxism does for the worker, and, in doing so grounds its critical discourse in a now critical insurgent ethics.

The right also articulates a resistance to the postmodern, astutely avoiding any reference that might convey the problematics of imperi-alism. In the right's traditional discourse, this possibility is always looked down upon as a "fictionalization" of the left, unless the impe-rial reference occurs with a warning to the socialist "monster," today a feeble warning indeed. Paradoxically, history, whose end is declared in the discourse of the right, comes back to life in order to account for the demise of the Socialist Empire. The right's rejection of postmodernism, different from what we have seen in the left, is grounded in the fear of a dangerous chaos that postmodernity seems to herald. The anarchy brought about by the postmodern challenges the working of absolute categories; it is a site with which the right is not willing to negotiate, for doing so would jeopardize the bases of its own hierarchical, differentiated, and self-legitimizing existence. Apart from social, historical, and political otherness I would also like to include the silenced otherness of the "aesthetic." For instance, in literature, the antielitist aftermath of the postmodern amounts to undermining the right's immaculate categories of "poet" and "author" and their practices, as long as postmodernity remains conscious of its own strength in the building of elitism.

The trajectory of the right in relation to this debate is evident in the work of one of its most distinguished speakers. In the newspaper *La Nación*, Vargas Llosa exposes postmodernism's frivolity, identifying it exclusively with the deconstructive trend, in fact, with a trivial version of deconstruction.[5] The kernel of his attack is articulated in the following instances:

> Hay una incongruencia absoluta entre una tarea crítica que comienza por proclamar la ineptitud esencial de la literatura para influir sobre la vida (o para ser influida por ella) y para transmitir verdades de cualquier índole asociables a la problemática humana y que luego, se vuelca tan afanosamente a desmenuzar -y a menudo con alardes intelectuales de inaguantable pretensión- esos "monumentos de palabras inútiles."[6]

I would like to bypass the commentary on the "intolerable pretension" that a genuine intellectual recognizes in the intellectual boastings of what Vargas Llosa sees as a pseudophilosophy. Rather, I concentrate on his belligerence towards the postmodern phenomenon, for I am claiming that deconstruction and postmodernism deserve a less "inept" reading.[7] Postmodernism, like deconstruction, recognizes an impure state of signification and cannot cease to participate in a system grounded on binary oppositions. This realization takes place in a conscious move to unveil the limitations of any valued critical judgment. It is not so much about the influence a critic, a writer, or for that matter *Literature* can have on life. The predicament of the postmodern moment preempts the possibility of this influence by dismantling the privilege space from which an intellectual practice could do so. Moreover, Vargas Llosa's assertion clearly separates creative and intellectual endeavors from life, as if these endeavors were not actually part of the "life" he mentions. In spite of this "contradiction," such discourses "are put to use diligently in the shattering" of various texts; yet, they aim towards a new (utopic) condition where oppositions, after a process of inversion, may eventually disappear.

BEYOND LEFT AND RIGHT

Until now I have been trying to justify postmodernism in the midst of a resistance from both the right and the left. I have done so by applying the same patterns of readaptation that characterize previous appropriations. If Latin American thought and criticism acquiesce to a dialogue with "foreign" concepts such as modernism, surrealism, Marxism, and avant-garde, to refer to local cultural phenomena, how could we deprive ourselves of the inescapable possibility of "thinking" in terms of the postmodern debate? Are we, Latin Americans, unqualified to think? Is it that Latin Americans are not fit to think postmodernity because it is foreign, Euro-North-American, and too advanced for our always borrowed and dependent talents?[8] Are Foucault, Derrida, Deleuze, and Lyotard's writings so radiant and hermetic that they conceal what was there since the beginning: western discourse and its will to master? In this exchange of ideas, we seem to retain these writings as mere "loans"—as Paz suggests—which prevents us from producing critical thought. The consequence of this claim is the characterization of Latin American critics who are receptive of the postmodern (García Canclini, Richard, Rincón, Casullo, Yúdice, Beverly, Colás, etc.) as naïve and untrained readers unable to detect the old trick of intellectual colonialism.

For instance, the Latin American critical community has demonstrated independence in articulating its position vis-à-vis a variety of cultural issues. This is evident in the manner in which, for example, the modern in Baudelaire differs from the modern in Darío. Hasn't the critical community that addresses this topic—native and foreign—demonstrated its commitment to understanding the implications of its critical task? Cannot Latin American criticism do the same with the postmodern? Therefore, Latin America must participate in this contemporary disagreement (*différend*). I am proposing here the possibility of thinking the postmodern, of merely voicing Latin America's right to participate, but not as a result of a permission gracefully granted by the Metropolis. This right is rather the consequence of the continuous articulation of heterogeneity as constitutive in the formation of Latin America. Although this hybridity is prior to the advancement of postmodernity, this presence does not determine the sterility of the postmodern in the promotion of the heterogeneous, a constitutive sign of Latin America's imaginary.

Latin American critics are clearly competent to problematize a thought. My assertive response can be confirmed by again alluding to Richard's and García Canclini's works; I would add to the list the contributions of Casullo, Oviedo, and Rincón and—among the non-native Latinamericanists— Beverly, Colás, and Yúdice. These critics' undertakings exemplify a thinking process that derives from the post-modern new ways to reconsider the modern-postmodern in Latin America, responding to our own needs and in consideration of our literary history and specific historiography.

The most distinct instances of this reflection are evident on two fronts: on one hand, we can see the rise of a trend that has gone beyond the dogmatic stagnation of the revolutionary sixties while still maintaining a radical vitality. I am thinking here of the *testimonio* and the new historical narration. On the other hand, we can verify a deconstructive drive when Latin American postmodernities dismantle the dichotomy between high and popular culture. Both examples indicate the revitalization of a "reflexión local sobre problemáticas nuestras: modernidad, cultura, democracia, etc."[9]

Revitalizing a differential political agency and building resistance to economic globalization in Latin America (the old neoliberal project remapped in the conception of a "Latin American free market") can be seen as some of the many imaginable contents of Latin American *postmodernities*. This available postmodernity, an important realization in this essay, attempts to diminish the movement towards regression peculiar to *academic* postmodernity. In the Latin American cultural debate, the postmodern assault (and the terminology that comes along with it: deconstruction, fragmentation, decentering, etc.) is subordinated to a critical, resistant, and reconstructive tendency, at odds with the regressive, ahistorical, and cool discourse of post-modernity so pervasive in some areas of the Euro-North-American postmodern phenomenon.

LATIN AMERICAN DIALOGIC POSTMODERNITY

My approach to postmodernity is not a vindication of purity in regards to its Latin American manifestation. The differential useful-ness of postmodern practice in Latin America is closely related to its dialogical nature. In the case of fictional writing (Piglia and Valen-zuela for example), we find an experience anchored in the disman-tling of the language-history dichotomy —a dichotomy intensified as a result of modernity. In what amounts to criticism, there is a call to relate to the objects of study as cultural artifacts. Although these can be examined in relation to an indiscriminate social-artistic constitu-tion, they are subsequently apprehended in relation to the necessary (new) project of democratic emancipation in Latin America (Arditi, Hinkelamert, Lechner).[10]

The dialogic articulation of the postmodern has initiated a ques-tioning of the exclusions and silences in Latin American postmod-ernism, revising the canonical taxonomies that were produced in the theorizing North. Right from the start, recognized scholars were quick to globalize the trend—a "justifiable" move in the logic of the postmodern. Barth, McHale, and Hutcheon came up with concurring catalogues, containing the same series of names: García Márquez, Cortázar, Vargas Llosa, and Fuentes.[11] The periphery reached a climax in a process of transmutation that ironically contradicts Paz's pronouncement: Latin America became the locus of the original.[12] In this view, the founder of literary postmodernity, someone with an indisputable "South American destiny," was born in Argentina. I am talking obviously about Jorge Luis Borges.[13]

Something extremely paradoxical is now taking place. At the moment that history is finished and the Utopia has failed, we are informed, from Europe and the United States, of a last hope. This optimism cannot be a political one since ideology has also perished, but at least we are blessed with a sort of aesthetic Utopia. There is a movement from the margin to the center, similar to the rearrangement experienced *avant la lettre* by barbarians tattooed with the signifiers of a period that they have yet to reach. Suddenly, we are projected into a privileged position by virtue of our "weakness": instability, fragmentation, chaos, incompleteness. What a costly price to pay for being finally considered occupants of a space in an expiring history! Our given location: the displaced center of a (Trans)-avant-garde. This "defective" cognition in the eyes of the Metropolis (and in our own distorted recognition) is the result of the totalizing, progressive, and linear project of modernity. Furthermore, this cognition becomes a sort of document, a statute, a "fundamental law" of the New Order that assigns to Latin America a new space in the planet, a mapping that finally contains us in a universal history. Oddly enough, our entry into history not only is tardy but, more remarkably, takes place once history is concluded, due to a process of erosion (Baudrillard), or as a result of an exhaustion of alternatives brought about by the triumph of liberal democracy (Fukayama). Latin America (and the so-called Third World) could be seen as the emblem of modernity's failure, but, at the same time and from a different point of view, also as the paradigm of instrumental modernity. Whichever position we embrace—the latter being "historically" more convincing—Latin American postmodernities (plurality is the first result of the previous questioning) could be utilized to surpass central modernity's imposition. We must try to exceed modernity in its attempt to banish Latin America to backwardness (premodernity and failure) but also in its universalization of the other in the celebratory discourse of ahistoric postmodernity (pseudomodernity and triumph).

POST-BOOM AND POSTMODERNITY

Context is perhaps the most obvious silence in the expansive system of Euro-North-American postmodernity. In this context, certain

names—Cortázar, Vargas Llosa, García Márquez, and Fuentes—
evoke a troublesome sound that threatens a previous, somehow noise-
less situation. This sound—Boom—shares with the postmodern the
fact that its detractors also see it as an empty "noise." Although the
problematic of the Boom in Latin American literature has been pro-
fusely studied, it is almost impossible to arrive at a stable formalization. Not only is it difficult to determine the nature of the phenomenon, the simple act of completing the list of its members becomes an
impossible task. There is however a partial agreement —according to
Liliana Heker—that includes the first three names mentioned above
in almost every list the Boom produced. Cortázar, Vargas Llosa and
García Márquez are also customarily included as postmodern in the
canonical articulation of Euro-North-American postmodernity; less
consistently, Fuentes is characterized under the same guise.

We aim here to create a relationship between the writers of the
post-Boom and the location of a postmodern literature in Latin
America. In the specific case of Argentina, writers like Piglia, Valen-
zuela, Soriano, Gambaro, and Villordo (de)construct the preceding
tradition in a process of critical continuation: the distorted Boom
sound. What do these authors (re)act against/with? In an attempt to
answer, we must arrive at an instrumental understanding of the
implication of the disputed "noise." With this aim in mind, we will
avail ourselves of Abelardo Castillos's words on the Boom. Although
we do not share entirely his words, they will be useful here to highlight the artificial nature of what Castillo sees as a simple noise:

> The Boom has nothing to do with Latin American Literature, actu-
> ally, quite the opposite. First, the word is an American ono-
> matopoeia for the bomb. The word is just a noise; let's put it this
> way—it is a foreign noise. As a cultural and sociological phenom-
> enon it relies exclusively on Europe's opinion of our writers. When
> in Paris or in Rome they realized that there was more to Latin
> America than *gauchos*, *mariachis*, and *rumba*, they discovered
> Borges, Rulfo, and Carpentier. Then, as a reflex, we also discov-
> ered them. . . . The Boom has much more to do with advertisement
> than with literature. This can be verified by examining whom we
> have "discovered": Carpentier, almost 70 years old; Borges, the
> traditional Nobel's candidate translated in every language;
> Asturias, who received the Nobel indeed and died; Rulfo, who has

refused, for more than 20 years, to publish anything new; Sabato, 65 years old and who sold more than a thousand copies of *On Heroes and Tombs* before the word boom was invented; Cortázar, who in his seventies had already written *Hopscotch* and *The Winners*, if we prefer not to mention his great stories published from 1951 on. In short, authors who have already written most, or, the best of their works. Writers to whom no boom was needed to be recognized but, only a bit of good education.[14]

I must not let go unnoticed the obvious familiarity between the logic of these words and the rejection of the postmodern grounded in the sort of imitative reflex discussed above. In particular, note the words "onomatopeya yanqui," "ruido extranjerizante" in the original Spanish and the phrases "Europe's opinion" and "the boom has much to do with advertisement" in my translation. Nevertheless, Castillo himself recognized the "reflexive" nature of "our" discovery by means of which we can dispute the "good education" of the Latin American reader. It is important, moreover, to keep in mind the logic just mentioned in order to articulate a critical understanding of the Boom that attempts to go beyond hegemonic constructions. It is evident that the conclusion should not be that of Castillo: "the boom has nothing to do with Latin American Literature"; but rather—without conclusive intentions—that Latin American literature does not perfectly fit the systematization of the so-called Boom, not even if we would be able to access a more autochthonous, less foreign onomatopoeia.

The canonical Boom's signifying scope—in spite of the limitations just mentioned—is closely related to the problematics of Latin American literary modernities and modernity in general. The explosion of the continent's narrative in the sixties can be interpreted as a sort of third independence movement, the second of a cultural nature, after turn-of-the-century *Modernismo*. Boom writers (Fuentes and Vargas Llosa are exemplary in that sense) saw themselves and were also perceived as vanguard initiators. This insight took place mostly in the metropolitan understanding of Latin American literature, which was in some cases still unaware of important names in this tradition. To name a few that will give us a perspective of a literature beyond the Boom, we could list Roberto Arlt, Macedonio Fernández, Felisberto Hernández, and Leopoldo Marechal. Some boom writers foster a teleological vision of the movement, the idea of a consummated arrival, the belief of an excursion into an unexplored territory: novelty, experimentation, a modern total abandonment rejecting the *Ancien Régime*—what was understood as the canon in Latin American literature (regionalism, *costumbrismo*, bourgeois realism, romanticism, etc.).[15] They set themselves up, sometimes apart from their proclaimed purpose, as the foundation of a movement that carries out—completes, if you will—the cultural as well as the political emancipation of a Latin America with capital letters. This revolutionary language articulates a modern approach *par excellance*. The implication of this ideology identifies with a concrete political situation: the "new man" of the Cuban revolution. Santiago Colás, in a work that we praised as an example of "resisting" postmodernism (to use his own logic), alludes to the significant absence of this revolution in the accounts of Latin American postmodernism drawn from Boom authors. This reticence in mentioning such an important contextual referent is astonishing, at least from the perspective of Latin America.

On the contrary, the correspondence between the modern utopia in Latin American revolution (embodied by revolutionary Cuba) and the literary utopia of the explosive Boom, prevents us from the erroneous identification of Boom authors (and particularly certain novels: *Hopscotch*, *Hundred Years of Solitude*, etc.) with postmodern fiction within the Latin American context. In the interrelation of these phenomena, it is possible to detect the same modern rhetoric of experimentation and innovation. Most importantly, this correspondence is informed by a familiar proximity between the ideas of "new man" and "new novel."[16] Avant-garde discourse in Boom literature has been identified with literary modernism. For the most part many of the critical approaches to the Boom repeat the authority of the same names (Faulkner and Joyce); and the complex list of traits is also very similar. The difficulty of creating a stable label for the Boom causes serious limitations in the construction of the category. However, the necessary classification emphasizes the following tracks: elitism, cosmopolitanism, universality, technical virtuosity, the writerly, antirealism, representation crisis—a series of paths that post-Boom writers will seek to *dis*mantle.[17]

To add to the confusion, a signifier that not long ago was simply a periodizing prefix intensifies the commotion. This new noise, in combination with the previous ones, refers to authors who came to be recognized after the Boom (this ingenuous periodization seems impossible nowadays). We witness then, an expansion of the debate in the piercing and diffuse expression "post-Boom." Some of us, probably confused by the profusion of noises, associate this restricted Latin American phenomenon with the tedious and inexhaustible debate about the "post." Such an association may be exemplified, for example, by *Artificial Respiration* (1983), a novel by Ricardo Piglia. This novel could be easily linked to a tendency of the post-Boom known as "New Historical Novel." In the critique of Menton and Shaw, paradoxically, this is the tendency where the rupture from the literature written by the Boom predecessors is more difficult to establish. The explanation is as follows: the novel—New Historical novels for the most part—repeats the same kind of skepticism about the possibility of accessing a transparent reality and explores structural and technical experimentation, signs that stabilize the post-Boom. We believe that the difference between "the state of affairs" before the concourse of our disturbing sounds and this new milieu, can be found neither in the emergence of neorealism nor in the presumed reader-friendliness of current novels—both of which are also informed by the mere preservation of the post-Boom as a fixed category. This difference occurs in the way history, but particularly histories, are considered, although deprived of modern scientific apprehension not granted the luxury of naïve withdrawal.

NOTES

1. Translation is mine from an interview, Horacio Machín, "Conversación con Fredric Jameson," *Nuevo texto crítico* 7 (1990): 3–19.

2. Nelly Richard, "Alteridad y descentramiento culturales," *Revista chilena de literatura* 42 (1993): 209. The Chilean critic typifies what Latin America has been ideally doing with that thing call postmodernity. Her conception, like my account, attempts to go beyond a simple rejection and assumes the prerogative of participation in a debate in which American reality cannot be ignored. America (the Americas) has an important role in the arrival of modernity despite the silencing of the Eurocentric discourse.

3. Iñaqui Urandibia, Gianni Vattimo, et al., *En torno a la posmodernidad* (Barcelona: Anthropos, 1994) p. 69.

4. For a better understanding of the process of transculturization that every discourse undergoes when it traverses Latin America's space, see Angel Rama, *Transculturación narrativa en América Latina* (México: Siglo XXI, 1982).

5. Vargas Llosa's elucidation of the postmodern is an adequate example of what Spivak describes to be the understanding of deconstruction in the United States: "The aspect of deconstructive practice that is best known in the United States is its tendency toward infinite regression. The aspect that interest me the most is, however, the recognition, within deconstructive practice, of provisional and intractable starting points in any investigative effort, its disclosure of complicities where a will to knowledge would create oppositions; its insistence that in disclosing complicities the critic-as-subject is herself complicit with the object of her critique; its emphasis upon 'history' and upon the ethico-political as the trace of that complicity—the proof that we do not inhabit a clearly defined critical space free of such traces; and finally, the acknowledgment that its own discourse can never be adequate to its example." Gayatri Chakravorty Spivak, *In Other Worlds* (New York: Methuen, 1987), p. 97

6. Mario Vargas Llosa, "Postmodernismo y frivolidad," *La Nación* 7 (May 1994): 1.

7. Spivak's reading appropriates deconstruction, from the perspective of the subaltern, to resist neocolonialism. After all, her deconstructive practice does not render dubious her Marxist feminist stance; on the contrary, deconstruction localizes her critique in the confines of her own critical task.

8. Octavio Paz appears to be one of those intellectuals that disputes the possibility of originality in this part of America. However, at the same time, he characterizes literary movements as transnational, *In/mediaciones* (México: Seix Barral, 1986), pp. 39, 45: "Todos los grandes movimientos literarios han sido transnacionales y todas las grandes obras de nuestra tradición han sido la consecuencia -a veces réplica- de otras obras." This seems to contradict his remarks about Latin America's lack of criticism: "Buena crítica literaria ha habido siempre; lo que no tuvimos ni tenemos son movimientos intelectuales originales. No hay nada comparable en nuestra historia a los hermanos Schlegel y su grupo; a Coleridge, Wordsworth y su círculo . . . [the list expands with Western artist, European and North-Americans] No es difícil adivinar la razón—o una de las razones—de esta anomalía: en nuestra lengua no hemos tenido un verdadero pensamiento crítico ni en el campo de la filosofía ni en el de las ciencias ni la historia. . . . Entre el pensamiento filosófico y científico y la crítica literaria ha habido una continua intercomunicación[in Europe and in the United States, not necessarily in the rest of the world]. . . . España, Portugal y sus

antiguas colonias son la excepción. Salvo casos aislados como el de un Ortega y Gasset en España, un Borges en Argentina y otros pocos poetas y novelistas dotados de conciencia crítica, Latinoamérica vive intelectualmente de prestado. Tenemos algunos críticos literarios excelentes pero en Hispanoamérica no ha habido ni hay un movimiento intelectual original y propio. Por eso somos una porción excéntrica de Occidente." Paz's descriptive diagnostic is as rightful as uncritical and contributes (unconsciously) to a division of labor in which the thinking portion of the world can discriminate between rational (original) and barbarian (derived).

9. Nelly Richard, "Alteridad y descentramientos culturales," p. 209.

10. See: Benjamín Arditi, "Una gramática postmoderna para pensar lo social," *Cultura política y democratización*, ed. Norbert Lechner (Santiago: CLACSO, 1987), p. 169. Franz Hinkelammert, "Frente a la cultura de la postmodernidad. Proyecto político y utopía," *David y Goliat* 17 (1987): 21–29. Norbert Lechner, "La democratización en el contexto de una cultura postmoderna," *Cultura política y democratización*, ed. Norbert Lechner (Santiago: CLACSO, 1987), p. 253.

11. See "Literature of Exhaustion" and "The Literature of Replenishment" in John Barth, *The Friday Book* (New York: Putnam, 1984). See also Linda Huthcheon, *A Poetics of Postmodernism* (New York: Routledge, 1988) and Brian McHale, *Postmodernist Fiction* (London: Routledge, 1991).

12. This revision might have serious consequences in a continent that has been accused of lack of originality. For Paz, the locus of intellectual activity and the original seems to reside in Europe. He has characterized "our America" as a continent without philosophy and philosophers but rich in poetry and poets that have mastered the art of embellishment.

13. According to Paz, Borges is one of the few Latin American artists that does not have a parasitic relation with Europe. It is remarkable that even in appreciating Borges's uniqueness, Paz seems to be subservient to an Eurocentric discourse that denies critical judgment to the periphery. For the Mexican, in addition to Borges, the other marvel in the "Hispanic" world is Ortega y Gasset, the two "originals" of this eccentric part of the West.

14. In Liliana Heker, "Posboom: una poética de la mediocridad," *El ornitorrinco* 14 (1986): 5.

15. It is precisely institutionalized criticism that is partially responsible for the formation of this canon, together with our stagnant reading conventions. As an example of a reading in confrontation with the Latin American canon—a canon in part advanced by some Boom writers—see the critical revision of a canonical text *par excellance* in Sylvia Molloy, "Contagio narrativo y gesticulación retórica en *La vorágine*," *Revista Iberoamericana* 53 (1987): 745–66.

16. Antiphallocentric accounts will became essential to the literature written after a Boom that was abundant in phallocentric discourses, unequivocally a remnant of its modern legacy.

17. I am following closely Donald Shaw's typology in "Towards a Description of the Post-Boom," *Bulletin of Hispanic Studies* 66 (1989): 87–94; and "The Post-Boom in Spanish American Fiction," *Studies in 20th Century Literature* 19 (1995): 7–27.

Pedro Lange-Churión

NEOBAROQUE
Latin America's Postmodernity?

"IT WILL NEVER BE KNOWN HOW THIS HAS TO BE TOLD"

> *It will never be known how this has to be told, in the first person or in a second, using the third person plural or continually inventing modes that will serve for nothing.*[1]

In "Blow Up," a story by Julio Cortázar, a narrator-photographer ponders the challenge to write a story about the odious plot of an imminent crime, revealed to him in the process of repeatedly blowing up a negative. In this process, the scenic subject of a randomly taken photograph swiftly changes as the photographer uncovers layers of foreboding details. If in photography, arguably the most faithful medium of iconic reproduction, the exactitude of representation becomes dependent on subjective and mechanical variables such as point of view and processes of film development; then, writing, because of the symbolic and (abstract) nature of language is, understandably, more limited than photography as a medium to record an increasingly elusive reality. Moreover, the inability to know "how this story will be told" is all the more ironic because there is no other way to tell "the story" but through a less than exacting medium of recording, writing.

Cortázar's story serves as a fitting image for an attempt to

253

address the crisis of representation intrinsic to postmodernity, to Latin America and to Latin America and postmodernity.

In this work, I will discuss elements in postmodernity and post-structuralism that point to a crisis of representation and identity; I will consider the (un)desirability of deploying postmodern strategies as interpretive schemes to account for the complex cultural reality of Latin America. After addressing the theoretical elements that have warranted the equivalence posmodernity-Latin America—and partly echoing Nelly Richard's words of caution against facile equations between Latin America and a theoretical practice that emerges from the center and exemplifies itself with the region's cultural products— I will propose a counterhegemonic reading. This reading suggests the notion that a similar crisis of representation to the one known today as postmodernity has been integral to Latin America from its entrance into Western history. In the waning of the fifteenth century, when Europeans had successfully carried out the mapping and con-quest of the new territories to the west of the Atlantic, the process of colonization had begun under the ethos of a European crisis: the baroque. This crisis found an original expression in the Latin Amer-ican baroque and has lingered in our days in the neobaroque. The neobaroque will be considered as an aesthetic epistemology whose theoretical underpinnings, as theorized by Severo Sarduy, José Lezama Lima, and Angel Rama, closely resemble the metaphysical decenteredness of the postmodern moment. A somewhat redemptive reading of the neobaroque in light of the postmodern will prove advantageous because the neobaroque hopefully can serve as an interpretive scheme for Latin America's crisis, an interpretive scheme which, contrary to the postmodern one, is enunciated from the periphery.

Risking redundancy (and who isn't any longer when it comes to writing about the postmodern?) I will briefly address some theoretical elements of postmodernity which, I hope, will help to better contex-tualize my discussion within the crisis of representation that is perti-nent to both Postmodernity and Latin America.

POSTMODERNITY AND THE
CHALLENGE OF REPRESENTATION

We can view postmodernity in part as a theoretical practice resulting from the West's skepticism towards the great narratives penned during the West's own modernity. These narratives served as models and prescribed more or less clear directives for a whole array of human endeavors and inquiries. The critique of their universal validity ended up corroding the epistemological foundations upon which they rested, thus *demolishing* or *weakening* the edifice of modernity. The difference between the demolition and the weakening of this edifice has to do with the already classic polarization between Lyotard and Habermas; whereas one affirms the existence of post-modernity as a *paradoxical surpassing* of modernity and the other negates the existence of postmodernity as a cultural determinant, affirming, rather, that the current crisis is symptomatic of a moder-nity that remains incomplete. One way or the other, be this crisis the result of the demolished Parthenon of modernity or of the still unfin-ished Babel, this end-of-the-century crisis is here to stay.

Fundamentally, postmodernity chips away at modernity's cer-tainties: there is one reason whose validity is imperative and categor-ical; one history traveling from East to West and reaching its zenith in Western Europe (specifically in Germany and England);[2] one uni-versal subject (white, European, and male). Conversely, in post-modernity, the categorical imperative of instrumental reason is chal-lenged (on ethical grounds) in light of the pernicious repercussions brought about by its implementation: from colonialism, through the proliferation of coercive institution to technological genocide. Onto-logical stability is set adrift as the universality of the Hegelian subject is challenged by the alterity of competing ontological projects that were either unheard or unvoiced up to this point. And a rejection of modernity's time-line leads to semiapocalyptic claims clamoring the end of history. Inextricably linked to postmodernity's lamentation about the end of history one also hears a murmur that speaks of the impossibility of aesthetic innovation. The artistic avant-gardes became ostensibly self-absorbed in a quest for innovation by means

of formal experimentation, lost in the conundrum of self-referentiality and incapable of communicating content to an increasingly
alienated viewer and reader, art relinquished the connotation of spiritual deliverance that was privy to its realm, according to the secular
division of labor introduced by modernity (the cognitive the moral
and the aesthetic).[3] In the wake of the avant-gardes' demise, postmodern art is content with renouncing altogether to innovation and
spiritual deliverance; therefore, it resorts to past aesthetics by paro-
dically citing them within the *parergon* of its artistic expressions.
Unable to go forward, to innovate, postmodern art becomes retro-
art.[4] The result is always ironic and certainly derisive of the artistic
aura evoked by Walter Benjamin and characteristic of modernity's
artists and their production. Postmodern aesthetics have also subverted the artistic hierarchies of modernity by including, within the
work of art, subgenres coming from popular culture; and within the
traditional spaces where great art had been solemmly revered
(museums, galleries, and editorials), "lesser genres" from mass media
and popular culture.

Poststructuralist writings, loosely connected to the student revolutions of 1968 in Europe and notably in France, have been connected to the crisis foregrounded by postmodernity and, to an extent,
have become the epistemological dimension of this cultural crisis. It
should not surprise us, then, that poststructuralist language has been
incorporated in postmodern discussions. Poststructuralist critique to
Western metaphysics has endowed postmodernity with a metaphysical dimension most evident in the writing of Jacques Derrida. For
Derrida the history of metaphysics was nothing more than the substitution of metonymies and metaphors, none of which could claim
structural centrality. Gone with structuralism is the notion of a central and universal signified (*episteme*) capable of coherently encom-
passing all variations within a particular structure or semiotic
system. In deconstruction, the *différance*, the difference whose presence within a particular system of signification has been differed as
marginal, becomes present by virtue of its very absence.[5] Texts that
are put to the test of deconstruction reveal their gaps because, in
them, the readers can read that which has been systematically

excluded. Deconstruction consists of a perspicacious act of reading whereby the reader becomes suspicious of such systematic exclusions; and, therefore, comes to realize that the very existence of the text is dependent on what has been excluded from it. To read deconstructively amounts to exercising a sort of hermeneutical irony, for one knowingly reads to find what is not there. The decentering of privileged signifieds and the consequent obliteration of metaphysical universalistic claims procures a new conception of the history of metaphysics as an ongoing interplay of difference, a continuous and ludic interplay of semiotic substitutions. It is in the inception of the ludic within the solemnity of philosophical discourse where Derrida finds the margins of philosophy's discursive regime. Being unable to claim and represent universal truths, philosophical discourse becomes as excessive and connotative as literature, its lesser counterpart; therefore, the classical binary opposition (philosophy/literature) is dismantled and philosophical discourse becomes riddled with the *literariness of the sign*. Discursive identities are thus disseminated in mere acts of writings: unqualified texts whose inexhaustible meanings are a function of potentially infinite acts of reading. Deconstruction of this opposition, as we will later suggest, has been achieved in Latin American literary practice, where writers have found a space for self-reflection and philosophical speculation, as—for instance—it is today evident in the works of Jorge Luis Borges.

Seminal to the issue of representation in the postmodern, we find the notion of the Kantian sublime as developed by Jean François Lyotard. Speculating on questions of aesthetics, Lyotard introduces the sublime in order to address the impossibility of representation in postmodernity. Briefly, the sentiment of the sublime occurs when the imagination, while capable of conceiving an object, cannot represent it.[6] Conception of the object in the subject's imagination can only be achieved by metonymic allusion because the subject must resort to the supplemental in order to represent the *absence* of that to which the signifier alludes. But when Lyotard affirms that "there is something of the sublime in capitalist economy,"[7] his cogent speculation on aesthetics aquires far-reaching implications. That *something* to which Lyotard obliquely refers has to do with the derealizing effect produced by capitalist economy: reality is devoid of stability as the identity of subjects and objects becomes interchangeable in the implacable logic of consumption and exchange that dominates the market. Entities collapse, erect and remap themselves in the wake of transactions where value is determined in reference to an empty signifier, currency. The vertiginous effect of this continuous derealizing process is, then, analogous to the workings of the sublime; this analogy bespeaks the impossibility of grasping a solid notion of identity, which would, in turn, serve as a solid referent for representation.

Jameson echoes this logic of derealization in identifying postmodernity as the cultural logic of late (transnational) capitalism.[8] The implication of Jameson's worldling is the following: transnational capitalism has globalized postmodernity as its cultural logic. The proliferation of signs promoted by mass media and technology is alluded to as an example of the globalization of postmodernity; nothing seems to escape the abysmal reproduction of signs, even reality itself is derealized by "*semiurgy.*" This technological semiosis is so pervasive that, in the midst of its unrelenting bombardment of representations of the real, the only manner by means of which the subject achieves cognition of himself/herself is through cognitive mappings, metonymic (partial) representations of the relation between subject, space, and time. Like in Virginia Woolf's *Jacob's Room*, where Jacob's subjectivity is a compilation of perspectives and discourses about space; or in Felisberto Hernández's narrators, who suffer from the impossibility of grounding subjectivity given the proliferation of increasingly deterritorialized and competing perceptions, these postmodern metonymic contrivances undermine the possibility of integral representation. This speculation about the representation of self in space approximates closely the notion of the sublime advanced by Lyotard in relation to postmodern aesthetics, a notion according to which the work of art "puts forward the unrepresentable in presentation itself."[9]

That these speculations flaunt an internal logic that is indeed seductive to theoreticians and philosophers is understandable. But once contextualized within the particularities of a world that the postmodern theoreticians seek to encompass in their totalizing discourses, a strategy to flatten difference appears to emerge from postmodernity's roaring celebration of plurality. If this strategy is embraced uncritically by Latin American intellectuals and theoreticians, the possibility for a postcolonial identity, as we shall see, would be seriously hindered.

INFIRMITIES OF THE POSTMODERN IN LATIN AMERICA

If the dynamics of representation in postmodern aesthetics are characterized by the sentiment of the sublime, wouldn't this sentiment, once postmodernity is linked to transnational capitalism as its cultural determinant, branch out beyond aesthetic concerns and surreptitiously insert its condition of irrepresentability into different aspects of reality? The fascination with the postmodern seems to elicit precisely from characteristics that contribute to produce the sentiment of the sublime: an exaltation of a diversity too vast to be grasped and to be represented by any one narrative.

In light of this pluralization, the failure of any one narrative to represent cohesively a socious that has become infinitely atomized, leads some to a cynical critique of metanarratives and ideologies whose appeal was based on a promise of utopian deliverance built upon egalitarian notions of wealth and power. Those who staunchly celebrate the end of ideologies, rejoice, for instance, in the end of the Cold War and the dissolution of the Socialist Bloc, for they claim that these events ratify the demise of ideological illusions. But with the disposal of utopian deliverance, the future, as it was inextricably linked to teleological notions of history, becomes redundant and the postmodern condition celebrates a perennial present, a present in which history becomes nothing but a parodic and stylish revival.

So, the emissaries of postmodernity recruit adherents who become seduced by what can be termed "cries of ends" (history, subject, ideologies, and innovation); this tendency has led critics of postmodernity to accuse postmodern theoreticians of being neoconservative. These criticisms are particularly poignant in Latin America where leftist theoreticians see in postmodernity an aesthetic veil

whose chaotic and sublime aura serves to justify the workings of an
equally unfettered and sublime capitalism, a capitalism solely dictated by the laws of the market, a capitalism whose vast dynamics
defy representation. Postmodernity, then, can serve as both: a fitting
euphemism for the advancement of neoliberalism, and as an interpretive scheme always ready to chastise state-regulated policies inim-
ical to the anarchic movements of the market and consumption. This,
of course, can have lethal consequences for Latin American societies,
where state-regulated policies for social welfare are needed, more
often than not, to ensure the subsistence of millions of socially and
economically marginalized human beings. But, as Latin American
countries exercise futility in an simultaneous attempt to service huge
foreign debts and develop their economies, subsistence becomes an
impossible task, because the potential for growth and development of
Latin American countries is drastically compromised by the stran-
gling economic measures imposed by the IMF and the World Bank. In
the midst of increasing human misery, these imposed economic measures protect the anarchic functioning of the market. Martin Hopenhayn sees clearly anarcho-capitalism when he states that "Postmodernist rhetoric has been profitably capitalized on by neoliberalism in
order to update its longed-for project of cultural hegemony."[10]

We need not go into details to realize that, if viewed solely from
this angle, postmodernity in Latin America is an ethically flawed
interpretive scheme; in light of the concrete infirmities suffered in the
continent, postmodern refinements are far too costly and irrelevant.
(César Vallejo's verses eloquently express the contrast between theoretical or aesthetic extravagance and a concrete instance of human
pain: "Un albañil cae de un techo, muere y ya no almuerza/¿Innovar,
luego, el tropo, la metáfora?")

But to dismiss postmodernity as a mere cover for market capitalism
would be to reduce its complexity and to ignore the fact that not
everyone that deploys it as an interpretive scheme of Latin American
realities can be labeled as neoconservative. There is, to be sure, a
democratizing impetus in the postmodern that has proven fruitful for
channeling alterity in Latin American, both within the continent's borders as well as vis a vis the center. There is a dialogizing aspect in the

postmodern which has served to foreground the cultural crisis brought about by dissenting micropolitics and their respective discourses in Latin America; Chiapas (as indicative in the fact that Beverley, Oviedo, and Arona's text *The Postmodern Debate in Latin America* closes with the EZLN's "Declaration from the Lacandon Jungle").[11] Latin American Feminisms, Ecological micropolitics and the promotion of Latin American Literature as a discursive space for collective reflection—a space privy to philosophical discourse—are but a few examples of spaces of alterity that are given representation by the postmodern debate.

It is well documented that the crisis of representation—and its relation to identity—has been a constant preoccupation for Latin American intellectuals and artists ever since 1492, when the *symbolic* constitution of the continent began to be coined by Europeans as a series of abstractions intended to represent and fulfill their own utopias. These abstractions were invariably embraced by Latin American elites as they struggled to forge a collective identity for the continent. In this sense, then, postmodernity as the crisis of representation that now haunts Europe and North America has been present since the very constitution of Latin America.

One must be suspicious, however, of theoretical discourses that attempt to deal with the Latin American crisis of representation in a manner that is too coherent. Instead, one ought to advocate a fluid politics of identity that, by virtue of its ductility, offers the possibility to negotiate and renegotiate notions of Latin American identities that arise from within the region's own cultural transformations as well as from "allegorizations" of Latin America constructed elsewhere.

If postmodernity has become an issue for Latin America, it is mainly because of the geographical, ethnic, and cultural plurality which comprise the region. This plurality produces the effects of postmodernity even before the word was coined as a theoretical construct. So, it seems that for the first time in its history, Latin America finds itself in the peculiar position of being at the avant-garde of Europe and North America. The crucial question that emerges here is "*avant whose lettre*" is Latin America Postmodern? Soon we realize that this position is relative to a theoretical practice exerted by the center. The challenge, then, is to articulate a practice whereby Latin America can take advantage of the postmodern "democratizing" impetus, without running the risk of being, once again, adumbrated by the "sophisticated economy of sameness" alluded to by Richard.[12]

For postmodernity to become a viable interpretive scheme for Latin American reality it ought not to stop at a simple celebration of the region's plurality. Rather it ought to pay close attention to how such plurality came about in order to thus produce a more effective reading of Latin America's heterogeneity.

Similarly, the heterogeneity that characterizes aesthetic production in Latin America comes from a process of textualization whereby Latin American artists and writers were able to appropriate technical innovations that originated in Europe in order to express local concerns. For instance, as economic elites in Latin America embraced radical modernist projects such as positivism, artistic elites developed a cultural movement partly inspired by European avant-gardes known as *Modernismo*. These aesthetic manifestations were able to think of themselves independently from the hegemony of European modernity and therefore subvert the constrictive notions of modernity espoused by the Latin American economic elites. In effect Iris Zavala argues that the "escapismo" levied against *Modernismo* is actually a genuine expression of cultural emancipation in the wake of the imperialist interventions of 1898.[13] Although Latin American *modernistas* went through a short-lived collective nihilism (see Dario's "Lo fatal"), the forthcoming avant-gardes were able to discard this nihilism in order to take advantage of the formal freedom of the European avant-gardes and thus reactualize heterogeneous realities and multitemporalities. Differently from the avant-gardes in Europe, whose exhaustion is the result of a quest of innovation based upon a construct of linear historical progression, Latin American writers like Alejo Carpentier take advantage of their experience with the European avant-gardes to rearticulate multiple traditions. Such is the case with his novel, *El reino de este mundo,* a nonmimetic novel that registers the fact that the first American emancipation is rooted not just in the prescriptions of the Enlightenment but also in those of Voodoo.

It is important to emphasize that this rearticulation does not propose a romantization of the traditional which would privilege the past

over the present, and would end up in an stringent binarism (tradi-
tional/contemporary). To do so would mean to acquiesce to the
manner in which the center frames and values our cultural production (the exotism of the primitive).

Surely, the plight of Latin America has not been one of the derealization of the real produced by the collapse of modernity's teleological
and universal projects. As pointed out, the Latin American predicament has little to do with nihilism as the inevitable consequence of the
capsizing of Reason; if anything, through the practice of colonization,
Latin America has been the test-ground of modernist utopias. In this
colonizing practice heterogeneous realities have been repressed and
far from being derealized they have thrived for survival in the only
way they could: they have hidden their signified under the guise of the
colonizer's signifier. An act of survival which, as Nelly Richard
asserts, involves an act of textualization and recycling.[14]

It could be argued that the postmodern as a label for Latin American cultural discourses must also be reappropriated with the purpose of inserting our own representational discourses within the
nuances of a global debate, always bearing in mind that the use of
such term preempts a hegemonic notion of postmodernity.

One can play with the rhetoric of postmodernity by inscribing it
within the Latin America's constitutive plurality, a ludic gesture that
appropriates *countermimetically* and in doing so undermines constrictive notions of a Latin American *autochthonous* reality.

It is by taking postmodernity's *grand recit* with a grain of salt—
by appropriating it in a carnavalesque gesture, by defusing the tendency for sameness exerted by the sublime and deconstructive strategies so characteristic of transnational postmodernity—it is by means
of these strategies that Latin America can participate in this supposedly "global" crisis of representation.

POSTMODERN OR NEOBAROQUE?

One manner of rethinking postmodernity from a Latin American perspective is by reading it in light of the Latin American neobaroque. To

be sure the equivalence baroque-postmodernity has been made, most notably in the excellent work by Christine Buci-Glucksmann, *Baroque Reason: The Aesthetic of Modernity*. Here Buci-Glucksmann argues that the baroque reason with its "logic of ambivalence is not merely another reason within modernity. Above all it is the *Reason of the Other*, of its overbrimming excess."[15] The baroque is, then, the uncanny of modernity, the region where modernity splits into a crisis. Moreover, the critic will argue that the prominent other of this reason is the feminine which always appears to problematize modernity's claims:

> But this night is one of potential desire and pleasure [*jouissance*], the night of an abyss which makes things visible. It is a baroque night—mystical perhaps. For it concerns that non-representable nothing which has perpetually haunted Western philosophy as its Oriental other, its limit, its difference. To this stage femininity has continually been summoned.[16]

Despite the poignancy of Buci-Glucksmann's work, it seems remarkable that allusions to the Latin American baroque are at best very oblique: "Imagine a city of several entrances, a labyrinthine proliferation of squares, crossroads, thoroughfares and side streets, a kind of multibody of the past and memory. In short a baroque town: Rome, Vienna, *perhaps* Mexico City."[17] Buci-Glucksmann's misgivings and omission are all the more reproachable because alluding to the Latin American baroque could only further her argument of the baroque as the reason of modernity's other. Has not Sor Juana Inés de la Cruz's femininity been summoned to the baroque stage, as evinced in the feminism *avant-la-lettre* contained in her ingenious *Respuesta a Sor Filotea de la Cruz*? But Buci-Glucksmann's omission of the Latin American baroque is questionable in a yet more profound sense. By marginalizing Latin America from her argument, she is actually marginalizing the embodiment of modernity's alterity, thus undercutting the ideological underpinning of her own thesis (i.e., to bring to the surface modernity's uncanny other). Dussel argues convincingly that European modernity, to be constituted, needed an Other to colonize and civilize under the dictums of modernity's universalizing claims: "The Other is a rustic mass dis-covered to be civilized by the European being (ser) of occidental culture, but this Other is in fact covered over (en-cubierta) in its alterity."[18] Latin America is, then, the ill-conceived product of European's modernity; it is the uncanny darkness of the enlightened projects, it was, from the moment of its inception in Western history, the prolepsis of modernity's collapse, a collapse now referred to by the center as post-modernity. If one can speak of a Latin American baroque, it is because the baroque as a European Christian crisis reached Latin America during colonization. That there is a Latin American baroque is an eloquent testimony of the fact that Latin American served as a test ground of European utopias. In no other colonized culture, in the long and painful history of European imperialism, can one find a baroque ethos as one does in Latin America. But Buci-Glucksman's exclusion of the Latin American baroque, an exemplar of the legiti-mate crisis of European modernity, is symptomatic of a Eurocentric cultural mapping that has lingered into the postmodern moment. To remap the cultural cartographies drafted in the center, we know turn to consider the Latin American baroque/neobaroque.

Unlike an allegory whose various meanings are nonetheless pre-scribed, a metaphor conjures up processes of decoding and active readings which will produce not one, but countless unencumbered meanings, thus attesting to the open-ended nature of this literary trope. According to Umberto Eco in *Opera Aperta*, the metaphor becomes a seminal element of baroque poetics and Eco identifies this historical-aesthetic period with the genesis of the open form in the work of art.[19] This baroque aperture disrupts the classical forms which were composed in relation to a central axis and which were prominent in Renaissance spatial configurations. The perception and hermeneutics of the baroque aesthetic object precludes a privileged perceptual stand; consequently, there are infinite possibilities to realize meaning. It all depends from which angle or context the work is being perceived. Such openness makes the baroque a semantically unstable and thus an inexhaustible aesthetic.

Severo Sarduy finds the baroque as the aesthetic correlate of a world vision whose notion of the universe had been radically chal-lenged by the shift that occurred from the Galilean to the Keplerian cosmic model: from Galileo's circle to Kepler's ellipsis, an ellipsis which is a decentered circle. In baroque aesthetics; the profusion of the decorative; the paratactic writing in poetry which sacrifices intelligibility (content) for music (form); the writing of metaphors which obscure their referents—all these are decentering strategies that will ultimately emphasize the primacy of the signifier and thus initiate the transit towards self-referentiality. This transit thwarts the possibility of *mimesis*: "El funcionamiento semiótico, sin punto de referencia, sin verdad última, grama móvil en constante traducción."[20]

Sarduy's theories on the collapse of referentiality in the baroque and neobaroque can be paralleled to Derrida's. Derrida brings about the collapse of the notion of structure by deconstructing the imperturbability of the epistemic center in Western metaphysics. The immediate repercussion of Derrida's poststructuralist argument is the disclosure of the itinerary of metaphysical certainties as a mere semiotic exercise prone to endless permutations. As a semiotic exercise, metaphysical discourse—previously anchored in the assurance of an unchallenged episteme—looses its metaphysical grounding and is therefore acknowledged as rhetorical representation. Thus, it lacks a platform for disqualifying literary discourse as frivolous, supplemental, nonserious, etc. For this reason, Derrida echoes Borges's dictum when the French philosopher asserts that "Borges is correct: Perhaps universal history is but the history of several metaphors."[21]

That Severo Sarduy and Lezama Lima posit the neobaroque as a aesthetic which carries metaphysical connotations, and that we can partly identify this metaphysical content with some of the characteristics of the postmodern as theorized by Jameson, Lyotard, and others has already been implicated in Buci-Glucksman's discussion on the baroque. But the equivalence that we are trying to establish here becomes relevant if we can also assert that the neobaroque as an aesthetic praxis is a distinctive Latin American expression.

Indeed, Angel Rama's analysis of the edification of baroque American cities suggests that the physiognomy of Latin America began to take shape at a juncture characterized by the semiotic circumstance advanced by *la logique de Port Royale* of 1662. This contingency was historically and qualitatively baroque, for at its core, one finds that "words began to separate themselves from things and the triple conjunction of ones and others . . . gave in to the binarism of the *Logique de Port Royale* which would theorize the independence of the order of signs."[22] Latin America originates and evolves out of this inherently baroque semiotic circumstance. It, therefore, began to exist as a vacuous signifier whose signifieds took turn: from the universalizing discourse of the *Orbis Christianus* to the imperative and also universalizing constructs of Reason.

Moreover, the semiotic baroquization of Latin America had a radically subversive consequence for the colonizing center. Reality was reduced to an interweaving of symbols which pervasively usurped their purported referent: "encomiendas," mapped cities, constitutions, and official grammars, all of which served as instruments of control to a distant absolute power that had no other resort than being represented via these signs. The traffic of these nonreferential signs ravaged the semiotic stability of the classical epistemic and aesthetic signs. These latter signs, nostalgically protracted into the "Enlightenment," became the bastions of modernity's *master narratives*, the purpose of which was precisely to hinder the irrevocable contingency born out of baroque Latin America: modernity's monologism was dialogized from its beginning by the contingency of its other; and if philosophical discourse, armed with the categorical imperative of Reason, attempted to repress modernity's contingency; the other of modernity (Latin America) attempted to challenge philosophical repression by means of the marginalized other of philosophy: baroque literature.

Georgina Sabat de Rivers's readings on the Latin American baroque illustrate the breaking down of discursive divisions between the aesthetic and the philosophical in baroque literature. It is in this literature where the configuration of the colonial subject and the colonial situation first emerges; and it is within this context that Sabat de Rivers reads the literary works of Balbuena, Domínguez Camargo, and Sor Juana. In their writings colonial alterity is formulated in terms of space and in terms of subjectivity; mainly in the case of Sor Juana who (as we know) considered the subalternity of the colonial subject in terms of the indigenous and feminine populations of Latin America. So, it is in the density of baroque poetry that the ontological configuration of a first Latin American subject begins to emerge. Indeed, Sabat de Rivers resorts to colonial poetry to chart the characteristics that distinguish the Latin American baroque from the Peninsular one. Here what is at work is an aesthetics that is concomitantly an epistemology and an ontology; thus, the divisions of spheres of knowledge advanced by modernity have collapsed in Latin America from its inception in the West. I will only refer here to some of the characteristics identified by Sabat de Rivers: "1. The initiation, independently from Peninsular influences, of baroque forms as well as an improvement over the Spanish baroque models: Balbuena, Domínguez Camargo, Sor Juana. 2. Importance of the literate city as the space where nationality begins to be forged. . . . 5. Contradictory and ambivalent discourse which carries within it the seed of the alterity of a nationalist consciousness. 6. Unconscious or disguised manipulation of the word for political ends: anti-hegemonic expressions. . . . 8. Proposal to displace Europe based on the American superiority as a vindicating process: *contra-conquista* (counter-conquest)."[23]

It is important to refer to the differentiation established by Sarduy in relation to the *primer barroco latinoamericano* and the *neobarroco*. Concomitantly with what Eco would argue, Sarduy sees, despite the structural openness of the baroque and its synchronic decenteredness, a diachronic harmony and coherence. The semantic absoluteness which engulfed the structural contingency of the first Latin American baroque was implicit in the two epistemic poles of the baroque century: God, and, as its terrestrial metaphor, the king. In the neobaroque, such semantic absoluteness no longer exists:

> Al contrario, el barroco actual, el neobarroco, refleja estructural-
> mente la inarmonía, la ruptura de la homogeniedad, del logos en
> tanto que absoluto, la carencia que constituye nuestro fundamento
> epistémico. Neobarroco del desequilibrio, reflejo estructural de un
> deseo que no puede alcanzar su objeto. [24]

At this point we return to ponder the equivalence we have previously introduced between the neobaroque and the postmodern. This equivalence is warranted not only by the fact that there is a coincidence between the theoretical claims advanced by the neobaroque (Sarduy) and poststructuralism (Derrida), as we have already mentioned; but it is also warranted by the fact that there have been attempts to use Sarduy's speculations as a model to interpret postmodern cultural products. This use, however, disregards the historicity of the term and its origins as a theoretical discourse produced in the periphery. Omar Calabrese in his book *Neo-Baroque* exemplifies this appropriation: "I intend to propose a different label for some of the cultural objects of our epoch. This label is the 'neobaroque'. . . . I should immediately like to make it clear that I have no particular affection for this term. It is simply a label like any other. It does, however, sum up the specific meanings that I intend to give to it."[25] The problem with Calabrese's statement is that the neobaroque is not just a label, it is not an empty signifier that can be pillaged and reformulated. By treating it as such he dispenses with the theoretical corpus developed by Sarduy and others, a theoretical corpus that is attentive to the historical dimension of the term and its relevance to Latin America. Calabrese's gesture—to explain the postmodern via an appropriated neobaroque—unveils a cultural neocolonialism, primarily because he does not take into account the peripheral cultural location from which the neobaroque is enunciated. He appropriates the neobaroque in the same fashion in which postmodern theoreticians appropriate Latin American cultural products to allegorically exemplify their theories. Surely, Calabrese does mention Sarduy, but he fails to acknowledge that it is Sarduy's notion of the neobaroque as a basic shattering of epistemic centrality that paves the way for his co-option of the neobaroque as a way of explaining postmodernity. Although Calabrese begins his work by referring to Foucault's conception of historiography as the writing of epistemic ruptures, he does not continue in this line. On the contrary, Calabrese specifies rigorously the scheme of his work as follows: "This is the procedure that we shall be using in these pages. *First*: to analyze cultural phenomena as texts, independently of a search for extra-textual explanations."[26] What follows from this structuralist premise is a mere taxonomy of formal characteristics to explain the aesthetic products of posmodernity; what is implied in his procedure is the dehistoricizing of the neobaroque as a cultural semiology that originates in the periphery of Europe's modernity (Latin America), one more *encubrimiento* as Enrique Dussel would argue.

If modernity's discursive division of labor (philosophy/literature) marginalizes Latin America's philosophy because it is embedded in literary discourse, the occlusion of Latin America's self-reflexive discourse is reactualized in the postmodern moment as the theoretical praxis emerging from the concrete cultural location of the Other. If the cultural products of Latin America (ostensibly its literature) display effects of pluralism, fragmentation, dissemination, pastiche, and self-referentiality, it is not because they are postmodern, or ahistorically neobaroque, which is the same thing. Rather, it is because these effects are neobaroque in as much as the neobaroque is historically rooted in the Latin American baroque. This historicity is disregarded by the North American and European postmodern theorizations. That the act of naming Latin America's cultural products and heterogeneous realities amounts to a colonial practice is obvious; an extensive bibliography already exists which deals directly with issues of postmodernity and postcolonialism in Latin America (Mignolo, Zavala, Yúdice, Richards, Canclini, Beverly, among many).

In the spirit of the Latin American baroque which is *contraconquista*,[27] as Lezama stated, we want simply to suggest a counter-hegemonic strategy that opposes postmodernity (philosophy) with the neobaroque (aesthetics). This opposition relativizes the relevance of hegemonic postmodernity; it also resists the neocolonial practice of the center in the recognition of a cultural semiology that is historically rooted in the very constitution of Latin America, and that is enunciated from the periphery by the periphery's subaltern subjects.

NOTES

1. Julio Cortázar, *Blow Up and Other Stories* (New York: Pantheon, 1977), p. 77.
2. Cited from Enrique Dussel, *The Invention of the Americas: Eclipse of the Other and the Myth of Modernity* (New York: Continuum Publishing Press, 1992), p. 20.
3. For a substantial discussion on modernity's divisions of labor and

their relationship to art in the Enlightenment and the avant-garde movements in the twentieth century, see Peter Bürger, *The Decline of Modernism* (Pennsylvania: Pennsylvania University Press, 1992), chaps. 1–3, pp. 3–48.

4. Commenting on Umberto Eco's Postcript to *The Name of the Rose*, Calinescu states: "The new element in Eco's treatment of the problem is his insistence that the postmodernist re-discovery of the past or of the 'already said' cannot be innocent and that this lack of innocence must be fully acknowledged. Irony, playfulness, parodic and self-parodic nostalgia are some of the ways of doing so." Matei Calinescu, *Five Faces of Modernity: Modernism, Avant-Garde, Decadence, Kitsch, Postmodernism* (Durham: Duke University Press, 1987), p. 277.

5. For a discussion on difference and deferral see Jacques Derrida, "Structure Sign and Play in the Discourse of the Human Sciences," in *Writing and Difference*, trans. Alan Bass (Chicago, 1978).

6. "The sublime is a different sentiment. It takes place . . . when the imagination fails to present an object which might, if only in principle, come to match a concept." Jean François Lyotard, "What is Postmodernity?" in *Postmodernism: A Reader*, ed. Thomas Docherty (New York: Columbia University Press, 1993), p. 43.

7. Lyotard, "The Sublime and the Avant-Garde," in Docherty, *Postmodernism: A Reader*, p. 255.

8. Frederic Jameson, *Postmodernism or, the Cultural Logic of Late Capitalism* (Durham: Duke University Press, 1991), chap. 1, pp. 1–54.

9. Lyotard,"What is Postmodernity," p. 46.

10. Matin Hopenhyan, "Postmodernism and Neoliberalism," in *The Postmodern Debate in Latin America*, ed. John Beverly, Jose Oviedo, and Michael Arona (Durham: Duke University Press, 1995), p. 98.

11. Ibid., pp. 311–13.

12. Addressing the deconstruction between center and periphery and Lyotard's disposition to celebrate difference as a positive aspect in postmodernity, Richard warns: "The fact is, however, that no sooner are these differences—sexual, political, racial and cultural posited and valued that they become subsumed into the metacategory of the 'undifferentiated' which means that all singularities immediately become indistinguishable and interchangeable in a new, sophisticated economy of 'sameness'." Nelly Richard, "Postmodernism and Periphery," in Docherty, *Postmodernism: A Reader*, p. 468.

13. Zavala makes this point clear at the outset of her work: "The focus of my reading consists in the following points: 1. That modernism is not a set of formal features in a given text, but a chronotope including both literary discourse and social life. . . . 4. That in that framework, in the Hispanic world, the contested field of modernism became an organic ideology at the turn of the century, creating a hegemony of cultural formalization founded

in the logic of identity, while bringing into questions modern forms of capitalist expansions." In Iris M. Zavala, *Colonialism and Culture: Hispanic Modernisms and the Social Imaginary* (Bloomington: Indianan University Press, 1992), p. 5.

14. "The periphery has always made its own mark on the series of statements emitted by the dominant culture and has recycled them in different contexts in such a way that the original systematization are subverted, and their claim to universality is undermined." Richard, "Postmodernism and Periphery," p. 470.

15. Christine Buci-Glucksmann, *Baroque Reason: The Aesthetics of Modernity*, trans. Patrick Camiller (London: Sage Publications,1994), p. 39.

16. Ibid., p. 130.

17. Ibid., p. 39. Emphasis added.

18. Dussel, *The Invention of the Americas*, p. 36.

19. For a comparison between the medieval allegory and the baroque metaphor, see Umberto Eco, *Obra Abierta*, trans. Roser Berdagué (Barcelona: Ariel, 1985), p. 77.

20. Severo Sarduy, *Barroco* (Buenos Aires: Editorial Sudamericana, 1974), p. 89.

21. Jacques Derrida, "Violence and Metaphysics," *Writing and Difference*, p. 9

22. Angel Rama, *La ciudad letrada* (Hanover: Ediciones del norte, 1984), p. 9. (My translation.)

23. Georgina Sabat de Rivers, *Estudios de literatura latinoamericana: Sor Juana Inés de la Cruz y otros poetas* (Barcelona: Promociones y Publicaciones Universitarias, 1992), p. 41.

24. Sarduy, *Barroco*, p.103.

25. Omar Calabrese, *Neo-Baroque* (Princeton: Princeton University Press, 1992), p. 14.

26. Ibid., p. 21.

27. "Repitiendo la frase de Weisbach, adaptándola a lo americano, podemos decir que entre nosotros el barroco fue un arte de contraconquista" Lezama Lima, *La expresion americana*, in *Obras Completas* (Mexico: Torre Agilar, 1977), vol. 2, p. 303. Like Buci-Glucksmann, Lezama sees in the contingency and arbitrariness that characterizes the baroque imagination a counter hegemonic stand which as Buci-Glucksmann has suggested becomes derisive of modernity's rationalism. In the following fragment by Lezama, the author writes ironically on Hegel's misreading of Latin American "desgano" and offers a counterhegemonic reading which stresses resistance: "Esa imaginación elemental propicia a la creación de unicornios y ciudades levantadas en una lejanía sin comprobación humana, nos ganaban aquel calificativo de niños , con que nos regalaba Hegel en sus orgul-

losas Lecciones sobre Filosofía de la Historia Universal, calificativo que se nos extendía muy al margen de aquella ganancia evangélica para los pequeñuelos , sin la cual no se penetraba al reino. Hay allí una observación que no he visto subrayada, que es necesario crear en el americano necesidades que levanten sus actividades de gozosa creación. Además de la función y el órgano, hay que crear la necesidad de incorporar ajenos paisajes, de utilizar sus potencias generatrices, de movilizarse para adquirir piezas de soberbia y áurea soberana `Recuerdo haber leído—dice Hegel con una displicencia casi exenta de ironía—que a medianoche un fraile tocaba una campana para recordar a los indígenas sus deberes conyugales' ?Han meditado en lo que implica la testadura afirmación de Hegel, de desarrollar en el americano el concepto y la vivencia de la necesidad? La gana española que pasa a nosotros como desgana, falta de rechazo y aproximación. La gana española es una manifestación de signo negativo; no tener ganas en el español es apertrecharse para una resitencia si alguien pretende sacarlo de sus apetencias. En el desgane americano hay como un vivir satisfecho en la lejanía, en la ausencia, en e frío estelar ganando las distancias dominadas por el impersonal rey del abeto." Ibid., pp. 297–98.

Nelly Richard

FEMINISM AND POSTMODERNISM

To unite these two fields of discourse, postmodernism and feminism, presents as a first inconvenience, the variety of definitions and situations to which each term confusedly refers to. Postmodernism combines theories and styles, forms and fashions which run indiscriminately through academic knowledge, quotidian aesthetics, and market policies; juxtaposing in a promiscuous mesh environmental signifieds which can be interpreted as a "reaction" (the neoconservative return to the fetichization of the capitalist order), as "resistance" (the emergence of new modalities of critical interventions that attack the social and cultural officiality. In the case of feminism, "what began as a vindication in the face of the exclusion and devaluation of women has rapidly become into a plurality of programs: liberal feminism, radical feminism and socialist feminism."[1] And also into a variety of theoretical options that cover from the essentialist and culturalist feminism to the poststructuralist and deconstructive feminism.[2]

The second problem for us consists in that the theoretical debates which articulate and confront these varieties of feminist and postmodernist options are debates which flaunt the international trademark of metropolitan thought and they should therefore be rearticu-

From Nelly Richard, *Masculino/Femenino: Prácticas de la diferencia y cultura democratia* (Chile: Francisco Legers Editor, 1993). Translated by Pedro Lange-Churión.

lated for the purpose of local self-signification in opposition to the centralizing paradigm of the Euro-North American theory.

POSTMODERN DEBATE AND THE STRATEGIC PROFITING FROM THE SYMTOMALOGY OF THE CRISIS

Many Latin American feminists believe that we should not think in terms of modernity/postmodernity, given that we have not been participants in the situation which originated and formulated the crisis of modernity in the postindustrial contexts where such crisis was established as a discourse and as a theory.[3] It is true that we have not been incorporated—and if we had only haphazardly—to the conceptualization and materialization of the dominant design of European modernity, neither as a sexual gender (woman), nor as a cultural identity (Latin America). It is also true that we have never been "strong" subjects of the tradition whose crumbling of values is presented as drama by a Western philosophy that today laments the fall of the exclusive and excluding privilege of its universal metalanguage. But I do not believe that because we are not part of the historical and geographical discursive perimeter where the crisis of postmodernity is diagnosed and discussed, we should be kept from the opportunity to pronounce ourselves in relation to the ambiguities of registers of such crisis, thus profiting from its most ductile figures.

Postmodern discourse is one that emerged in the interior of a culture that always sought to administer linearly the consecutivity of the "pre" and the "post" form the *unique* point of view of its historically dominant rationalization. These abuses of viewpoints culminate today in the postmodern operation of the metropolitan synthesis of economic and cultural power, and of the combinations of series globally ramified by multinational capitalism. But postmodern discourse, like any other discourse, offers discontinuities and textual openings that help take strategic advantage of the fractures of its perspectives, in favor of a critical refunctionalization (Latin American) of the most insurgent vocabularies related to the crisis' narrative.[4]

Already, some of the postmodern utterances shed a bouncing light on some of our areas of cultural tension either not verbalized until now, or lacking eloquence for not having been faced yet with questions that would compel them to mark and unmark themselves so intensively. Thus it happens with various areas of contradiction which form *pliegues* (folds) in the discourse of Latin American modernity. A first postmodern suggestion encourages the rereading of modernity from what is denied by modernity itself, or from what in its interior resists the classical guidance of its pure enlightened reason: what hides in the most shady areas of its "unreasonable reason" (Buci-Glucksmann). These rereadings already favor a perception of Latin American modernity as a pluralistic interplay of uneven rationalities. And they bring us closer to a *heterodox* comprehension of the residual modernity of peripheral Latin American: a modernity which joins and disjoints heterogeneous times and spaces plurally stratified for discordant tendencies (myth and progress, orature and telecommunication, folklore and industry, traditions and the market place, ritual and simulacrum). A modernity, then, whose inbreedings and transplants bring it closer to the *impurity* of collage (and its interplay of diverse textures and surfaces) than to the purity of an ethical-religious rituality that will remain as an nonpolluted *bedrock* because "it preserves without modifications its original nuclei of values."[5]

Another postmodern unveiling of these areas of "unreasonable reason" teaches us that "the archeology of the modern has been obsessed with the feminine": the baroque metaphor of an alterity and a heterogeneity that always threatened to make unstable the I-identity of classical rationalism.[6] It is for this reason that in each phase of crisis there appears along with "the question of modernity" the question of woman and the question of "the feminization of culture." That other area of plural negativity of the modern reemphasized by the critical move of postmodernity help us analyze "the series of correlations to be built among the culture of crisis . . . the deconstruction of the self-aware classical masculine subject and the re-questioning of the masculine/feminine schism."[7]

But it is necessary to go beyond the benefit brought about by these suggestions of postmodern rereadings of the modernity that celebrates the blending and scrambling of the hybrid languages of Latin American transculturization, or that unfold the baroque twist of the hidden fold (*pliegue*) of the feminine. Other arguments also in favor of the potentiality of critical performance that justifies the transference and peripheral recontextualization of one of the postmodern themes are the notions of discenteredment and alterity.

The antiauthoritarian modalities of a new thought, attracted by the explosion and pulverization of categories such as system, center and hierarchy, have made the figure of the *margin* one of utmost critical tension. A figure which is nurtured on the postmodern idea of the *center's dehierarchization* (of the images of the Center) in order to redistribute the values between the canonical and the anticanonical, the dominant and the minority, the hegemonic and the subaltern, etc., in favor of what has been hitherto dispensed with and debased by the hierarchies of official culture (logocentric, phalocentric-eurocentric, etc.). The fact that "the position of women is structurally inscribed" in the marks of "the absence, the periphery and the Other" has persuaded a number of postmodern theoreticians that "feminism is the paradigmatic political discourse of postmodernity."[8]

Undoubtedly, Latin American feminism must be alert and must generate resistances to the manner in which the Euro-North American theory usually vindicates the figure of the Other in order to *administer its rhetoric* as an internationalist privilege: the decentered center speaks in representation of the Other, but it does so by denying its *others* (those in the periphery) the opportunity to fight against the mechanisms of discursive and institutional intervention and confrontation that would constitute and institute them in *subjects* rather than objects of the discourse of otherness.[9] But, apart from exercising surveillance on the stratagems of this "aestheticizing marginocentrality" (Yúdice), Latin American feminism must also worry about knowing where the grooves and interstices are of the metropolitan theory that can be taken advantage of in order to twist or deviate in its favor the paradigm of the Other. And it also must determine what alliances could and should be reached between certain peripheral discourses and certain metropolitan theories: the ones willing to explore the cartographies of an "alternative postmodernity,"[10] those that trespass the preestablished borders of official postmodernity.

In this sense, to venture into the crossroads of the postmodern debate and feminism is not only an exciting prospect, but it is also a necessary one, since these crossroads discussions are vital for Latin American feminism: discussions about identity and power (about margins and centers; about centers, decenteredments, and recenterement of cultural power), but also discussions about strategies of the theoretical and political inscription of difference (woman, periphery) in the problematic of "the Difference" as a way to dialogue with and at the same time question the postmodernist theorization of the Other that are validated in the international centers.

It is true that many of the official comentators of postmodernism were not energetic enough in maintaining critical oppositions to the conservative regainings of the cultural institution, conservative regainings that profited from the antimodernist slogan about the death of the avant-gardes in order to return to the idealist-bourgeoise tradition that characterizes academic culture. It is also easy to prove that the slogan about the failure of utopian radicalisms and the revolutionary ideologies, about the discredit of leftist militancy, usually operates as an alibi that is utilized to celebrate the return to a real-socius, freed from critical interventions and transformed, once again, into an object of narcissistic contemplation. The same postmodern slogan about the plural (plurality and pluralism) is usually underpinned by an annulment of a judgment which makes differences serve passively the conformist aloofness of the *"todo vale"* (anything goes), now freed from the market of goods and messages.

But along with the demobilizing force of skeptical relativism and contemplative nihilism that characterize a particular postmodern style, there exist, within the very postmodern field, tendencies whose confrontational energy highlight projects of critical and social interventions. And rather than simply lamenting and condemning those postmodernist declinations (perhaps the most visible ones) that serve as ideological disguises to the market's scams in transnational capitalism, or that function as perverse allies to the neoliberal rightist move, "we should try to rescue postmodernity from its collusion with neoconservatism, wherever such operation would seem possible. We should also try to reflect whether postmodernity conceals productive contradictions and a critical and oppositional potential. If the postmodern is a historical and cultural condition (no matter how incipient), then the oppositional and strategic practices should be located *in the interior* of postmodernity, not of course in its shining facades."[11]

The postmodern register emerges from the crisis of the totalizing metanarratives based upon the lineal configuration subject-reason-science-progress of the philosophical and historical thought of modernity. That crisis can be interpreted—and it is to our advantage to do so—as the product of the fractures in the authority of the omnipotent rationality of the transcendental subject of universal modernity. It can be interpreted as a fissure zone of the great narratives of modernity's epistemology, an epistemology that today sees weakened its claim to ground the absolute subject of sovereign truth.

Postmodernity as the register of "a crisis of cultural authority, specifically the authority conferred upon western European culture and its institutions,"[12] supposes the questioning of many of the conceptions which determined a model of cultural identity: that based upon the omni-comprehensive totalizations of the finite systems of historical and social exegesis. The notions of *totality* came into crisis (the disintegrated fragment replaces the completeness of the Whole), of *centrality* (there is not anymore a fixed point to justify the superior dominance of an absolute reference), of unity (the monological thought of the One has been defied by the scattered heterogeneity of the multiple).

In theorizing the fracture of modernity's universal rationalism, a rationalism which made absolute the consciousness of the dominating-universal subject as the only one possessing knowledge, the postmodern incision in fact dismantles the archetypes of representation which centered its authority in the primacy of the white-educated-metropolitan-male subject. The delegitimation and dehierarchization of this colonial subject opens new possibilities of signification and participation for identities and practices so far censored by the absolute truth implicit in the male-western representation.[13] These marginal identities and practices press against the hegemonic configurations of the central culture in order to make unstable its dominant view point. Women and periphery, along with the respective debates that emerge from these identities (feminism, third-worldism, and poscolonialism), are part of this theoretical and cultural landscape of new expressions that have nothing to loose—and that have much to gain—from the erosion and fractures of the normative identity of universal modernity.

The postmodern problematic of the "other" is one we could *resharpen* by means of a gesture that takes advantage of the fissures generated in the system of cultural authority in the central thought. To discern, amidst the flow of propositions originating in the metropolitan culture, those already sensitive to the discussion of its vices of authority, thus displaying a selective ability which favors the periphery by giving it elements to thus *reintentionalize* the meaning of the center's failures. In this sense the disintegration of the totalizing paradigms of the dominant European modernity motivates the construction of alternative and dissenting expressions whose defiant virtuality should not be abandoned by the periphery because the articulation of such disintegration has been theoretically drafted in the center. It is possible to rearticulate the postmodern discourse of discenteredment in new poetics and politics emerging from the margins; these would in turn incite the subaltern voices to strike a blow to the canon of cultural authority, basing themselves upon the conflicting points of view unraveled in the center by the social actors which denounce and respond to the dominant narratives of the superior culture. The critical potential of these new positions (positions that by virtue of being subversive against the regime of institutional capture, destabilize its hegemonic repertoire) must be utilized reinterpreted by the cultural periphery in its disputes against the center's reterritorializations.

FEMINISM OF EQUALITIES AND FEMINISM OF THE DIFFERENCE(S)

In order to describe the relation of feminism to the change of scenarios modernity/postmodernity, one can allude to the passage between a feminism of "equality" which is conceived as emancipation in the historical matrix of modernity and based upon the vector of social progress as corroboration of human justice, and a feminism of "difference" which answers in a postmodern fashion to the disbelief in the universal notion (modern) of Identity as a historical and philosophical metareference.

But the feminism of "difference" is not a field of positions that is harmonized in relation to the defense of arguments which are concomitantly postmodern. There exists a contradictory variety of meanings for "difference" which separate the diverse feminism grouped under this name.[14] One could state the following:

—difference as *difference among women*, seeking to correct the a-historical tendency which represents *the* woman without properly specifying experiential variables (race, ethnicity, class) which in turn diversify each group outside the gender coordinate.

—difference *as difference between men and women* (a biological-sexual difference culturally reinterpreted by the gender mark), which is based upon a division-opposition between masculinity and femininity taken as separate models of experience and culture.

—difference as *relational and positional signified of identity*, which indicates to us that masculinity and femininity are subjective *modes* of construction and strategies of critical manipulation of the codes of symbolic and cultural representation.

If it is true that these three signifieds (meanings) coexist under the designation of "feminism of the difference," the term ostensibly carries the mark of the antiessentialist and deconstructive feminism: a feminism which has resorted intensively to psychoanalysis, to semiotics, to deconstruction, thus contradicting the well-known suspicion of radical feminism that has always mistrusted theory, considering it an apparatus of clear masculine domination. Such feminism of "difference" originates in the postmetaphysical tenet which asserts that identity is not anymore the self-sufficient and unified reference of transcendental idealism, but the stage where psychological and social forces intersected and *decentered* the fiction of an I transparent and identical to itself. For such poststructuralist feminism, the fissures and disintegration of the One-subject makes it nonviable to continue thinking femininity as the fixed and constant value of a homogeneous substance. Beyond inquiring about the feminine in terms of *interiority*, such feminism goes on to reflect upon the *exteriority* of *signs* (representations) that construct and socially transmit the images of femininity with which the subjects assemble their identities, either by repetition or by negation, deriving and selecting roles and forms of subjectivity from the changing and multiple repertory of culture.

But the theoretical validity of these gender-feminine redefinitions of "identity" now thought as "difference" cannot cancel out the historical significance of the feminist struggles for sexual equality: "If we opt for the egalitarian feminism of the Enlightenment, . . . if we abide by it, we will reproduce a culture prone to erase differences, a culture that simply regulates the progress of women's conditions in relation to the progress of men's condition. We will remain thus on the surface of professional, cultural and political conditions ending up in an internalization of the masculine model. But if we limit a feminism of the differences we risk reproducing a hierarchy, we risk disregarding the forms of political syndicalist and professional struggle with the excuse that women, in as much as they are different and in order to affirm such gender difference, does not need to antagonize men in all these arenas."[15]

The relations between feminism of equality and feminism of difference point to a zone of complex tensions among the different positions which simultaneously direct and divide the problematics of today's feminism:

1. The position to continue advancing in the social and political struggle for the suppression of the inequalities that continue to oppress women at various levels of patriarchal domination=struggle for equality.

2. The position not to sacrifice in the equality man/woman the specificity and differentially of the feminine, since annulling such differentiation subsumes women within the general category of the

human and disempowers (by neutralizing it) its critique against the masculine as universal vindication of difference.

3. The position to avoid the separatism implied in "difference," a separatism that isolates the culture of women as a separate culture, and which reessentializes the absolute feminine leaving the system of polar identities untouched=rejection of the opposition identity/difference and *multiplication of the differences* as "differences which confuse, disorganize and make ambiguous the meaning of any fixed binary opposition."[16]

The complexity of this game of critical operation which articulates and disarticulates itself, seems to recommend that the new political strategies of feminism ought to learn to alternate and combine these positions, always tacitly judging "the usefulness of certain arguments" (in favor of equality, difference or differences) "within certain discursive contexts" without implying the invocation of "absolute qualities in women and men."[17]

The relativization of categories not thought of as fixed substances, but as flexible constructions, is perhaps on of the theoretical repostulations of feminism; it works best in synchrony with certain postmodern propositions, those related to the pluralization of meaning, the fragmentation of identity and the dissemination of power.

Pluralization of sense: the Text, history and society as texts ceased to obey a transcendental meaning which made the comprehension of the real subordinate to its unique and hierarchical code of reading. Signs, then, proliferate and disseminate themselves horizontally, in provisory and transitory routes of signification.

Fragmentation of the identities: the subject owner of itself—homogenous and transparent—of metaphysical rationalism disintegrated in various "I's" which unsteadily combined plural markers of sexual, social, and cultural identification. Dissemination of power: there is not anymore either a homogenous polarity or a fixed representation that places power in *one* center but in diffuse networks which multiply and scatter their points of contention and lines of confrontation. Such detotalizing of the categories of sign, culture, and power invites feminism to reformulate its antipatriarchal critique with the support of new "theories that would allow us to think in terms of pluralities and diversities in place of unities and universals";[18] with these in mind, these new theories would purposely forge alliances with those postmodern formulations which criticize the monological identities of totalizing reason.

The appropriation made by a certain feminism sympathetic with poststructuralist theory emphasizes "identity" as *construction, position, and relation.* In other words, it emphasizes an active transformation of the first piece of information of biographical corporality by means of which the cultural symbolizations, changing and changeable, revoke the supportive tenet of an identity defined in and of itself once and for all.

Taking this deessentializing tendency to extremes risked that the abandonment of gender (sexuality) in favor of the feminine as subject's position (textuality) would have a completely deactivating effect in the assumption of a feminist consciousness and its willingness for social change: if women only existed abstractly, as positionalities of discourses, rather than existing concretely as sex, there would be nothing worth fighting for, in the name of women's liberation against the material and symbolic violence of patriarchy.[19] But the vindication of the subject as position and discursive strategy has no reason to distance itself from the material analysis that questions the conditions of signification and power in which the *politics of identity* is concretely articulated and disarticulated; "the question of how texts, images and other cultural artifacts constitute the subjectivity of a historical question"[20] and also of a sexualized question. There is no reason to understand that the emphasis on the *positionality* of the feminine (in the *game of the localizations* of the sign of sexual difference whose mobility trespasses the ontological tenet of the referent "body") necessarily implies the degendering of sexual difference. It is possible to combine, in its respective levels of efficacy, the move to keep advancing gender as a platform of social vindication that springs from the signifier "woman," with the other move that consists of confronting the codes of symbolic and interpretive power from a mobile plurality, a plurality of positions-postures of critical subjectivity which displaces and spins the constellation of "minority futures" of the "feminine."

To approach the question of the feminine not so much as the expression of an I that assumes surreptituosly (because of its biographical and corporeal substratum) the representation of a total and absolute femininity, but as a *problematic of subjectivity*, demands in any case from feminism that it work out a theoretical articulation that recognizes each subject as being transversed by a conflictive multiplicity of pulsation of identity and logics of power. Only a feminism that theorizes the feminine as force of intervention in / of the politics of identity, responds to the necessity that "in neocolonized countries the submission of women be studied in terms of global relations of power."[21]

The Latin American context is characterized by the fact that the mechanisms of oppression and repression are always multiple (colonialist, neoimperialist, militaristic, and patriarchal, multicapitalistic, etc.) and they interweave its mechanisms *diagonally*: the masculine-patriarchal ideology goes through subjects, discourses, and institutions, tying knots (in intersections and superpositions) with other mechanisms of power which are then combined in hybrid formation of utterances. It is convenient to eviscerate the imbrication of these multiple figures of systems, given that the points of major symbolic violence are the ones saturated by the coactive exercise of the various logics of domination which strengthen and gain power from each other. To move from one figure to another in order to disentangle the nets of tacit complicity subjecting the different utterances, implies that the "feminine" displaces with a great plurality of critical movements in order to dismantle the inner workings of reasons and powers which search, among other things, fasten us to fixed categorizations of homogeneous identities: *the* feminine identity, *the* Latin American identity, etc. To contradict these categorizations not only makes sense to the theoretical analysis: It is proven daily that "there are feminine bread-winners, nurturing males, feminist mothers and house wives; many middle class white males who teach black and feminist literature; in short, there is confusion and quite a number of gender transgression in our daily commitments." These transgressions not only make us believe that the old discourse of absolute masculinity and femininity has become outdated, but they also make us look again at "the normative content of the feminist argument,"[22] in terms of the multipositionality of the subject which has begun to acquire concrete forms in accordance with the present diversification and complexity of the sexual and social roles which tip over the divisive hierarchies and frontiers of the traditional notion of identity. A nonnormative revision of militant feminism antipatriarchal slogan, a revision that would in turn be consist in allowing dimensions such as creativity, fantasy and pleasure, taste and style, to mix *aesthetic pulsation* with *will to change* in order to intertwine the repertories of figure and the techniques of *seduction* and *sedition*.

NOTES

1. Jean Franco, "If you let me talk: the struggle for the interpretive power," *Casa de las Americas* no. 171 (Cuba-1988).

2. Teresa de Laurentis speaks of the Anglo-American feminist tendency to "typologize," define, and mark the various "feminisms" by means of an ascendant scale of theoretical and political sophistication where the "essentialism gravitates heavily in the lowest point"; "the essentialism in as much as a belief in a "feminine nature," is associated with cultural feminism, the "separatist" feminism, radical feminism (with it innuendoes), and occasionally, liberal feminism while socialist feminism and nowadays poststructuralist and deconstructive feminism appear in the highest point of the scale." This citation belongs to her text: " the essence of the triangle or taking seriously the risk of essentialism: feminist theory in Italy, U.S.A. and Great Britain," *Debate Feminista*, no. 2 (México-1990).

3. I refer as an example the following citation by Raquel Olea: "The controversy Postmodernity/Modernity cannot be part of our Latin American feminist discourse, a discourse whose ambiguous integration into the cultural processes originating in eurocentricism impedes its positioning in relation to its own reality. . . . Moreover, we women have not been subjects neither of the modernist project, nor of this project crises."
This citation belongs to a fragment of her article "Feminismo una utopía que tiene lugar" delivered in the Conference *"Modernidad/Postmodernidad: una encrucijada latinoamericana"* jointly organized by ILET in Buenos Aires and *Revista de Crítica Cultural de Santiago de Chile* (University of Chile—Mayo 1990).

4. This argument is incorporated in my text "Latinoamérica y la Postmodernidad." *Revista de Crítica Cultural* no. 3, de Santiago de Chile (Universidad de Chile—Mayo 1990).

5. This citation from "Ritual y Palabra" by Pedro Morandé (Centro

Andino de Historia 1980 Lima) is taken from the text by Sonia Montecino/Mariluz Dussuel/Angélica Wilson, "Identidad Femenina y Modelo Mariano en Chile," in *Mundo de mujer, Continuidad y Cambio* (Santiago de Chile-Cem-1988), p. 505. As a counterpoint (complement) to the thesis of Pedro Morandé (as reformulated by Sonia Montecino), I refer the reader to José Joaquín Brunner and Nestor García Canclini's reflections on the "cultural heterogeneity" or the "multitemporal heterogeneity" of Latin American modernity: José Joaquín Brunner, *Un espejo trizado* (Santiago de Chile Flacso 1988) y Nestor García Canclini: *Culturas híbridas* (México-Grijalbo-1989).

6. Christine Buci-Glucksmann, *La raison baroque: De Baudelaire a Benjamin)"* (Paris-Ed Galileé-1984), p. 34.

7. Ibid., p. 33. My translation.

8. Laura Kipnis, "Feminism: The political Conscience of Postmodernism?" in *Universal Abandon?* ed. Andrew Ross for Social Text (Minneapolis: The University of Minnesota Press, 1989), p. 160. My translation.

9. "What we must eliminate are systems of representation that carry with them the kind of authority which, to my mind, has been repressive because it doesn't permit or make room for interventions on the part of those represented. . . . The alternative would be a representational system that was participatory and collaborative, non-coercive, rather than imposed, but as you know, this is not a simple matter. We have no immediate access to the means of producing alternative systems. Perhaps, it would be possible through other, less exploitative fields of knowledge. But first we must identify those social/cultural/ political formations which would allow for a reduction of authority and increased participation in the production of representations, and proceed from there." Edward Said, "In the shadow of the west; an interview with Edward Said," in *Discourses: Conversations in Postmodern art and culture* (New York: The New Museum of Contemporary Art, 1990), p. 95.

10. George Yúdice in "El conflicto de postmodernidades," *Nuevo Texto Crítico*, no. 7 (Stanford University, 1991).

11. Andreas Huyssen, "Guía del Posmodernismo," in *El debate modernidad/posmodernidad*, compilación y prólogo de Nicolás Casullo (Buenos Aires-Punto Sur-1989), pp. 289, 290.

12. Craig Owens, "El discurso de los otros: Las feministas y el posmodernismo," in *La posmodernidad*, selección y prólogo de Hal Foster (Barcelona-Kairos-1985), p. 93.

13. To foreshadow optimistically these opportunities must not make us forget the following:

"Si uno de los aspectos más sobresalientes de nuestra cultura posmoderna es la presencia de una insistente voz feminista . . . , las teorías del posmodernismo han tendido ya sea a hacer caso omiso de esa voz, ya sea a reprimirla. La ausencia de comentarios sobre la diferencia sexual en los escritos acerca del posmodernismo, así como el hecho de que pocas mujeres han participado en el debate modernismo/posmodernismo, sugiere que éste podría ser otra invención masculina maquinada para excluir a las mujeres." ["If one of the most outstanding aspects of our postmodern culture is the presence of an insistent feminist voice . . . , postmodern theories have been inclined to either disregard this voice, or repress it. The absence of comments on sexual difference in postmodern writings, and the fact that only a few women have participated in the debate modernity/postmodernity, suggests that this [postmodernity] could be one more masculine invention devised to exclude women."] Owens, "El discurso de los otros," p. 100.

14. Michéle Barret, " El concepto de diferencia," in *Debate Feminista,* no. 2 (México-1990).

15. Jacques Derrida, "Feminismo y De(s)construcción," in *Revista de Crítica Cultural,* no. 3 (Santiago de Chile-1991).

16. Joan W. Scott, "Igualdad versus Diferencia: Los usos de la teoría postestructuralista," in *Debate Feminista,* no. 3 (México-1992).

17. Ibid.

18. Ibid.

19. The same thing happens when one takes too seriously certain modernist-postmodernist statements related with the "death of the subject," despite the fact that such statements have been formulated in order to attack the bourgeois idealism which consecrated the metaphysical subject: In fact, we must ask ourselves if the slogan "the death of the subject" "is not sabotaging the possibility of defying an *ideology of the subject* (white, male, of middle strata) and of developing differing and alternative notions of subjectivity." Huyssen, "Guía del Postmodernismo," p. 304.

20. Ibid.

21. Kemy Oyarzún, "Edipo, autogestión y producción textual: Notas sobre cítica literaria feminista," in *Cultural and historical grounding for hispanic and lusobrazilian feminist literary criticism,* ed. Hernán Vidal (Minneapolis Minnesota: Institute for the study of Ideologies and Literature, 1989), p. 593.

22. Kate Soper, "El postmodernismo y sus malestares," *Debate Feminista,* no. 3 (México-Marzo 1992).

Guillermo Gómez-Peña

END-OF-THE-CENTURY
TOPOGRAPHY REVIEW

FIRST WORLD

a tiny and ever shrinking conceptual archipelago from which 80 percent of the resources of our planet are still administered and controlled

SECOND WORLD

aka "geopolitical limbo," includes Greenland, the Antarctic continent, the oceans, the mineral world, and the dismembered Soviet Bloc

THIRD WORLD

the ex-underdeveloped countries, and the communities of color within the ex-First World

From Guillermo Gómez-Peña, *The New World Border: Prophecies, Poems, and Loqueras for the End of the Century* (San Francisco: City Lights, 1996), pp. 244–45. Reprinted with permission.

FOURTH WORLD

a conceptual place where the indigenous inhabitants of the Americas meet with the deterritorialized peoples, the immigrants, and the exiles; it occupies portions of all the previous worlds

FIFTH WORLD

virtual space, mass media, the U.S. suburbs, art schools, malls, Disneyland, the White House, and La Chingada

QUESTIONS FOR THE READER:

Where exactly is the United States located?

In which world (or worlds) are *you* located?

Has your community been left out of the above categories?

For which world does your art speak?

Are you experiencing an identity crisis?

BIBLIOGRAPHY

Abellán, Manuel. *Censura y creación literaria en España (1939–1976)*, Barcelona: Península, 1980.

Abu-Lughod, Janet. *Before European Hegemony: The World System A.D. 1250–1350*. New York: Oxford University Press, 1989.

Adorno, Theodor W. *Negative Dialectics*, New York: Continuum, 1983.

———. *Philosophy of Modern Music*, New York: Seabury Press, 1983.

Ainsa, F. *De la Edad de Oro al El Dorado: Génesis del discurso utópico Americano*. México: F.C.E., 1992.

Alcoff, Linda Martí, and Eduardo Mendieta. *Thinking from the Underside of History: Enrique Dussel's Philosophy of Liberation*. Lanham: Rowman and Littlefield, 2000.

Amin, S. *El desarrollo desigual. Ensayo sobre las formaciones sociales del capitalismo periférico*, Barcelona: Fontanella, 1974.

Amin, Samir. *L'accumulation à l'échelle mondiale*, Paris: Anthropos, 1970.

Arditi, Benjamín. "Una gramática postmoderna para pensar lo social." In *Cultura política y democratización*. Edited by Norbert Lechner. Santiago: CLACSO, 1987.

Anzaldúa, Gloria. *Borderlands/La Frontera: The new Mestiza*, San Francisco: Spinsters/Aunt Lute, 1987.

Aubert, Jacques D. *Rhetoric and Culture in Lacan*. Cambridge: Cambridge University Press, 1996.

Barret, Michéle. "El concepto de diferencia." *Revista de Crítica Cultural* 2 (México, 1990).

Barth, John. "Literature of Exhaustion." In *The Friday Book*. New York: Putnam, 1984.

———. "The Literature of Replenishment." In *The Friday Book*. New York: Putnam, 1984.

Baudrillard, J. *Crítica de la Economía Política de Signo*. Madrid: Siglo XXI, 1972.

Bell, Daniel. *The Cultural Contradictions of Capitalism*. New York: Basic Books, 1976.

Bell, Daniel. *The Coming of Post-Industrial Society*. New York: Basic Books, 1973.

Benet, Juan. *La inspiración y el estilo*. Madrid: Revista de Occidente, 1966.

Bernal, Martin. *Black Athena: The Afroasiatic Roots of Classical Civilization*. New Brunswick: Rutgers University Press, 1989, t.I.

Bertaux, Pierre. *Africa. Desde la prehistoria hasta los Estados actuales*. Madrid: Siglo XXI, 1972.

Blanco Aguinaga, Carlos, Julio Rodríguez-Puértolas, and I. M. Zavala, eds. *Historia social de la literatura española (en lengua castellana) I-III*. Madrid: Castalia, 1978–1979.

Blaut, J. M., ed. *1492: The Debate on Colonialism, Eurocentrism, and History*. Trenton, N.J.: Africa World Press, 1992.

Braudel, F. "Monnaies et civilisation: de l'or du Soudan à l'argent d'Amérique," en *Annales ESC* t.I/1 (1996): 12–38.

Brenner, Rober. "Das Weltsystem. Theoretische und Historische Perspektiven." In *Perspektiven des Weltsystems*. Edited by J. Blaschke, Frankfort: Campus Verlag, 1983, pp. 80–111.

Britto-García, Luis. "Critiques of Modernity: Avant-Garde, Counterculture, Revolution." *The South Atlantic Quarterly* 92 (1993).

Brunner, J. J. "Cultura Popular, industria cultural y modernidad." In *América Latina: cultura y modernidad*. México: Editorial Grijalbo, 1992.

———. "Notas sobre la modernidad y lo postmoderno en la cultura latinoamericana," *David y Goliath*, 1987.

———. "Un espejo trizado." In *América Latina: cultura y modernidad*. México: Editorial Grijalbo, 1992.

Buci-Glucksmann, Christine. *La raison baroque (de Baudelaire a Benjamin*. Paris: Ed. Galileé, 1984.

Buchloh, H. D., S. Guilbaut, and D. Solkin, eds. *Modernism and Modernity: The Vancouver Conference Papers*. The Nova Scotia Series, vol. 14. Halifax, N.S.: Press of the Nova Scotia College of Art and Design, 1983.

Butler, Judith. *Bodies that Matter: On the Discursive Limits of "Sex."* New York: Routledge, 1993.

Cacho Viu, Vincente. *Els modernistes i el nacionalisme cultural. Antologia*, Barcelona: Ed. De La Magrana, 1984.

Calhoun, Craig. *Critical Social Theory*. New York: Blackwell, 1995a.

———. *Critical Social Theory: Culture, History, and the Challenge of Difference*, Oxford: Oxford University Press, 1995b.

Canclini, Nestor García. "Memory and Innovation in the theory of Art." *The South Atlantic Quarterly* 92 (1993).

Canclini, Nestor García. *Culturas híbridas: Estrategias para entrar y salir de la modernidad*, México City: Grijalbo, 1989.

Cardoso, Ciro F. S. *Historia económica de América Latina*. Barcelona: Crítica, 1979, t.1–2.

Casas, Bartolomé de las. *Obras escogidas de Fray Bartolomé de las Casas*. Madrid: Biblioteca de Autores Españoles, t. 1 (1957)–5 (1958).

Castro-Gómez, Santiago. *Crítica de la Razón Latinoamericana*. Barcelona: Puvill Libros, S. A., 1996.

Cerutti Guldberg, H. "Posibilidades y límites de una filosofía de la liberación." *La filosofía en América. Trabajos presentados en el IX Congreso Interamericano de Filosofía. Vol. 1.* Caracas: Sociedad Venezolana de Filosofía, 1979.

Chakabarty, Dipesh. "Provincializing Europe: Postcoloniality and the Critique of History." *Cultural Studies* 6, no. 3 (1992).

Chaunu, Pierre. *Séville et l'Atlantique (1504–1650)*. Paris: SEVPEN, t. 1 (1955)–7 (1959).

Chaunu, P. *Conquête et exploitation des nouveaux mondes(XVIe. siècle)*. Paris: PUF, 1969.

Chaudhuri, K. N. *Trade and Civilisation in the Indian Ocean. An Economic History from the Rise of Islam to 1750*. Cambridge: Cambridge University Press, 1985.

Chen, Kuan-Hsing. "Voices from the outside: towards a new internationalist localism," *Cultural Studies* 6, no. 3 (1992).

Chomsky, N. *Year 501: The Conquest Continues*. Boston: South End Press, 1992.

Copjec, Joan. *Read My Desire: Lacan against the Historicists*. Cambridge and London: MIT Press, 1995.

Coronil, Fernando. "Transculturation and the Politics of Theory: Countering the Center, Cuban Counterpoint." Intoduction to Fernando Ortíz's *Cuban Counterpoint*. Durham: Duke University Press, 1995.

Davidson, Ned. *The Concept of Modernism in Hispanic Criticism*. Colorado: Pruett Press, 1966.

Dean, Carolyn. "Law and Sacrifice: Bataille, Lacan, and the Critique of the Subject." *Representations* 13 (1986).

de Bary, William Theodore. *Self and Society in Ming Thought*. New York: Columbia University Press, 1970.

de Imáz, J. L. "¿Adiós a la teoría de la dependencia? Una perspectiva desde la Argentina." *Estudios Internacionales* 28 (1974).

de Laurentis. "The essence of the triangle or taking seriously the risk of essentialism: feminist theory in Italy, U.S.A., and Great Britain." *Debate Feminista* 2 (México, 1990).

Deleuze, Gilles, and F. Guattari. *On the Line*. New York: Semiotext(e), 1983.

de Man, Paul. *Blindness and Insight: Essays in the Rhetoric of Contemporary Criticism*. Minneapolis: University of Minnesota Press, 1983.

Derrida, Jacques. "Feminismo y De(s)construcción." *Revista de Crítica Cultural* 3 (Santiago, 1991).

———. *L'Ecriture et la Différence.* Paris: Seuil, 1967a.

———. *De la Grammatologie.* Paris: Minuit, 1967b.

Descartes, René. *Oeuvres et Lettres de Descartes.* Paris: La Pléiade, Gallimard, 1953.

de Torre, Guillermo. *Historia de las literaturas de vanguardia.* Madrid: Guadarrama, 1965.

Diemer, Alwin. *Philosophy in the Present Situation of Africa.* Wiesbaden, 1981.

Diemer, A. Hountondji, P. *Africa and the Problem of its Identity.* Frankfurt, 1985.

Ducrot, Oswald. *Le dire et le dit.* Paris: Minuit, 1984.

Dussel, Enrique . *El dualismo en la antropología de la Cristiandad.* Buenos Aires: Editorial Guadalupe, 1974a.

———. *1492: El encubrimiento del Otro. Hacia el origen del mito de la modernidad.* Madrid: Nueva Utopía, 1993a (hay trad. al inglés Continuum Publishing Group, New York, 1995; al alemán Patmos Verlag, Düsseldorf, 1993; al francés Editions Ouvrières, Paris, 1993; al italiano La Piccola Editrice, Brescia, 1993; al portugués, Vozes, Petropolis, 1994; al gallego, Santiago de Compostela, 1992).

———. "Eurocentrism and Modernity." *Boundary 2* 20, no. 3 (1992). Published in *The Postmodernism Debate in Latin America.* Edited by J. Beverley and J. Oviedo. Durham: Duke University Press, 1995.

———. *Filosofía Ética Latinoamericana.* Vols. 1–3. México: Edicol, 1977.

———. "General." In *Historia General de la Iglesia en América Latina.* Salamanca: Sígueme, 1983, t.1, pp. 1–724.

———. *Método para una Filosofía de la Liberación.* Salamanca: Sígueme, 1974b.

———. *Para una de-strucción de la historia de la ética.* Mendoza: Ser y Tiempo, 1973b.

———. *Philosophy of Liberation,.* Orbis: Maryknoll, 1985.

———. "World Systems, Politics, and the Economics of Liberation Philosophy." In *The Underside of Modernity: Apel, Rorty, Taylor, and the Philosophy of Liberation.* Translated and edited by Eduardo Mendieta. Amherst, N.Y.: Humanity Books, 1996.

Eagleton, Terry. "Capitalism, Modernism, and Post-modernism." *Against the Grain: Selected Essays.* London: Verso, 1986.

Erlich, Bruce. "Amphibolies: On the Critical Self-Contradictions of 'Pluralism'." *Critical Inquiry* (1986).

Escobar, T. "Postmodernismo/Precapitalismo." *Casa de las Américas* 168 (1988).

Fanon, Frantz. *The Wretched of the Earth.* 1961. Reprint, New York: Grove Weidenfeld, 1991.

Fals Borda, O. "El nuevo despertar de los Movimientos Sociales." *Ciencia propia y colonialismo intelectual. Los nuevos rumbos.* Bogotá: Carlos Valencia Editores, 1987.

Fell, Claude. "Panamericanismo a iberoamericanismo: el debate entre los intelectuales latinoamericanos." *Mexico* (Universidad Autónoma de México, 1986): 112–25.

Follari, R. *Modernidad y posmodernidad: una óptica desde América Latina.* Buenos Aires: Rei, 1991.

Fokkema, Douwe W. *Literary History, Modernism, and Post-modernism.* Amsterdam: John Benjamins, 1984.

Fokkema, Douwe W., and H. Bertens, eds. *Approaching Postmodernism.* Amsterdam: John Benjamins, 1984.

Franco, Jean. "If you let me talk: The struggle for the interpretive power." *Casa de las Americas.* Cuba, 1988.

Frank, A. G. "A theoretical Introduction to 5000 years of World System history." *Review* (Binghamton) 13, no. 2 (1990): 155–248.

Foster, Hal, ed. *The Anti-Aesthetic: Essays on Postmodern Culture.* Port Townsend, Wash.: Bay Press, 1983.

Foucault, M. *Archäologie des Wissens.* Frankfurt: Surkamp, 1973. (French original: *L'archéologie du savoir*, 1969.)

———. *Die Ordung de Diskurses.* Frankfurt: Fischer, 1991. (French original: *L'ordre du discours*, 1972.)

———. *Las palabras y las cosas. Una arqueologia de las ciencias humanas.* Barcelona: Planeta-Agostini, 1985.

———. *Les mots et les choses: Une archeologie des sciences humaines.* Paris: Gallimard, 1966.

———. *Power/Knowledge: Selected Interviews and Other Writings, 1972–1977.* Edited by C. Gordon. New York: Pantheon, 1980.

Fukayama, F. "El fin de la historia. El más frío de todos los monstruos fríos." *Revista Foro* 18, Santafé de Bogotá, 1992.

Galeano, Eduardo. *Las Venas abiertas de América Latina.* Montevideo: Universidad de la República, Departamento de Publicaciones, 1971.

Galilei, Galileo. *Il Saggiatore.* In *Le opere di Galileo Galilei.* Firenze, 1933, t.6.

García Delgado, D. "Modernidad y posmodernidad en América Latina. Una perspectiva desde la ciencia política." In *Modernidad y posmodernidad en América Latina.* Edited by D. J. Michelini, J. San Martín, and F. Lagrave. Río Cuarto: ICALA, 1991.

Gehlen, A. "Ende der Geschichte?" In *Geschichte schreiben in der Postmoderne.* Edited by Ch. Konrad and M. Kessel. Stuttgart: Reclam, 1994.

Gicovate, Bernardo. "El modernismo y su historia." *Hispanic Review* 323 (1964).

Gilroy, Paul. *Black Atlantic: Modernity and Double Consciousness.* Cambridge: Harvard University Press, 1993.

Godinho, V. M. "Création et dynamisme économique du monde atlantique (1420–1670)." *Annales ESC* (1950) t.V/1, enero-marzo.

González, Erlinda. "La deslatinización del pueblo neomexicano." In *La latinidad y su sentido en América Latina.* México, 1986.

Goytisolo, Juan. *El furgón de cola.* Paris: Ruedo Ibérico, 1967.

Graff, Gerald. "The Myth of the Postmodernist Break-Through." *Tri-Quarterly* 26 (1975).

Grewal, Inderpal, and Caren Kaplan, eds. *Scattered Hegemonies: Postmodernity and Transnational Feminist Pracitices.* Minneapolis: University of Minnesota Press, 1994.

Guadarrama González, Pablo. "La malograda modernidad latinoamericana." In *Postmodernismo y crisis del marxismo.* México: UAEM, 1994.

Guillén, C. *Entre lo uno y lo diverso. Introducción a la literatura comparada.* Barcelona: Crítica, 1985.

Habermas, J. *Der philosophische Diskurs der Moderne,* Frankfurt: Suhrkamp, 1988. (Ed. castellana Taurus, Buenos Aires, 1989.)

———. "Die Moderne: ein unvollendetes Projekt." *Philosophische-politische Aufsätze, 1977–1990.* Leipzig: Reclam, 1990.

———. *Theorie des kommunikativen Handelns.* Frankfurt: Suhrkamp, 1981, t.1–2. (Ed. cast. Taurus, Madrid, t.1–2, 1987.)

Hall, A. R. *The Scientific Revolution.* Londres, 1954.

Hall, Stuart. "The Local and the Global: Globalization and Ethnicity." "Old and New Identities, Old and New Ethnicities." In *Culture, Globalization, and the World-System.* Edited by A. D. King. Minneapolis: University of Minnesota Press, 1997.

Hammarström, D. Ingrid. "The *price revolution* of the sixteenth century." *Scandinavian Economic History* 5, no. 1 (1957): 118–54.

Hassan, Ihab. "Pluralism in Postmodern Perspective." *Critical Inquiry* (1986).

Hassan, Ihab, and Sally Hassan, eds. *Innovation/Renovation: New Perspectives on the Humanities.* Madison: University of Winsconsin Press, 1983.

Hegel, G. W. F. *G. W. F. Hegel Werke in zwanzig Bänden. Theorie Werkausgabe.* Frankfurt: Suhrkamp, t.1 (1971)–10 (1979).

Heidegger, Martin. *Die Frage nach dem Ding,* Tübingen: Niemeyer, 1963. (Ed. cast. Sur, Buenos Aires, 1964.)

Heker, Liliana. "Posboom: una poética de la mediocridad." *El ornitorrinco* 14 (1986).

Hinkelammert, Franz. *Crítica a la razón utópica.* San José de Costa Rica: CEI, 1984.

——— . *Dialéctica del desarrollo desigual. El caso latinoamericano.* Santiago: Centro de Estudios de la Realidad Nacional, 1970b.

———. "Frente a la cultura de la postmodernidad: proyecto político y utopía." *El capitalismo al desnudo.* Bogotá: Editorial El Búho, 1991.

————. *Ideologías del desarrollo y dialéctica de la historia.* Santiago de Chile: Ediciones Nueva Universidad, 1970a.

Hodgson, Marshall. *The Venture of Islam.* Chicago: University of Chicago Press, 1974, t.1–3.

Hopenhayn, M. *Ni apocalípticos ni integrados. Aventuras de la modernidad en América Latina,* Santiago: F.C.E., 1994.

————. "Postmodernism and Neoliberalism in Latin America." In *The Postmodernism Debate in Latin America.* Edited by J. Beverley, J. Oviedo, and M. Aronna. Durham: Duke University Press, 1995.

Human Development Report 1992. Development Programme, United Nation. New York: Oxford University Press, 1992.

Huntington, Samuel P. "The Clash of Civilizations." *Foreign Affairs* (1993).

Hutcheon, Linda. *A Poetics of Postmodernism.* New York: Routledge, 1988.

Huyssens, Andreas. "Guía del Posmodernismo," In *El debate modernidad/posmodernidad.* Compiled by Nicolás Casullo. Buenos Aires: Punto Sur, 1989.

Ilie, Paul. *The Surrealist Mode in Spanish Literature.* Ann Arbor: University of Michigan Press, 1969.

Jameson, Fredric. "El posmodernismo o la lógica cultural del capitalismo tardío." *Casa de las Americas* 26 (1986): 155–56.

————. *Fables of Aggression. Wyndham Lewis: The Modernist as a Fascist.* Berkeley: University of California Press, 1979.

————. *Marxism and Form: Twentieth Century Dialectical Theories of Literature.* Princeton: Princeton University Press, 1971.

————. "Marxism and Historicism." *New Literary History* 11 (1979).

————. *The Political Unconscious: Narrative as a Socially Symbolic Act.* Ithaca: Cornell University Press, 1981.

————. *Posmodernism: Or the Cultural Logic of Late Capitalism.* Durham: University Duke Press, 1991.

————. "Progress versus Utopia: Or, Can We Imagine the Future?" *Science-Fiction Studies* 9 (1982).

————. "Reification and Utopia in Mass Culture." *Social Text 1* (1979).

Kant, Immanuel. *Kant Werke,* Darmstadt: Wissenschaftliche Buchgesellschaft 1968, t.1–9.

————. *Observations on the Feeling of the Beautiful and the Sublime* (1764). Translated by J. T. Goldwhalte. Berkeley: University of Califonia Press, 1960.

Kaplan, Caren. *Questions of Travel: Postmodern Discourses of Displacements.* Durham: Duke University Press, 1996.

Kennedy, Paul. *The Rise and Fall of the Great Powers.* New York: Random House, 1987.

Khatibi, Abdelkebir. *Maghreb pluriel.* Paris: Denoel, 1983.

Kipnis, Laura. "Feminism: The Political Conscience of Postmodernism?" In

Universal Abandon? Edited by Andrew Ross. Minneapolis: University of Minnesota Press, 1989.

Krauss, Rosalind. "Poststructuralism and the 'Paraliterary'." *October* (1980).

Kuhn, Thomas. *The Structure of Scientific Revolutions.* Chicago: University of Chicago Press, 1962.

Lacan, Jacques. *The Ethics of Psychoanalysis.* London: Routledge, 1992.

———. *The Four Fundamental Concepts of Psychoanalysis.* New York: Norton, 1981.

———. *La identificacion. Seminario X.* Unpublished seminar.

———. *The Psychoses.* London: Routledge, 1993.

———. *Television: A Challenge to the Psychoanalytic Establishement.* Edited by Joan Copjec, translated by Denis Hollier, Rosalind Krauss, and Annette Michelson. New York: Norton, 1990.

Laclau, Ernesto. *Emancipations.* London: Verso, 1996.

———. "Politics and the Limits of Modernity." In *Universal Abandon? The Politics of Postmodernism.* Edited by Andrew Ross. Minneapolis: University of Minnesota Press, 1988.

———. "Universalism, Particularism, and the Question of Identity." In *The Identity Question.* Edited by John Rajchman. New York/London: Routledge, 1995, pp. 93–108.

Laclau, Ernesto, and C. Mouffe. *Hegemony and Socialist Strategy: Towards Radical Democratic Politics.* London: Verso, 1985.

Laclau, Ernesto, ed. *Making of Political Identities.* London: Verso, 1994.

Lambert, Richard D. "Blurring the Disciplinary Boundaries: Area Studies in the United States." *American Behavioral Scientist* 33, no. 6 (1990).

Lattimore, Owen. *Inner Asian Frontiers of China.* Boston: Beacon Press, 1962.

Lazzarato, Maurizio. "Immaterial Labor." In *Radical Thoughts in Italy: A Potential Politics.* Edited by P. Virno and M. Hard. Mineapolis: University of Minnesota Press, 1996.

Lechner, N. "La democratización en el contexto de una cultura posmoderna." *Los patios interiores de la democracia.* Santiago: F.C.E., 1990.

Levenson, Michael L. *A Genealogy of Modernism: A Study in English Literary Doctrine 1908–1922.* Cambridge: Cambridge University Press, 1984.

Levin, Harry. "What was Modernism?" *Massachusetts Review* 1 (1960).

Litvak, Lily. *La musa libertaria. Antología.* Barcelona: A. Bosch, 1981.

Llorens, Vicente. *La emigración Republicana de 1939. I. El exilio español de 1939.* Madrid: Taurus, 1976.

López, Julio. *Poesía épica española (1950–1980),* Madrid: Pluma Rota, 1982.

Lopez, Milagros. "Post-Work Society." In *Social Text* 34 (1994).

Luhmann, Niklas. *Soziale Systeme. Grundriss einer algemeinen Theorie.* Frankfurt: Suhrkamp, 1988. (Trad.cast. *Sistemas Sociales,* Alianza Editorial, México, 1991.)

Llosa, Mario Vargas. "Postmodernismo y frvolidad." *La Nación*, 7 May 1994.

Lyotard, Jean-François. "Answering the Question: What is Postmodernism?" In *Innovation/Renovation: New Perspectives on the Humanities*. Edited by Ihab Hassan and Sally Hassan. Madison: University of Wisconsin Press, 1983.

———. *Der Winderstreit*. München: Wilhelm Fink Verlag, 1987. (French Original: *Le Différend*, 1983).

———. *Economie Libidinale*. Paris: Minuit, 1974.

———. *La condition postmoderne*. Paris: Minuit, 1979.

———. *La condition postmoderene: Rapport sur le savoir*. Paris: Minuit, 1979.

———. *Le différend*. Paris: Minuit, 1984.

———. "Reescribar la modernidad." *La polémica de la postmodernidad*. *Revista de Occidente* 66 (1986).

Machín, Horacio. "Conversación con Frederic Jameson." *Nuevo texto crítico* 7 (1990).

McNeil, William. *The Rise of the West*. Chicago: University of Chicago Press, 1964.

Mansilla, Hugo Felipe. "Las utopías sociales y sus consecuencias totalitarias." *La Cultura de autoritarismo ante los desafios del presente. Ensayos sobre una teoríca critica de la modernización*. La Paz: CEBEM, 1991.

Mann, Michael. *The Sources of Social Power: A History of Power from the Beginning to A.D. 1760*. Cambridge: Cambridge University Press, 1986, t.1.

Marcuse, Herbert. "Liberación respecto a la sociedad opulenta." In *The Dialectics of Liberation*. Edited by David Cooper. London: Penguin Books, 1968 (trad.cast. Siglos XXI, México, 1969, pp. 183–92).

Marquard, Odo. *Abschied vom Prinzipiellen*. Stuttgart, 1981.

Marx, K. *Das Kapital*, I, en *MEGA*, II, 6 (1987).

———. *Grundrisse der Kritik der politischen Oekonomie*. Berlin: Dietz, 1974.

Martí, José. *Política de Nuestra América*. México City: Siglo XXI, 1979.

———. "Versos Sencillos." In *Poesía Completa: Edición Crítica*. Vol. 1. Havana: Centro de Estudios Martianos y Editorial Letras Cubanas, 1993.

McHale, Brian. *Postmodernist Fiction*. London: Routledge, 1991.

McNeil, William. *The Rise of the West*. Chicago: University of Chicago Press, 1964.

Melo e de Castro, E. M. *As vanguardas na poesia portuguesa do século vinte*. Lisboa: Ministério de Educacâo en Ciència, 1980.

Mignolo, Walter . "Colonial and Postcolonial Discourse: Cultural Critique of Academic Colonialism?" *LARR* 28, no. 3 (1992c).

————. "Colonial Legacies and Postcolonial Theories: Cultural Critique or Academic Colonialism." In *Latin American Research Review* 28 (1993).

————. *The Darker Side of the Renaissance: Literacy, Territoriality, and Colonization.* Ann Arbor: University of Michigan Press, 1995a.

————. "Espacios geográficos y localizaciones epistemológicas o la ratio entre la localización geográfica y la subalternización de conocimientos." *Disenso* no. 3 (1997).

————. "Semiosis Colonial: La dialéctica entre representaciones fracturades y hermenéuticas pluritópicas." In *Cultura y Tercer Mundo.* Edited by Beatriz González Stephan. Caracas: Nueva Sociedad, 1992d.

Minervini, G., and K. Renna. "Dossier: Dire Dio dopo Auschwitz, durante Ayacucho. Dialogo tra Jürgen Moltmann e Gustavo Gutiérrez." *mosacio de pace* 4 (1993).

Modelski, George. *Long Cycles in World Politics.* Londres: Macmillan Press, 1987.

Molloy, Sylvia. "Contagio narrativo y gesticulación retórica en *La vorágine.*" *Revista Iberoamericana* 53 (1987).

Montecino, Sonia, Mariluz Dussel, and Angélica Wilson. "Identidad Femenina y Modelo Mariano en Chile." *Mundo de mujer. Continuidad y Cambio.* Santiago: Cem, 1988.

Moreiras, Alberto. "The End of Magical Realism: Arguedas's Passionate Signifier." Lecture Canada 1997.

Mouffe, Chantal. *The Return of the Political.* London: Verson, 1993.

Morón Arroyo, Ciriaco. *El sistema de Ortega y Gasset.* Madrid: Alcalá, 1968.

Morris, C. B. *Surrealism in Spain: 1920–1936.* Berkeley: University of California Press, 1972.

Mudimbe, V. Y. *The Invention of Africa: Gnosis, Philosophy, and the Order of Knowledge.* Bloomington: Indiana University Press, 1988.

Needham, Joseph. "The Chinese contributions to vessel control." In *Scientia* XCVI, 98 (abril 1961):123–28, (mayo 1961):163–68.

————. "Commentary on Lynn White *What accelerated technological change in the Western Middle Ages?*" In *Scientific Change.* Edited by A. C. Crombie. New York: Basic Books, 1963, pp. 117–53.

————. "Les contributions chinoises à l'art de gouverner les navires." In *Colloque International d'Histoire Maritime.* Paris, 1966, pp. 113–34.

Nicholson, Linda. *Feminism and Postmodernism.* New York: Routledge, 1990.

O'Gorman, Edmundo. *La invención de América.* México: FCE, 1957.

Olea, Raquel. "Feminismo una utopía que tiene lugar." Paper delivered for the conference "*Modernidad/Postmodernidad: una encrucijada latinoamericana*" jointly organized by ILET in Buenos Aires and *Revista de Crítica Cultural* de Santiago de Chile, 1990.

Ortíz, Fernando. *Cuban Counterpoint: Tobacco and Sugar.* Durham: Duke University Press, 1995.

Owens, Craig. "El discurso de los otros: Las feministas y el posmodernismo," *La posmodernidad*, Barcelona: Kairos, 1985.

Oyarzún, Kemy. "Edipo, autogestión y producción textual: Notas sobre crítica literaria feminista." In *Cultural and Historical Grounding for Hispanic and Lusobrazilian Feminist Literary Criticism.* Edited by Hernán Vidal. Minneapolis: Institute for the Study of Ideologies and Literature, 1989.

París Pombo, M. D. *Crisis e identidades colectivas en América Latina.* México: Plaza y Valdéa S.A., 1992.

Paz, Octavio. *El laberinto de la soledad.* México: Cuadernos Americanos, 1950.

———. *In/mediaciones.* México: Seix Barral, 1986.

———. *Signos en rotación.* Madrid: Alianza, 1983.

Perloff, Marjorie. *The Dance of the Intellect: Studies in the Poetry of the Pound Tradition.* Cambridge: Cambridge University Press, 1985.

Perus, Francois. *Literatura y sociedad en América Latina: El modernismo.* México: Siglo XXI, 1976.

Picón Garfield, Evelyn, and Ivan S. Schulman. *"Las entrañas del vacío" Ensayos sobre la modernidad hispanoamericana.* México: Cuardernos Americanos: 1984.

Pletsch, Carl E. "The Three Worlds, or the Division of Social Scientific Labor, circa 1950–1975." *Comparative Studies in Society and History* 23, no. 4 (1981).

Rama, Angel. *Rubén Darío y el modernismo: circustancia socioeconómica de un arte americano.* Caracas: Universidad Central de Venezuela, 1970.

———. *Transculturación narrativa en América Latina.* México: Siglo XXI, 1982.

Ramón Jimenez, Juan. *El modernismo: Notas de un curso (1953).* Edited by R. Gullón and E. Fernández Méndez. México: Aguilar, 1962.

Ramos, Samuel. *Profile of Man and Culture in Mexico.* Translated by P. G. Earle, Austin: University of Texas Press, 1973.

Ramsden, H. *The 1898 Revolution in Spain. Towards a Reinterpretation.* Manchester: Manchester University Press, 1975.

Retamar, Roberto Fernández. *Caliban and Other Essays.* Translated by E. Baker. Minneapolis: University of Minnesota Press, 1989.

Ribeiro, Darcy. *Las America y la civilizacion. Proceso de formacion y causas del desarrollo desigual de los pueblos americanos.* Caracas: Ayacucho Library, 1992.

Rich, Adrienne. "Notes Towards a Politics of Location." *Blood, Bread, Poetry: Selected Prose, 1979–1985.* New York: Norton, 1986.

Richard, Nelly. "Alteridad y descentramiento culturales." *Revista chilena de literatura* 42 (1993).

———. "Latinoamérica y la Postmodernidad." *Revista de Crítica Cultural* 3 (1990).

———. "Latinoamérica y la postmodernidad." In *Postmodernidad en la periferia. Enfogues de la nueva teoría cultural.* Edited by H. Herlinghaus and M. Walter. Berlin: Langer Verlag, 1994.

———. "The Latin American Problematic of Theoretical-Cultural Transference: Postmodern Appropriations and Counterappropriations." *The South Atlantic Quarterly* 92 (1993).

———. "¿Tiene sexo la escritura?" *Debate Feminista* (México City) 9 (1994).

Rivera Cusicangui, Silvia. "Liberal Democracy and *Ayllu* Democracy in Bolivia: The Case of Northern Potosi." *The Journal of Development Studies* (1990).

Roig, A. A. "Posiciones de un filosofar: Diálogo con Raúl Fornet-Betancourt." *Rostro y filosofía de América Latina.* Mendoza: EDIUNC, 1993.

———. "¿Qué hacer con los relatos, la mañana, la sospecha y la historia? Respuestas a los postmodernos."

Rooney, Ellen. "Who's Left Out? A Rose By Any Other Name is Still Red: Or, The Politics of Pluralism." *Critical Inquiry* (1986).

Rossabi, Morris. *China Among Equals: The Middle Kingdom and its Neighbors 10–14th Centuries.* Berkeley: University of California Press, 1982.

Rorty, Richard. *Philosophy and the Mirror of Nature.* Princeton: Princeton University Press, 1979 (trad.cast. Cátedra, Madrid, 1989).

Rowe, W., and V. Schelling, eds. *Memory and Modernity: Popular Culture in Latin America.* London: Verso, 1991.

Said, Edward. *Culture and Imperialism,* New York: Knopf, 1993.

———. "In the shadow of the West; and interview with Edward Said," *Discourses: Conversations in Postmodern Art and Culture.* New York: The New Museum of Contemporary Art, 1990.

———. "Intellectuals in the Post-Colonial World," *Salmagundi* 70–71 (1986): 43–64.

———. "Opponents, Audiences, Constituencies and Communities." In *The Anti-Aesthetic: Essays on Postmodern Culture.* Edited by Hal Foster. Port Townsend, Washington: Bay Press, 1983.

Salecl, Renata. *The Spoils of Freedom.* London: Verso, 1994.

Sánchez Vázquez, A. "Posmodernidad, posmodernismo y socialismo." Havana: *Casa de las Américas* 175, (1989).

Sarlo, Beatriz. "Basuras culturales, simulacros políticos." In *Postmodernidad en la periferia.* Edited by Herman Herlinghaus and Monika Walter. Berlin: Langer Verlag, 1994.

Scharlau, B., ed. *Lateinamerika denken. Kulturtheoretische Grenzgänge zwischen Moderne und Postmoderne.* Tübingen: Gunter Narr Verlag, 1994.

Schutte, Ofelia. *Cultural Identity and Social Liberation in Latin American Thought.* Albany: SUNY Press, 1993.

Schwartz, Sanford. *The Matrix of Modernism: Pound, Eliot, and Early 20th-Century Thought*. Princeton: Princeton University Press, 1985.

Scott, Joan W. "Igualdad versus Diferencia: Los usos de la teoría postestructuralista." *Debate Feminista* (México) 3 (1992).

Shaw, Donald. *The Generation of 1898 in Spain*. New York: Barnes & Noble, 1975.

———. "The Post-Boom in Spanish American Fiction." *Studies in 20th Century Literature* 19 (1995).

———. "Towards a Description of the Post-Boom." *Bulletin of Hispanic Studies* 66 (1989).

Sombart, Werner. *Der Bourgeois*. München: Duncker, 1920.

———. *Der moderne Kapitalismus*. Leipzig: Duncker, 1902.

Soper, Kate. "El postmodernismo y sus malestares." *Debate Feminista* (México) 3 1992.

Spivak, Gayatri. "Can the Subaltern Speak." In *Marxism and the Interpretation of Culture*. Edited by C. Nelson and L. Grossberg. Urbana: University of Illinois Press, 1988.

———. *In Other Worlds*. New York: Methuen, 1987.

Stavarianos, L. S. *The World to 1500: A Global History*. Englewood Cliffs: Prentice Hall, 1970.

Subirats, E. "Transformaciones de la cultura moderna." In *La polémica de la postmodernidad*. Edited by Tono Martínez. Madrid: Ediciones Libertarias, 1986.

Suleri, Sara. *The Rhetoric of English India*. Chicago: Chicago University Press, 1992a.

Taviani, Paolo Emilio. *Cristoforo Colombo. La genesi della scoperta*. Novara: Isstituto Geografico de Agostini, 1982.

Thompson, William. *On Global War: Historical-Structural Approches to World Politics*, Columbia: University of South Carolina Press, 1989.

Tilly, Charles. *Big Structures. Large Processes*. New York: Russell Sage Foundation, 1984.

Toynbee, Arnold. *A Study of History*. Vol. 1. New York and London: Oxford University Press, 1946.

Troeltsch, Ernst. *Die Soziallehren der christlichen Kirchen und Gruppen*. Tübingen, 1923.

Ulmer, Gregory L. "The Object of Postcriticism." In *The Anti-Aesthetic: Essays on Postmodern Culture*. Edited by Hal Foster. Port Townsend, Wash.: Bay Press, 1983.

Urandibia, Iñaqui, and Gianni Vattimo, et al. *En torno a la posmodernidad*. Barcelona: Anthropos, 1994.

Valentí, Eduard i Fiol. *El primer modernismo literario catalán y sus fundamentos ideológicos*. Barcelona: Ariel, 1973.

Varga, Kibédi, ed. *Littérature et postmodernité, Crin* 14 (1986).

Vargas Lozano, G. "Reflexiones críticas sobre modernidad y postmodernidad." ¿Qué hacer con la filosofía en América Latina? México: UAM/UAT, 1991.

Vattimo, Gianni. La fine della Modernità. Milán: Garzanti, 1985.

Vicens Vives, Jaime. Approaches to the History of Spain, Berkeley: University of California Press, 1970.

Viswanathan, Gauri. Masks of Conquest. New York: Columbia University Press, 1989.

Wallerstein, Immanuel . The Modern World-System. New York: Academic Press, t.1 (1974)–3 (1989) (ed. cast. Siglo XXI, México, t.1 ([1979]).

———. Open The Social Sciences. Report of the Gulbenkian Commission on the Restructuring of the Social Sciences. Palo Alto: Stanford University Press, 1996.

———. The Politics for the World-Economy. Cambridge: Cambridge University Press, 1984.

Wallis, Brian, ed. Art After Modernism: Rethinking Representation. New York: The New Museum of Contemporary Art, 1984.

Waugh, Patricia. Metafiction: The Theory and Practice of Self-Conscious Fiction. London: Methuen, 1984.

Max Weber. The Protestant Ethic and the Spirit of Capitalism. Translated by Talcott Parsons. New York: Charles Scribner's Sons, 1958.

Welsch, Wolfgang . Unseres postmoderne Moderne. Berlin: Akademie V., 1993.

———. Vernunft. Die Zeitgenösische Vernunftkritik und das Knozept der transversalen Vernunft. Frankfurt: Suhrkamp, 1995.

Wohl, Robert. "The Generation of 1914 and Modernism." In Modernism: Challenges and Perspectives. Edited by Monique Chafdor, R. Quiñones, and Albert Wachtel. Urbana: University of Illinois Press, 1986.

Wolf, Eric. Europe and the People without History. Berkeley: University of California Press, 1982.

Yndurain, Domingo, ed. Historia y crítica de la literatura española. Epoca contemporánea. 1939–1980. Barcelona: Crítica, 1981.

Young, Howard T. "The Exact Names." Modern language Notes 96 (1981):2.

Young, Robert J. C. Colonial Desire: Hybridity in Theory, Culture, and Race. New York: Routledge, 1995.

Yúdice, George. "El conflicto de postmodernidades." Nuevo Texto Crítico 7 (1991).

Yúdice, G., J. Franco, and J. Florez, eds. On Edge: The Crisis of Contemporary Latin American Culture. Minneapolis: University of Minnesota Press, 1992.

Zavala, Iris M. "The Baroque as Point the Capiton." Lecture Canada 1997.

———. Colonialism and Culture. Hispanic Modernisms and the Social Imaginary. Indiana University Press, 1992.

————. "1898, Modernismo and the Latin American Revolution." *Revista chicano-Riqueña* 3–4 (1975).

————. *Fin de Siglo: Modernismo, 98 y bohemia.* Madrid: Cuadernos para ed Diálogo, 1974.

————. *Illuminaciones en la sombra.* Madrid: Alhambra, 1985.

————. "The Manuscript and Its Interpreters: Notes on the 'Omnisicent Reader' of the Poetics of the Lyric." In *Approaches to Discourse, Poetics and Psychiatry: Papers from the 1985 Utrecht Summer School of Critical Theory.* Edited by Iris M Zavala, T. A. van Diuk, and M. Díaz-Diocaretz. Amsterdam: John Benjamins, 1987.

Zea, L. "Modernización y Estado en Latinoamérica." In *Modernidad y posmodernidad en América Latina.* Edited by D. J. Michelini, J. San Martín, and F. Lagrave. Río Cuarto: ICALA, 1991.

Žižek, Slavoj. *Everything You Always Wanted to Know About Lacan (But Were Afraid to Ask Hitchcock).* London: Verso, 1994a.

————. *For They Know Not What They Do.* London: Verso, 1996.

————. *The Metastases of Enjoyment.* London: Verso, 1994b.

Zunzunegi, J. "Los orígenes de las misiones en las Islas Canarias." *Revista Española de Teología* 1 (1941): 364–70.

CONTRIBUTORS

JORGE LUIS BORGES (Argentina) is perhaps the most significant Latin American writer ever and certainly one of the most influential writers in contemporary literature. His short stories, collections of essays and poetry have been translated into numerous languages. Borges's texts have been influential beyond literary studies and they have been constantly cited in contemporary philosophy and scientific theory. The following are among the most representative works: *Ficciones*, *EL Aleph*, *Other Inquisitions*, among others. After sharing the Fromentor prize with Samuel Beckett in 1961, a compilation of his works was published for English readers under the title *Labyrinths*.

SANTIAGO CASTRO-GÓMEZ (Colombia) has studied philosophy at the Universidad de Santo Tomás de Bogota and in the University of Tubingen. He is the coeditor of the journal *Dissens*. Apart from having published numerous articles on themes related to philosophy, cultural studies, and Latin American thought, he has recently published a book entitled *Critica de la razon Latinoamericana*.

ENRIQUE DUSSEL (Argentina, Mexico) is one of the major philosophers associated with liberation theology in Latin America. He has authored over twenty books on religion, sociology, history, and law. His most recent works include *The Invention of the Americas* and *The Underside of Modernity*. A political refugee from his native Argentina,

Dussel has lived in Mexico since 1975 and is currently Professor of Philosophy and Ethics at the Universidad Autonoma de Mexico.

GUILLERMO GÓMEZ-PEÑA (Mexico, U.S.) is an internationally acclaimed multimedia performance artist, social and cultural critic, and author. He first came to the United States in 1978. Since then he has been exploring crosscultural issues in his artistic performances and writings. He is a regular contributor to the national radio news magazine "Latino USA" and a contributing editor at *High Performance Magazine* and the *Drama Review*. His *New World Border* (San Francisco: City Lights Bookstore, 1996) won the 1997 American Book Award granted by the American Book Association.

PEDRO LANGE-CHURIÓN (Venezuela) is an Associate Professor of Latin American literature at the University of San Francisco. He has published several articles and reviews about Latin American literature and culture. He has also written on film. His book entitled *Felisberto Hernández: la traza del deseo en lo extraño* is accepted for publication (Rodopi: Amsterdam). Currently he is writing a book on representations of space in aesthetic discourses. Professor Lange-Churión is also a filmaker.

EDUARDO MENDIETA (Colombia, U.S.) is Assistant Professor of Philosophy at the University of San Francisco. He is the editor and translator of Enrique Dussel's *The Underside of Modernity*, which also contains essays by Karl Otto Apel and Paul Ricouer. He co-edited *Liberation Theologies, Postmodernity and the Americas* (New York: Routledge, 1997), and *Thinking from the Underside of History: Enrique Dussel's Philosophy of Liberation* (Lanham: Rowman & Littlefield Publishers, Inc., 2000). Currently he is writing a book entitled *The Geography of Utopia: Modernity's Spatio-Temporal Regimes*.

WALTER MIGNOLO (Argentina, U.S.) is Professor of Romance Studies, Cultural Anthropology and the Graduate Program in Literature at Duke University. His books include *Writing without Words: Alterna-*

tive Literacies in Mesoamerica and the Andes (Duke University Press, 1994), and *The Darker Side of the Renaissance: Literacy, Territoriality, and Colonization* (University of Michigan Press, 1995), which was awarded the Katherine Singer Kovacs Prize from the Modern Languages Association, and *Local Histories/Global Designs: Coloniality, Subaltern Knowledges, and Border Thinking* (Princeton University Press, 2000).

MARCELO PAZ (Argentina) is an Assistant Professor of Spanish and Latin American literature at the University of Evansville. He is the author of articles and reviews on Argentinian literature. Currently he is working on a book entitled *Una historicidad insolita en la narrativa argentina de la dictadura militar*.

OCTAVIO PAZ (Mexico) is a Nobel Prize laureate in literature (1993). He is arguably among the most important Latin American poets and intellectuals. His literature is ranked along the works of Neruda and Borges. Octavio Paz has been quite concerned with the question of modernity and Latin America. Some of the works that bring to the fore this aspect of his intellectual preoccupation include *The Labyrinth of Solitude* and *Children of the Mire: Modern Poetry from Romanticism to the Avant-Garde*.

NELLY RICHARD (Chile) is the editor of the *Revista de Critica cultural* in Santiago de Chile and among the most renowned theorists of Postmodernism in Latin America. She was closely involved in the activities of the Chilean artististic avant-garde in opposition of the Pinochet dicatatorship. Her books include *Margenes e instituciones* (1986), *La estratificacion de los margenes* (1989), and *Masculino/femenino: Practicas de la diferencia y cultura democratica* (1993).

OFELIA SCHUTTE (Cuba, U.S.) is an Associate Professor of Philosophy and affiliate at the center for Latin American Studies at the University of Florida. In 1993 she published an important work titled *Cultural Identiy and Social Liberation in Latin American Thought*.

IRIS M. ZAVALA (Puerto Rico) is Professor and Chair of the Spanish Department at the University of Utrecht. She is the author of over ninety articles on literary history; social and political history; history of ideas; Spanish, Latin American, and Caribbean literatures and cultures; literary theory; semiotics; Bakhtin; and popular culture. She has written over thirty books, including *Ruben Dario bajo el signo del cisne*, which was awarded the Literary Prize of the Institute of Puerto Rican Culture, and *Colonialism and Culture*.

LEOPOLDO ZEA (Mexico) is perhaps the foremost contemporary Latin American philosopher and thinker. He is a Professor at the Universidad Autonoma de Mexico. Among his works: *America en la historia* (1957), *Dialectica de la conciencia americana* (1975), and *Discurso desde la marginacion y la barbarie* (1988).

INDEX